WHERE'S THE REST OF ME?

RONALD REAGAN WITH RICHARD G. HUBLER

Where's the Rest of Me?

THE RONALD REAGAN STORY

APPLEWOOD BOOKS
Carlisle, Massachusetts

To Honey with Love

CHAPTER

1

The story begins with the closeup of a bottom in a small town called Tampico in Illinois, on February 6, 1911. My face was blue from screaming, my bottom was red from whacking, and my father claimed afterward that he was white when he said shakily, "For such a little bit of a fat Dutchman, he makes a hell of a lot of noise, doesn't he?"

"I think he's perfectly wonderful," said my mother weakly. "Ronald Wilson Reagan."

Those were their first opinions of me. As far as I know, they never changed during their lifetimes. As for myself, ever since my birth my nickname has been "Dutch" and I have been particularly fond of the colors that were exhibited—red, white, and blue. I have not been uncomfortable on the various occasions when I have had an overwhelming impulse to brandish them. I have heard more than one psychiatrist say that we imbibe our ideals from our mother's milk. Then, I must say, my breast feeding was the home of the brave baby and the free bosom. I was the hungriest person in the house but I only got chubby when I exercised in the crib; any time I wasn't gnawing on the bars, I was worrying with my thumb in my mouth—habits which have symbolically persisted throughout my life.

In those early days I was sure I was living the whole life of Reagan. When any Irishman, who generally knows quite well how to live, believes that, he is usually right. It was not until thirty years later that I found part of my existence was missing.

3

It came with the making of a picture called *King's Row* for Warner Brothers in 1941. In this I played the role that first made me a motion picture star.

It certainly was one of my best pictures. Based on the novel of the same name by Henry Bellamann, it was a slightly sordid but moving yarn about the antics in a small town, something I had more than a slight acquaintance with. I took the part of Drake McHugh, the gay blade who cut a swathe among the ladies. I had inherited a good deal of money, the story ran, but the head of the bank had absconded with it. On my upper-crust uppers, I made the most of it.

My key scene was to be played in a bed. This environment was the result of the plot which had me injured in an accident in the railroad yards. Taken to a sadistic doctor (who disapproved of my dating his daughter and felt it was his duty to punish me), I recovered consciousness in an upstairs bedroom. I found that the doctor had amputated both my legs at the hips.

It was the portrayal of this moment of total shock which made the scene rough to play. Coming from unconsciousness to full realization of what had happened in a few seconds, it presented me with the most challenging acting problem in my career. Worst of all, I had to give my reaction in a line of no more than five words.

A whole actor would find such a scene difficult; giving it the necessary dramatic impact as half an actor was murderous. I felt I had neither the experience nor the talent to fake it. I simply had to find out how it really felt, short of actual amputation.

I rehearsed the scene before mirrors, in corners of the studio, while driving home, in the men's rooms of restaurants, before selected friends. At night I would wake up staring at the ceiling and automatically mutter the line before I went back to sleep. I consulted physicians and psychologists; I even talked to people who were so disabled, trying to brew in myself the caldron of emotions a man must feel who wakes up one sunny morning to find half of himself gone.

4

I got a lot of answers. I supplied some more for myself. None of mine agreed with any of theirs. Theirs did not agree with each other. I was stumped. I commenced to panic as the day for shooting came nearer.

The night before I could not sleep. I appeared wan and worn on the sound stage, still not knowing how to read the line. Without hope, with make-up pasted on and in my nightshirt, I wandered over to the set to see what it looked like. I found the prop men had arranged a neat deception. Under the gay patchwork quilt, they had cut a hole in the mattress and put a supporting box beneath. I stared at it for a minute. Then, obeying an overpowering impulse, I climbed into the rig. I spent almost that whole hour in stiff confinement, contemplating my torso and the smooth undisturbed flat of the covers where my legs should have been.

Gradually the affair began to terrify me. In some weird way, I felt something horrible had happened to my body. Then gradually I became aware that the crew had quietly assembled, the camera was in position, and the set all lighted. Sam Wood, the director, stood beside me, watching me sweat.

"Want to shoot it?" he said in a low voice.

"No rehearsal?" I begged. Somehow I knew this one had to be for real.

God rest his soul—fine director that he was, he just turned to the crew and said, "Let's make it."

There were cries of "Lights!" and "Quiet, please!" I lay back and closed my eyes, as tense as a fiddlestring. I heard Sam's low voice call, "Action!" There was the sharp *clack* which signaled the beginning of the scene. I opened my eyes dazedly, looked around, slowly let my gaze travel downward. I can't describe even now my feeling as I tried to reach for where my legs should be. "Randy!" I screamed. Ann Sheridan (bless her), playing Randy, burst through the door. She wasn't in the shot and normally wouldn't have been on hand until we turned the camera around to get her entrance, but she knew it was one of those scenes where a fellow actor needed all the help he could get and at that moment, in my mind, she was Randy answering my call. I asked the question--the words that had been haunting me for so many weeks—"Where's the rest of me?"

There was no retake. It was a good scene and it came out that way in the picture. Perhaps I never did quite as well again in a single shot. The reason was that I had put myself, as best I could, in the body of another fellow. Five years later, under different circumstances than make-believe, I had to ask myself the same question. And since that time, no single line in my career has been as effective in explaining to me what an actor's life must be.

So much of our profession is taken up with pretending, with the interpretation of never-never roles, that an actor must spend at least half his waking hours in fantasy, in rehearsal or shooting. If he is only an actor, I feel, he is much like I was in *King's Row*, only half a man—no matter how great his talents. I regard acting with the greatest affection; it has made my life for me. But I realize it tends to become an island of exaggerated importance. During my career on the screen I have commanded excellent salaries, some admiration, fan mail, and a reputation—and my world contracted into not much more than a sound stage, my home, and occasional nights on the town. The circle of my friends closed in. The demands of my work—sometimes as much as fourteen hours a day—cut me off even from my brother Neil, who lived within half a mile of my apartment.

I began to feel like a shut-in invalid, nursed by publicity. I have always liked space, the feeling of freedom, a broad range of friends, and variety (not excluding the publication). Now I had become a semi-automaton "creating" a character another had written, doing what still another person told me to do on the set. Seeing the rushes, I could barely believe the colored shadow on the screen was myself.

Possibly this was the reason I decided to find the rest of me. I loved three things: drama, politics, and sports, and I'm not sure they always come in that order. In all three of them I came out

6

of the monastery of movies into the world. In sports, though I could no longer play top football, I could still swim or ride horseback or simply watch. In motion pictures or television, I could do more than a competent job. In politics, I found myself in the middle of the biggest tohubohu of my life.

As a first-line Irishman, I relished it. There seems to be something blarney-green in the blood of most Sons of the Old Sod—as proved by the recent political history of the country—that gives zest to the shillelagh psyche. I had been lauded as a star in sports and had been praised in movies: in politics I found myself misrepresented, cursed, vilified, denounced, and libeled. Yet it was by far the most fascinating part of my life.

I suppose my desire to mix into public life was the result of cross-bred genes from both my father and mother. My father was John Edward Reagan (always pronounced Ra-gan), a first-generation black Irishman. He loved shoes. He sold them as a clerk, managed shoe departments and his own stores. He even studied correspondence courses about how to sell more sabots, and spent hours analyzing the bones of the foot. He was a man who might have made a brilliant career out of selling but he lived in a time—and with a weakness—that made him a frustrated man.

I was eleven years old the first time I came home to find my father flat on his back on the front porch and no one there to lend a hand but me. He was drunk, dead to the world. I stood over him for a minute or two. I wanted to let myself in the house and go to bed and pretend he wasn't there. Oh, I wasn't ignorant of his weakness. I don't know at what age I knew what the occasional absences or the loud voices in the night meant, but up till now my mother, Nelle, or my brother handled the situation and I was a child in bed with the privilege of pretending sleep.

But someplace along the line to each of us, I suppose, must come that first moment of accepting responsibility. If we don't accept it (and some don't), then we must just grow older without quite growing up. I felt myself fill with grief for my father at the same time I was feeling sorry for myself. Seeing his arms

7

spread out as if he were crucified—as indeed he was—his hair soaked with melting snow, snoring as he breathed, I could feel no resentment against him.

That was Nelle's doing. With all the tragedy that was hers because of his occasional bouts with the dark demon in the bottle, she told Neil and myself over and over that alcoholism was a sickness—that we should love and help our father and never condemn him for something that was beyond his control.

I bent over him, smelling the sharp odor of whiskey from the speakeasy. I got a fistful of his overcoat. Opening the door, I managed to drag him inside and get him to bed. In a few days he was the bluff, hearty man I knew and loved and will always remember.

Jack (we all called him by his nickname) was a handsome man —tall, swarthy, and muscular, filled with contradictions of character. A sentimental Democrat, who believed fervently in the rights of the workingman—I recall him cursing vehemently about the battle at Herrin in 1922, where twenty-six persons were killed in a massacre brought about by a coal-mine strike—he never lost his conviction that the individual must stand on his own feet. Once he caught me fighting in the schoolyard, surrounded by a circle of eggers-on. He stopped the fight, tongue-lashed the crowd —then lifted me a foot in the air with the flat side of his boot. "Not because you were fighting," he said, "but because you weren't winning." That was my first sample of adult injustice. I *had* been winning.

He believed literally that all men were created equal and that the man's own ambition determined what happened to him after that. He put his principles into practice. On the occasion when that early film classic, *The Birth of a Nation,* came to town, my brother and I were the only kids not to see it. "It deals with the Ku Klux Klan against the colored folks," Jack said sternly, "and I'm damned if anyone in this family will go see it." Years later in the dark depression years when he was trying to earn a buck on the road as a shoe salesman, he checked into a small-town

8

hotel. "Fine," said the clerk, reversing the register and reading his name. "You'll like it here, Mr. Reagan. We don't permit a Jew in the place."

My father picked up his suitcase again. "I'm a Catholic," he said furiously, "and if it's come to the point where you won't take Jews, you won't take me either." Since it was the only hotel in town, he spent the night in his car in the snow. He contracted near-pneumonia and a short time later had the first heart attack of the several that led to his death.

He was a restless man, burning with ambition to succeed. When I left home at seventeen to go to college, we had never lived in a house we owned; it was twenty years afterward that I was able to bring him out to Hollywood and present him with the clear deed to a small house and lot, the first piece of real estate he had ever owned. It was the most satisfying gift of my life.

He had a wry, mordant humor. He was the best raconteur I ever heard, especially when it came to the smoking-car sort of stories. But Jack always made clear to us that there was a time and place for this kind of anecdote; he drew a sharp line between lusty vulgar humor and filth. To this day I agree with his credo and join Jack and Mark Twain in asserting that one of the basic forms of American humor is the down-to-earth wit of the ordinary person, and the questionable language is justified if the point is based on real humor.

If my father was Catholic, my mother was Protestant. If he rebelled against the universe, she was a natural practical do-gooder. If he was Irish, she was Scots-English. If he was occasionally vulgar, she tried to raise the tone of the family. Perhaps she never understood the reason for his week-long benders once or twice a year, any more than he understood her cultural activities, but they put up with each other.

Nelle Wilson Reagan—small, with auburn hair and blue eyes —had the conviction that everyone loved her just because she loved them. My father's cynicism never made the slightest impression on her, while I suspect her sweetness often undermined his

9

practical viewpoint about the world. Neither she nor my father had ever graduated from any school but the elementary grades. No diploma was needed for kindness, in her opinion, just as my father believed energy and hard work were the only ingredients needed for success.

My mother arranged regular readings for the various ladies' societies. She set up weekly schedules for herself to visit the prisoners in the local jails. Years later, when she came to California, she discovered an indigent tuberculosis sanitarium and made it her pet charity and visitation point. Months after her death, at a movie banquet, a waiter soft-shoed up behind me and whispered in my ear, "You want a steak instead of that rubber chicken?" I admitted I would be very grateful. He brought me a juicy sirloin that made the evening memorable. I figured he was a real fan and tried to thank him but he shook me off. "Just tell me how your mother's doing," he blurted, identifying himself as an old TB patient who had been cured but had never forgotten my mother's visits.

Ours was a free family that loved each other up to the point where the independence of each member began. For as long as I can remember we were on a first-name basis with each other. I came into it more than two years after my brother, John Neil Reagan, and this characteristic appeared at an early age. By the time I was nine years old, we had lived in a succession of small towns west of Chicago, as well as in the city itself. The beginning for my brother and me was Tampico, then a little country town with the usual Civil War cannon and pyramided cannon balls in a lush green park just across from our house. The fascination of the railroad tracks and station lay just beyond—too much to resist. In a toddling expedition, my brother and I crawled under a train snorting steam in the station. We got to the other side just before it gave a mighty jerk and chuffed out. Our narrow escape would have been all right except that Nelle saw us. She nearly collapsed in the kitchen. She caught up with us as we were swiping bits of ice from the ice wagon (our target for the day) and earlifted us home.

That same year we moved to the South Side of Chicago, near the university campus. Neil and I promptly got into one of our inevitable difficulties. This time, Jack had gone out to work. Nelle was absent on one of her periodical goodwill trips. We got scared, with twilight coming on, and went to scour the city for our parents—after first carefully blowing out the gas lamp. We never found them, getting engaged in a debate with a friendly drunk who thought we shouldn't be out so late. Nelle arrived just in time to agree with him. Nelle had almost lost her mind, coming home to a gas-filled house with us missing. She did lose her temper and stood as a figure of righteous wrath while Jack clobbered us.

From Chicago, we moved to Galesburg, Illinois. I was deeply impressed with the big green trees and the dark red brick streets; they fitted into a picture of bright-colored peace, the way some primitive lithographs do. I have a whole set of these stereoscopic memories in my head—beginning with Tampico—that I can bring into focus exactly the way we used to do in the parlor, running them back and forth in my memory. In Galesburg I changed my living habits from the Chicago flat to a bungalow and, finally, to a rented house with an attic. Here I ran across a forgotten, enormous collection of birds' eggs and butterflies. The colors and textures—and most especially the fragility—of these objects fascinated my imagination. They became gateways to the mysterious, symbols of the out-of-doors they represented. Here, in the musty attic dust, I got my first scent of wind on peaks, pine needles in the rain, and visions of sunrise on the desert.

I could sit for hours in that wonderful attic, looking at those glass-encased collections—stored there as the property of the mysterious landlord who owned this, our home. To me the house was tremendous in size, and directly across the street—between our neighbors and family friends, the McGowans and the Tennerys—was an open field shaded by a row of poplar trees. Here too was nature in the raw, where you could even find a shiny emerald-green grass snake. Years later a pilgrimage back to those haunts reduced the house to a very modest size, and the field turned out to be an empty lot with no more than a sixty-foot width.

World War I was being fought and there was an excitement in the air for even a five-year-old. One day I would learn that Jack had been first in line to enlist, but fathers of two weren't being taken. He always protested his bad timing at being a between-wars generation—too young for the Spanish-American and too old for "Over There." But I didn't know about his long-ing as I would sit on Neil's secondhand bike, hanging onto a hitching post in front of the house. My timing was better than Jack's because I was always there at noon when he came home for lunch. He would push me around in the street for a few exhilarat-ing circles. I never asked him to, but it seemed that he was able to figure out what was on my mind.

Even before I started school, at the age of five, I learned to read. I can't claim special talent; it came about simply because my mother took the time to sit down every night and read books to us, following each word with a finger, while we watched over her shoulder. One evening all the funny black marks on paper clicked into place. I was lying on the floor with the evening paper and Jack asked what I was doing—so I told him. "Reading." He said, "Well, read me something," and I did. Nelle was proud enough to canvass the neighbors and get them to come in while I proudly recited such events as the aftermath of a bomb that had exploded in San Francisco during a parade and the exciting details of the $40,000,000 two-dead Black Tom explosion in New Jersey.

Some time after first grade—no kindergarten in those days—we moved again, this time to Monmouth, to spend a year or two. We rented a house just off the campus of Monmouth College—a scenic place, with respectable hills, even for Illinois. We used the

12

hills for roaming in summer and sledding in winter. At the age of seven, I saw the coming of the Armistice of World War I. The parades, the torches, the bands, the shoutings and drunks, and the burning of Kaiser Bill in effigy created in me an uneasy feeling of a world outside my own. And the coming of the dread plague of influenza that year settled my conviction that other powers existed besides my father and mother. Nelle got the flu—as did hundreds of others in the neighborhood—but she survived. I have always attributed her almost miraculous recovery (in those times, the flu had a reputation like the bubonic plague of the Middle Ages) not as much to the candles that my father paid for in the church as to a primitive use of yet-undiscovered penicillin. A gruff old family-type doctor, after doing all he could for her, gave this magic advice, "Keep her stuffed to the gills with old green cheese, the moldier the better."

After her wobbly recovery, we moved again. My father got an excellent job as the manager of the general store back in Tampico. Away we went in the most fortunate shift of my life. My existence turned into one of those rare Huck Finn-Tom Sawyer idylls. There were woods and mysteries, life and death among the small creatures, hunting and fishing; those were the days when I learned the real riches of rags. Out of town, one way, there was a clear-bottomed creek; the other way, there was a deep and treacherous canal which we always used for swimming. It was dangerous to those who could not handle themselves in water; several times I can recall the hushed mood of the town when they brought a small covered burden home from the canal.

That big gap of two years between Neil and myself was pretty apparent by this time, and we were each traveling our own paths. Hence this was the beginning time for friends of the inseparable buddy type. With mine I covered the countryside. We had the usual number of narrow escapes and minor triumphs over nature. None was more narrow than the one Monkey Winchell and I went through. Monkey was the son of the store owner opposite my father's emporium; in those times, all proprietors and managers lived just over their stock in trade. One Saturday night I visited my friend—who got his nickname for his insatiable curiosity—ostensibly to study our Sunday School lessons. But Monkey discovered his father's pump shotgun in the closet. For no reason except curiosity, he put the butt on the floor with the barrels pointing upward and pulled the trigger. Nothing happened. Whereupon I could not stay out of the act. I pumped it once and gave it back to Monkey, telling him to try it again. Butt on the floor and pointed toward the ceiling—we knelt down and Monkey tried it again.

There was a blast like doomsday. Monkey rolled on the floor, too scared to cry. A hole had appeared in the plaster, showering down bits of mortar and lath. We heard the thunder of feet on the stairs, the yells of alarm coming rapidly nearer. When our parents came puffing up the stairs, they saw Monkey and myself on the couch in a cloud of smoke, huddled together, frantically reading our Sunday School quarterly. Above us the vast gape in the ceiling bled white drops on our heads.

My worst experience as a boy, however, was not the licking I got for that. It was a thousand times worse: the day my father bought a carload of secondhand potatoes for a personal speculation. My brother and I were ordered to the siding to sort the good potatoes from the bad. It was a unique experience. No one who has not sat in a stinking boxcar during hot summer days, gingerly gripping tubers that dissolve in the fingers with a dripping squish, emitting an odor worse than that of a decaying corpse, can possibly imagine the agony we suffered. We did this hideous chore for days. At last we got so queasy at the very look of spuds that we simply lied about the rest and dumped them all, good or bad. My father made a little money on the proposition. We got a near permanent dislike for potatoes in any form. Anyone having trouble staying on a diet should take one whiff of a spoiled potato.

Some of these tribulations were compensated for by the jeweler and his wife next door. An elderly childless couple, they took a special fancy to me. I had no grandparents and this sort of spoil-

14

ing was delightful. The jeweler's wife gave me ten cents a week as an allowance (a magnificent sum in those days) plus cookies and chocolate every afternoon. The best part was that I was allowed to dream. Many the day I spent deep in a huge rocker in the mystic atmosphere of Aunt Emma's living room with its horsehair-stuffed gargoyles of furniture, its shawls and antimacassars, globes of glass over birds and flowers, books and strange odors; many the day I remained hidden in a corner downstairs in Uncle Jim's jewelry shop with its curious relics, faint lights from gold and silver and bronze, lulled by the erratic ticking of a dozen clocks and the drone of the customers who came in.

Nelle was the dean of dramatic recitals for the countryside. It was her sole relaxation from her family and charitable duties; she executed it with the zest of a frustrated actress. She recited classic speeches in tragic tones, wept as she flung herself into the more poignant, if less talented, passages of such melodramas as *East Lynne,* and poured out poetry by the yard. Occasionally she descended to low comedy such as "Levinsky at the Wedding," but those readings were rare. Naturally I was pressed into protesting service—usually as the thing in a sheet at the Sunday School pageant with a character name such as "The Spirit of Christmas Never Was." It may be argued that my dramatic yen started at this point; my own opinion is it had a somewhat stunting effect—since it took me away from my beloved sports.

The rough reality of disorganized play had gradually invaded my dream world, supplanting relics and stuffed animals (my idol was the local taxidermist). Out in the fields, I disliked beating snakes to death because they seemed to suffer but I got a wild exhilaration out of jumping feet first into a pile-up. We played football for the first time in those years, just before I was ten. We used the immemorial rules that are standard for any gang of boys on their own.

An older and better-heeled kid got the first lopsided football in the town. We scoured the neighborhood, collecting as many

15

friends and enemies as we could—the latter being useful as opponents—and invaded the park. There was no field; no lines, no goal. Simply grass, the ball, and a mob of excited youngsters. We chose up sides, backed up to the limits of the field, and one of us kicked off. Then, screaming and waving our arms, we descended on the unlucky kid who caught it. Everyone piled on top of him, sometimes including his own team. I worshiped the wild charge down the field and the final melee—but being underneath it all, once or twice, gave me my first taste of claustrophobia. I got frightened to the point of hysteria in the darkness under the mass of writhing, shouting bodies.

I never thought seriously about retiring from the junior mayhem, but I managed to time my charge so that I was in one of the upper layers of bodies. The lure of sweat and action always pulled me back to the game—despite the fact that I was a scrawny, undersized, underweight nuisance, who insisted on getting in the way of the more skillful (such as my brother). As a result, I had a collection of the largest purplish-black bruises possible. More than once, I must have been a walking coagulation. Those were the happiest times of my life.

CHAPTER

2 Fresh in my memory is getting off the train in the middle of the snow at Christmas time to meet my aunt and uncle, who had a farm near Morrison, Illinois. We'd climb into the sleigh with hot bricks at our feet, buffalo robes over our legs, and drive off with bells jingling and the frosty wind slashing the blood into my cheeks until it seemed they would burst. In the summertime, I rode in a buggy with a fringe on top and a dashboard below to prevent the mare from kicking her heels into my lap. I remember sitting with a dozen others in a little room with breathless attention, a pair of earphones attached tightly to my head, scratching a crystal with a wire. I was listening to raspy recorded music and faint voices saying, "This is KDKA, Pittsburgh, KDKA, Pittsburgh."

When I was nine, we moved to Dixon. It was ninety miles from Chicago, ten times as big as Tampico, with the Rock River running through the middle. A small town of ten thousand—to me it was a city. It was to be home to me from that moment on until I was twenty-one. All of us have to have a place we go back to; Dixon is that place for me.

There was the life that has shaped my body and mind for all the years to come after. Sitting in the Family Theatre, watching the marvelous flickering antics of Tom Mix and William S. Hart as they foiled robbers and villains and escorted the beautiful girls to safety, waving back from their horses as they cantered into the sunset. Weeping and laughing boisterously from the second balcony at the touring plays like *What Price Glory?* that projected real emotion from a shambles of scenery over a hushed audience. Going on reading binges in the public library or in the park. Waiting and hoping for the winter freeze without snow so that we could go skating on the Rock River—a rink two hundred yards wide and endlessly long, as clear and smooth as glass—and the trick of skating for miles against the wind and then spreading the coat for the pleasure of letting the wind blow you back. Swimming and picnics in the summer, the long thoughts of spring, the pain with the coloring of the falling leaves in the autumn.

It was a good life. I never have asked for anything more, then or now. Probably the best part of it all was playing football. Sure, I played basketball, went out for track and swimming; but those were games. Football was a matter of life and death.

We lived on the south side of the Rock River, on Hennepin Avenue. We practiced football from the end of summer until past the first snow flurries, every moment we could steal from school. Across the street we punished the lawn of the O'Malleys (Eddie was my age, though George and Neil were classmates). When the O'Malleys tired of taking it, the four of us used our side lawn until that sixth sense warned us it was time to go back to the O'Malleys'. How do four kids play football? Easy—one center, one ball carrier, and two men in the defensive line. But never family against family.

By the time I got into the Dixon High School, I was panting to perform. My poor eyesight had a great deal to do with my love for football. It never occurred to me that I was dreadfully near-sighted; I simply thought that the whole world was made up of colored blobs that became distinct when I got closer—and I was sure it appeared the same way to everyone else.

My eyes were my big handicap in sports. I never cared for baseball, for example, because I was ball-shy at batting. When I stood at the plate, the ball appeared out of nowhere about two feet in front of me. I was always the last chosen for a side in any game. Then I discovered football: no little invisible ball—just another guy to grab or knock down, and it didn't matter if his face was blurred. I sat in the front row at school and still could not read the blackboard; I bluffed my lessons and got fairly good marks, considering.

What finally alerted the family to my condition was an afternoon when we were riding in the country. My brother could read the highway signs and I couldn't. I thought this was odd. I borrowed my mother's glasses. Putting them on, I suddenly saw a glorious, sharply outlined world jump into focus and shouted with delight. After that—if only to get her own back—my mother had me fitted out with huge black-rimmed spectacles.

When I picked up my mother's glasses, the miracle of seeing was beyond believing. I was astounded to find out trees had sharply defined separate leaves; houses had a definite texture and hills really made a clear silhouette against the sky. But the miracle, as miracles do, wore off. I began to hate the big glasses I had to wear; I hate them to this day.

My other liabilities were that Neil had been at Dixon High School before me and had become a regular end; also that I stood five feet three and weighed 108 pounds with weights in my pockets. They had no pants small enough to fit me. My assets, however, were one of a kind. I was one of the better ones in town at playing "Little Al" on the ice of the river in winter. The game was assassination hockey, to escape being tagged. It made me an excellent skater and even better at maneuvering my weight and sliding home-free on my back or belly; in any scrimmage, I knew my way around. But that first year, with three teams competing, I couldn't make the scrub. What was worse, two of my best friends, Dick McNicol (now vice-president of one of the better-known cereal companies) and Harold Marks (now a doctor in California) had both matured physically ahead of me and were in serious contention for team assignments, at least as high as second string.

At my size scrimmage was denied me, but I never missed a practice. Somehow, instinctively, I knew that I'd grow up someday and in the meantime I'd learn the fundamentals.

It was midseason of that third year when it happened. There

was some kind of hanky-panky going on in the center section of the "big" team and I found myself learning plays at guard among my heroes. All week long I figured I was being used to discipline or scare the regular guard into more effort. I can never describe the feeling on the following Saturday when I heard the coach in that impressive pre-game locker room hush come to right guard in the starting lineup. His next word was Reagan.

I had a good day—particularly on defense—and there I was at last, and for the rest of the season, a "regular."

Even in summer, my mind was on football. When I was fourteen, I picked up a job with a construction contractor. In those days there was no such thing as specialization, or mechanical helpers. Unions were something you only read about. One man did everything: laying floor, painting, plumbing, shingling. This particular entrepreneur paid me thirty-five cents an hour for a ten-hour day, six-day week. He put me to work digging foundations in heavy clay soil, work guaranteed to stick beef in the biceps and deltoids, and ennui in the soul. This brought about the incident which my father always called "the damnedest exhibition of laziness I ever saw in my life." He had come to pick me up at lunch hour, just as the whistle blew. At that moment I had my pick raised in the air. Without moving it another inch, I simply opened my hands, walked out from under it, and let it fall. The pick dropped behind me and stuck in the ground—an inch or so from the toes of my boss who had been checking on me. He turned around and bawled to my father, "This kid of yours can get less dirt on a shovel than any human being that's human!" But he didn't fire me. That summer of 1925 I made about two hundred dollars, my first real spending money, but already I knew it was for something else—college, if ever I was to get there.

The next summer I got a job I was to keep for seven summers; that of a lifeguard at Lowell Park, one of the two recreation areas which fronted on the river. A three-hundred-acre, naturally forested park, it was named after the poet James Russell Lowell, who wrote his famous "Ode to a Waterfowl" in the vicinity.

The Lowell family willed the park to the city. My job was not owed to any fowl but to the fact that I was willing to take fifteen dollars a week to save the lives of all and sundry.

Lifeguarding provides one of the best vantage points in the world to learn about people. During my career at the park, I saved seventy-seven people. I guarantee you they needed saving —no lifeguard gets wet without good reason. In my case it really took an emergency because my job was seven days a week, and from morning until they got tired of swimming at night. A wet suit was a real hardship and I was too money-conscious to have a spare. Not many thanked me, much less gave me a reward, and being a little money-hungry I'd done a little daydreaming about this. They felt insulted. The only money I ever got was ten dollars for diving for an old man's upper plate that he lost going down our slide.

I got to recognize that people hate to be saved: almost every one of them later sought me out and angrily denounced me for dragging them to shore. "I would have been fine if you'd let me alone," was their theme. "You made a fool out of me trying to make a hero out of yourself."

As a matter of fact, the water in the Rock River off Lowell Park was a fairly difficult spot to swim. There was a dam downstream which, when the sluices were opened, gave the ordinarily slow current a quicker tempo and deeper thrust. The bottom sloped swiftly into deep water not too far from the edge. An additional hazard was the other bank, about six hundred feet away: swimming across was a challenge—only, once started, you had to go all the way, or else. I learned the lesson that all lifeguards teach themselves—to watch for the unexpected but to keep my eye mainly on the two or three places where trouble would begin: downstream from the dock or between dock and raft.

Football, lifeguarding—I knew there was something else to that idyllic life: love and lessons. As we might have expected, Dick —my best friend, quarterback and captain of the football team— and I fell for the same girl. She was Margaret Cleaver, a sparkling brunette, the daughter of the minister of the Christian Church. Since Dick was a mere Methodist and I was one of her father's congregation, this gave me an undeserved edge. I used to look at her more than I listened to the sermons.

There was no girlish playing of one against the other by Margaret. She was (strange as it sounds) grown up enough to know we weren't any of us grown up enough to call this anything but friendship, and on that basis it was perfectly natural to accompany one or the other of us to the prom or the football banquet. Me!—I was in love and if it hadn't been for her common sense I could easily have wallowed in juvenile jealousy. Youth being what it is, however, there came a day when Margaret's feelings for me underwent a change. We *were* in love, as much as that is possible at such callow years. Now with her innate honesty, the problem of our mutual friend Dick had to be faced—but, as I say, he was and is a rare person. He had seen what we thought was hidden. The senior banquet was coming up and it was his turn to be Margaret's escort, by the terms of our arrangement. With a simple honesty that could solve a lot of adult problems, if only adults could be so grown up, Dick came to me and said, "I think Margaret has made her choice and you should ask her to the banquet." Disappear triangle, but add one very wonderful friendship.

At that time college was far from the accepted thing. The country was sagging a little. But jobs were plentiful, though beginning to tighten up. The notion had not yet appeared that education was a fad in which everyone should join; a Bachelor of Arts seemed very far away and a Doctor of Philosophy was revered as something almost unattainable. The difference, of course, was one of economics: colleges cost money. Many folks reasoned, maybe the children weren't worth the $3,600 investment and the four years thrown away when a man could be out on a real job. My brother Neil, for one, thought college was a waste of time; also an impossibility, if you had to do it on your own.

But I had enough of working, except for my beloved lifeguarding during the summer. Even in that summer when the newspapers were trumpeting about the good days ahead, the lower echelons of workers were hurting. Ever since my first job at age fourteen I had been saving for college—in fact, for a particular college. While still in those grade school days, my hero had been the high school fullback and captain, one Garland Waggoner, son of the minister Margaret's father was later to replace. He went to Eureka College, where for four more years he starred in football. I had never seen Eureka College but it was my choice. I don't know what might have happened if Margaret had chosen another school, but I didn't have that problem to face. Her older sisters had gone to Eureka and she was slated to go there, too, probably because of her father and the fact that Eureka was a Christian Church college of the same family group as Texas Christian University—but there the family resemblance ends.

Eureka had about 250 students—roughly 130 boys and 120 girls, enough to make any sex competition interesting. It was situated in the small town of Eureka, about twenty miles from Peoria. Poor and struggling, it was top-heavy with tradition. It had been founded by one Ben Major, who had led a wagon train from the East to the very spot. The legends said that old Ben had sunk an ax into the stump of the first tree he hewed down and said, "Here we'll build our school!" So they did: the first college building was finished before any of the settlers' houses were completed. Eureka had the reputation of being the oldest coeducational institution west of the Alleghenies.

I arrived at Eureka in the fall of 1928, which was the period marking the end of raccoon coats and things called collegiate. Thanks to Margaret's folks and the boyfriend of one of her sisters, I wasn't making a cold entrance but was already slated for the Teke house—Tau Kappa Epsilon, one of the several national fraternities on the campus.

I fell head over heels in love with Eureka. I still think, after years of crisscrossing the United States, that it is one of the love-liest colleges in existence. It seemed to me then, as I walked up the path, to be another home. There were five big main buildings, arranged in a semicircle, built of red brick with white-framed windows, a style that is an American reminiscence of English Georgian architecture. Walls were covered with friendly ivy, and the whole framed with huge elms and rolling green lawns.

I wanted to get in that school so badly that it hurt when I thought about it. The obstacle was money—not my marks. I had never bothered to do much more in Dixon than remain eligible for the athletic teams—but in those days a diploma was all you needed and I had that. I was broke. Nevertheless, I had some reputation as a swimmer and some as a football player. The tuition was $180 a year and I had brought with me about $400 from my few summers' earnings.

As it happened, things went my way. The officials gave me a scholarship for half my tuition and a job for board. This was the maximum in help because of the need for spreading jobs over as many students as possible. Payment for my room would have to come out of my savings. My job was washing dishes in the fraternity house, later a somewhat more romantic post called "cleansing tableware" in a girls' domitory. In my junior and senior years I managed to earn my way as the swimming-pool life-guard and official coach.

In that yesterday of which I speak, small schools like ours competed with the biggest for talent and there wasn't a great gap between. Bradley Tech could play Iowa of the Big Ten on even terms, and a week later we'd be forcing Bradley to the limit for a fourth quarter win. No conference furnished more players to big-time pro ball than did that league of prairie colleges. In basketball I don't think a Big Ten team had ever beaten a Little Nineteen team. A measure of quality was the fact that in my sophomore year Wesleyan beat Eureka by two points for the title, and that Wesleyan team was chosen to play the University

24

of Pittsburgh National Champions in an exhibition for the Coaches Association meeting.

At Eureka, I was getting ready to save the day. Dixon High School wasn't tiny and football was pretty important. Eureka had gone through two disastrous seasons, so I anticipated quite a welcome. Someone once said, "If you don't remember your freshman year in college and get a little red around the ears, you didn't have a normal freshman year." Mine must have been normal as hell.

It's tough to go from lordly senior to lowly freshman and even tougher to go from first string end to the end of the bench before the whistle blows for the first game. I managed to accomplish this all by myself. But in my mind I had help—heaven forbid I should take the blame! I told everyone who would listen that the coach didn't like me, I was the victim of unreasoning prejudice. I needed a damn good kick in the keister, but how can you kick something that's permanently planted on a bench?

My sin would haunt me until graduation, but I really waited thirty-five years for the chance to do a little something to square the debt and diminish some of the red around my ears.

Not too long ago I journeyed from California to Northern Illinois University, where I spoke at a testimonial dinner marking Ralph McKinzie's retirement from coaching. He was finishing his career at this university after many years at Eureka, where he had played as well as coached and where he was a legend in his own time. A farm boy from Oklahoma, Mac had followed his high school coach to Eureka. World War I interrupted his education but he returned in 1920 to win twelve letters for football, basketball, and baseball—as well as a collection of gold balls symbolic of championship. Eureka still cherishes the Peoria headline that proclaimed in two-inch type MCKINZIE BEATS BRADLEY, 52 TO 0, and he had, scoring every one of the fifty-two points himself. When Coach Pritchard (for whom Eureka's gynmasium is named) retired, it was inevitable that "Little Mac" should be named coach.

We had a special spirit at Eureka that bound us all together, much as a poverty-stricken family is bound. Like so many small colleges with church affiliations, Eureka was perpetually broke. Tuition fees, of course, made no pretense of covering the actual cost of an education—these schools exist to serve. Church contributions, gifts from alumni and friends, and proceeds from an inadequate endowment are supposed to make up the difference. When the depression dried up these sources we were to see our professors go for months without pay and the small town merchants extend credit for the necessities of life. Sometimes the college paid something on account with actual produce and foodstuffs from a farm which was part of the endowment.

The new president of Eureka tripped over the panic button and announced a plan for saving the college. He favored a plan which called for such a drastic cutback academically that many juniors and seniors would have been cut off without the courses needed for graduation in their chosen majors. Needless to say, the faculty would have been decimated and Eureka would have lost its high academic rating.

Looking back, I realize now that he sincerely felt his course was proper. However, he had persuaded the board of trustees to go along without any thought of consulting students or faculty. They, knowing this was equivalent to cutting out the heart of the college, responded with a roar of fury. That was how I came to participate in my first strike.

I'm afraid I get a bit smug when I contrast that collegiate strike to some of the "panty raids" and fevered picketing of these more modern times. Ours was no riotous burning in effigy but a serious, well-planned program, engineered from the ground up by students but with the full support and approval of almost every professor on the campus. A counterplan was offered to and rejected by the president. Then a petition was presented to the board, demanding his resignation. The board met on the last Saturday before Thanksgiving vacation.

The football team met Illinois College that afternoon. It was

26

one of the best games no one ever saw. I was on the bench as usual, but the team on the field—which had had a good season without me—played one of those thrilling, "if anybody makes a mistake that's it" games. Lump Watts, a classmate of mine—a colored boy who had been all-state fullback at Kewanee High—set a conference record by punting one that carried over eighty yards in the air. Late in the fourth quarter he won the game with a drop kick of better than fifty yards. Through some technical error regarding registering of the feat, this kick has been kept out of the national records, but he did it for three points. To digress for a moment, I often daydream of what the next three years might have been if Lump hadn't dropped out of school—a depression victim. Today he has his own successful trucking company.

I wasn't exaggerating much when I said no one saw the game. The crowd was there, all right, but our academic controversy had attracted the attention of the metropolitan papers. In the second half, newsboys hit the stands with extras headlining the fact that our petition to the board had been denied. Looking back from the bench was like looking at a card stunt: everyone was hidden by a newspaper. A few even showed up along the bench. The win over Illinois was the least-celebrated victory a hungry Eureka would ever know.

My participation on the strike committee was as a representative of the freshman class and, as such, I was far from a ringleader. Nevertheless, Sunday was not a day of rest and a lot of us got our first taste of running from persistent reporters. Don't ask me about our spy system, but we had informers—and most of us on the committee never knew their identity. Word came that the next move would be a long board meeting the night before Thanksgiving vacation, at which the trustees would adopt the president's plan. All of us would be home for a week, and we'd return, with passions cooled, to a *fait accompli*. Sure enough, the president and the board met—but not a student left for home. We all remained on the campus, waiting until midnight for the summit conference to break up.

CHAPTER

3

When the trustees came out that night with
gloomy dachshund faces, our committee was waiting. We buttonholed them for the news. They
told us the facts, their intended reticence overcome by surprise. The old college bell started
tolling—it was as prearranged as Paul Revere's
ride. From dormitories and fraternity houses the students came,
almost all of the faculty from their homes—until the chapel was
filled. Everyone but our committee was clad only in nightclothes
under hastily donned overcoats. And this was my moment to
come off the bench. It had been decided that the motion for putting our plan into effect should be presented by a freshman, because the charge could be made that upper classmen had a selfish
interest.

Very simply, our plan was that we would go home on vacation
and we would return to the campus on the day vacation ended,
but no one would attend a single class, and this strike would
continue until our demands were met. The plan was simple, but
I'm afraid my motion wasn't. I'd been told that I should sell the
idea so there'd be no doubt of the outcome. I reviewed the history
of our patient negotiations with due emphasis on the devious
manner in which the trustees had sought to take advantage of
us. I discovered that night that an audience has a feel to it and, in
the parlance of the theater, that audience and I were together.
When I came to actually presenting the motion there was no
need for parliamentary procedure: they came to their feet with a

roar—even the faculty members present voted by acclamation. It was heady wine. Hell, with two more lines I could have had them riding through "every Middlesex village and farm"—without horses yet.

Back in Dixon on vacation, another incident was to take place that would be a beginning link in a later pattern. Margaret's family took us to a nearby larger city one night to see the supposedly original London company play *Journey's End*. War-weary, young but bitterly old Captain Stanhope carried me into a new world. For two and a half hours I was in that dugout on the Western front—but in some strange way, I was also on stage. More than anything in life I wanted to speak his lines to the young replacement officer who misunderstands and sees callousness in his effort to hide grief. That deep silence, the slow coming to his feet, then the almost whispered, "My God, so that's it! You think I don't care! You bloody little swine, you think I don't care—the only one who knew—who really understood." He was, of course, referring to the death that day of the beloved older officer. If I had only realized it, nature was trying to tell me something—namely, that my heart is a ham loaf.

After Thanksgiving, we put our strike plan into effect. It was the essence of simplicity. Few students attended any classes at all. All the professors attended them, marked all the absentees present, then went home. The college ground to a standstill. Snow came: we indulged in skating and sledding and tobogganing but nary a class. Every afternoon the strike committee sponsored a dance. It ended at four o'clock for basketball practice.

Not once did we neglect our studies. To have done so would have been to contradict the whole spirit of what we were fighting for. The committee set up regular study hours and enforced them; we concocted our own assignments and worked them out (and in some cases were ahead of the regular study schedule).

News of our unique strike spread. It hit the headlines locally and spread across the country. Reporters swarmed over the campus. Unperturbed, the strike committee set up a regular press headquarters and a public relations office. The president and the students fought a battle of the mimeograph. We had a faculty-student panel to issue regular bulletins on our progress.

The publicity helped, but in the end it was our policy of polite resistance that brought victory. After a week, the new president resigned. A high-level conference was held. Eureka got back into the business of education, with the faculty agreeing to withhold any salary demands for an indefinite period.

The results of our winning that strike were notable. The four classes on the campus became the most tightly knit groups ever to graduate from Eureka. Campus spirit bloomed. A remarkably close bond with the faculty developed. The marks of the strikers were not notably improved by our layoff, but we found we achieved a lot more personal attention—plus an education in human nature and the rights of man to universal education that nothing could erase from our psyches.

At Eureka, I had assumed I would play basketball. I went to the first practice, looked through the door, adjusted my glasses, looked again, turned, and walked away. I saw fellows doing things with a basketball I just didn't believe. This was my introduction to basketball as it was played in the southern tip of Illinois and Indiana. One boy on our squad never saw a football until he came to college. His high school played schedules of more than eighty games a season and practiced the year round. One small high school scrounged up fifteen men for their team total. They entered two invitational tournaments, sending eight men to the hardest and seven to the other—each team captained by one of a pair of brothers. They won both. One of those brothers was now a freshman at Eureka.

I completed my freshman year but only just. I went back to Lowell Park and lifeguarding that summer. When the fall came, I had decided that Eureka was a nice place but it would have to struggle along without me. I wasn't going back. First of all, I was still sulking over football and McKinzie and, second, I had only the two hundred dollars I'd earned that summer. Eureka's total help could only cover board and half tuition—therefore my two hundred dollars wasn't enough.

Once again fate stepped in with a kindness I've never believed I deserved. In a sad last date, I'd said good-bye to Margaret the night before her departure for Eureka. The next morning didn't dawn, it floated in—and surveyor's crews don't work in the rain. That doesn't make much sense unless I tell you I'd gotten a job as rodman with a surveyor who'd talked to me about a scholarship to Wisconsin (his alma mater) for rowing, if I stayed out of school a year.

One quick call to Margaret and I was a passenger in their car for the trip to Eureka—just for a visit. By the time we got there the rain was gone, the air zinged every time your breath touched it, and somehow it kept smelling like liniment and football.

McKinzie (that fellow who hated me) showed me the new football uniforms for the season. Suddenly I lost my taste for rowing one of those narrow-gauge rowboats at Wisconsin—but I was stuck with my two hundred dollars and no job. God bless little schools. In twenty minutes I was offered a job washing dishes in the girls' dormitory, the college volunteered to defer their half of the tuition until after graduation (my first experience with credit), and I made a call home to tell them I was going to college.

"I've got news for you," Nelle said. "Your brother Neil doesn't think college is a joke any more. He doesn't want to work, he wants to be educated. He wants to come to Eureka."

I couldn't believe it—my brother (who was Neil only to our mother; he had picked up the nickname Moon in high school and it follows him to this day) was a sophisticate in my eyes. I could see him at some large university where a speakeasy wasn't out of reach, but not in the mellow, small-town, ivy-covered atmosphere of Eureka, where not too many years before dancing had been prohibited on the campus. But Nelle was convinced and, in turn, convincing. I promised to call her back.

Over to the gym I went on a second trip. I laid it on the line to McKinzie. Moon had played end on a championship team and now had been out of school three years. When I called home again, Moon had a job in the Teke house kitchen, which meant he would be pledged in that fraternity, and the college would defer his tuition. That bothered me a little because he'd never paid me back any small loan in his life, and I didn't like to think he might someday treat Eureka the same way. As it turned out, I didn't have to worry—three years in a cement plant had been quite a course in growing up.

I was a long time finding out all that had happened to change Moon's mind about going to college. Working in a grimy atmosphere of limestone dust, he was teamed with an elderly immigrant who could barely manage our language. This oddly assorted pair became friends and exchanged information as men will about their families and backgrounds. The old man constantly queried Moon as to why he wasn't in college as I was. Then one day very quietly he presented Moon with the alternative to college. "Look at me—ve'll alvays vork together, chust you and me, and zomeday you'll be chust like me—isn't that nize?" He never mentioned it again—he didn't have to.

That sophomore year everything seemed to brighten all across my life. Unexpectedly I fell into one of the great experiences, one of the kind that takes you over if you will let it, until you lose all sense of time and space. I came into tempo with the curious rhythm which is college life, the silly, the serious, and the sentimental. I said Eureka was bound by tradition but traditions aren't all noble—some are just fun and funny.

There was the big gala watermelon hunt. We herded a few carefully indoctrinated freshmen out into the country by night and indicated a plot where we could swipe some of the bulging fruit from the vine. Tiptoeing through the patch to build up suspense, and at a prearranged location, the place exploded with light. A shotgun blast went off. An upper classman near me collapsed with a scream, gripping his chest, red fluid flowing slowly between his fingers. "I'm shot," he screamed. "My God, I *am* shot!" To add to his overacting, a flashlight gave a quick look at his catsup-covered midsection. A well-trained supporting cast, using some version of subliminal selling, shoved the freshmen toward the road, screaming, "Get help—a doctor—run back to town!" Other things were said, but these were the key words, repeated often enough to stick.

The frosh took off like leaves before the wind, propelled by fear and charity. We ran a few steps, then let them get ahead and watched them disappear. We hiked back to town by another and shorter road.

This particular night the freshmen ran nearly eight miles, probably setting some unofficial records (we never bothered to time them). But one fellow had retained his wits long enough to duck into a farmhouse on the main road halfway back to the college. He had wakened the old boy and they phoned a doctor in town, giving the location of the shooting and all the lurid details. Through the night, on his errand of mercy, sped the doctor. The slower return trip gave him time to do a little two-plus-two-comes-up-college type of figuring. At the end of that month, each fraternity on the campus received a bill. It read: "For battle, murder, and sudden death at the watermelon patch—$10." Each fraternity paid without protest.

There was the custom of "kegging." Eureka was the only place I've ever known where you could walk down a street with your girl on one arm and a blanket on the other without starting a scandal. You headed for open country and that wasn't hard to find because any point in that lovely little town was only a short walk from plowed ground. Of course food was taken, and a picnic supper was part of the evening program.

Dances in the gym and various fraternity houses were fun, but finding privacy for philosophic discussions and such always presented a problem. Local geography contributed to Eureka's traditional solution for this problem—the cemetery was a three-minute walk from the campus. Everyone had his favorite grave, usually with a large enough tombstone to provide a backrest for two and a sizable pool of shadow.

Personally, I'm sure that the ghosts that must have always hovered over us looked down in a kindly way, perhaps simpering over our worldly visit. But if we felt they didn't, we could always turn it to advantage by telling our date for the night a few grisly tales; she usually gripped the teller hard enough to substitute for a hug. One of the minor ceremonies attached to such a night was the fraternity whistle. Some brother might feel lonely or scared; if he did, all he had to do was to pucker up for a trill. It was wonderful to hear the response from all parts of the cemetery, to see the tousled little heads popping up from places you were sure were deserted except for katydids.

Oh, it was a small town, a small school, with small doings. It was in a poor time without money, without ceremony, with pleasant thoughts of the past to balance fears of the uncertain future. But it somehow provided the charm and enchantment which alone can make a memory of a school something to cherish. Those were the nights when we spent all of twenty cents on a date: two big cherry phosphates at the drug counter (with the big colored jars of water lighted up) and a walk home. Or when we danced in somebody's house or in the fraternity living rooms under the dimmest of lights, while the chaperones—always old Eureka grads who had met each other this way themselves—took a turn around outside or just dozed. Or when we devoured home-made cake and repressed heartburnings of a different sort as we strolled under the campus elms. And there was the wonderful thing of inviting older people who knew some jokes and the ways of the world and how to talk to us without condescending; scrambling eggs before an open fire and talking about Hoover and his calm statements on prosperity; whipping up the hot chocolate and shaking our heads over this upstart Franklin D. Roosevelt who was beginning to criticize from New York.

The start of my sophomore year was the year of the great market crash, but the only crash Eureka was interested in was that of body against body—and the bodies were getting bigger and

34

better. As I've already indicated, the depression didn't wait until the black of October, 1929, to actually begin. Out in the farm belt jobs had been disappearing as money grew harder to come by. The result was that a number of onetime college dropouts and guys like Moon who had passed up college for weekly paychecks were choosing the campus over the breadline.

With a student body of 250, divided roughly half and half between girls and boys, there was plenty of room in the grandstand because we had five full teams on the field—and I was on number five. My attitude had changed but not for the better. Now I was mad, and in my anger had decided the only way to revenge myself on Mac was to make the team. I was not only nearsighted: my vision was limited to one square yard of turf—the one occupied by the right guard on the first team, next to Captain Pebe Leitch, right tackle, fraternity brother, and something of an idol. I'm a sucker for hero worship to this day, and teaming with Pebe in mayhem on various and sundry opponents was my dream of Valhalla. He was an older than average senior, having spent a few years at work before coming to college. He could have played on any team in the country.

Among the new enrollees that autumn, and typical of the freedom of our conference, was one Enos "Bud" Cole. You knew immediately that Bud had a big-time flavor, even though it was concentrated in a small package. He had earned his freshman numerals at Northwestern and then had absented himself from school while he played three years of pro ball. One of Mac's generation had steered him to Eureka, and he had the quarterback post sewed up on arrival.

Our fraternity had pledged him and we were friends as well as potential "brothers in the bond." Once again I was to know the blessing of a helping hand at a key moment in my life. A scrimmage was scheduled between the first and second teams with frequent switches in the lineups to provide a kind of audition for some of the aspirants. Bud Cole was sidelined by an old knee injury so that when, in the course of events, I was tagged to play

35

right end on the second team, he became a personal coach for me. Now, however, Bud made the decisions and I became a purely physical means to the ends he dictated. Watching the signal caller and the still rusty backs on the varsity, he would whisper, "Knife in—they are going the other way." Doing as he ordered, I was in on the ball carrier three plays in a row. "Now," he hissed, "go straight across—they'll try a reverse to suck you in." Of course he was right, and by following his orders I was as effective as a traffic light in halting all movement around end.

That night as Pebe and I left the locker room to start our twilight walk to the Teke house, we met Mac. He and Pebe exchanged a few observations and as we parted, Mac (my enemy) turned to me. "Keep it up," he said. "You are doing fine." Don't ask me why, but I couldn't speak for the next few blocks—not with a football-sized lump in my throat. I don't know what Mac majored in, but I'll give him A in Psychology. The next day I was guard on the second team, but this still wasn't the place for the "lived happily ever after" line.

The first game was won without me. The team was winning—why change the lineup? Of course, I didn't endorse that philosophy, but no sulking now. There were seven games left and I meant to play in all of them.

The following week it rained. In a cold drizzle we worked at learning a new set of plays. Over and over, against no opposition, we ran through these plays, fixing our individual assignments in our memories. One play in particular, a wide end sweep, depended on the right guard backing out of the line and leading the interference—his target the defensive halfback. This was an era of watch-charm guards, created from converted backs and ends in an effort to get the speed necessary for running interference. At Notre Dame, Rockne was to make history with a 158-pound All-American guard named Metzger. It didn't make me feel too small at all at 175.

Every coach has a few unofficial helpers and Mac was no exception. A former "great" who had followed his Eureka career by

36

playing three years at Oregon State spent his autumn afternoons as a volunteer advisor and coach. (If the above line leaves you puzzled, remember this was a day when Army and Navy, as well as many engineering and agricultural schools, legally played college graduates.)

Mac was quite emphatic in his instructions to me that the play could only work if the right guard upended the defensive half. Suddenly our "old grad" galloped over into the center of a rain-slick, skinned baseball diamond that intruded on our practice field. "Here I am," he called, "I'm the defensive half—come get me!" I was walking on eggs at this point, fearful that any wrong move on my part could upset my chance of making the first team. Anxiously I turned to Mac. "You just want me to go out there?" I asked. "You don't really want me to hit him, do you?" Before Mac could answer, the "old grad" called the turn. "Sure, take me down, if you can. That's what I'm here for!" he yelled. Mac said nothing.

The ball was snapped, and we rolled out to the right. Now I was in the lead, angling toward the sideline. Ahead of me and on a collision course was still-agile, two hundred odd pounds of "old grad." Our paths were forming two sides of a thirty-degree angle. Some place between the pitcher's mound and third base I took off. Never before or since did I throw such a block. I hit him solidly. It seemed as if the unofficial coach was in the air long enough for me to recite "Mary had a little lamb." He came down in the vicinity of the third base coaching box and there he stayed, while I returned, wordless and scared, to the huddle. Then he rose and quietly limped off the field. Mac seemed to be having a coughing spell over at the corner of the bleachers. On the following Saturday, I started—and for the next three seasons averaged all but two minutes of every game.

I was investigating a new, wonderful world, possibly more fascinating than any other, the world of drama. In the Dixon High School I had been lucky enough to be under the instruction of a new English teacher named B. J. Fraser. He was a bespectacled, slim, rather quiet man, with a wry sense of humor. He had the chore of teaching drama, together with English. From him I learned almost all of what I know about acting today (and if the people back there will quit shouting, "That's not much!" I'll be quite happy). Fraser had the knack of quietly leading us into a performance, of making us think our roles instead of acting them out mechanically.

Our class was the guinea pig for this revolutionary idea. I got my best role when I was a high school junior. I played Ricky, the young son in Philip Barry's play, *You and I*. My father was Dick McNicol. We had surprise on our side since our parents weren't prepared for the change of pace in the usual high school dramatic presentations—but even so the reaction was a tribute to B. J. and his confidence in a bunch of teen-age kids.

The next year I was the villain in George Bernard Shaw's *Captain Applejack,* and I learned that heroes are more fun. As old Eddie Foy once said, "Sing pretty, act pretty, pretty things they enjoy." All of this commenced to create in me a personality schizo-split between sports and the stage. The fact was, I suppose, that I just liked showing off.

At Eureka I had continued much the same career by joining the dramatic society and enrolling in the dramatics course which was part of the curriculum in English. Here too I was lucky because a new teacher, Miss Johnson, was a sister-under-the-skin to B. J., as far as the stage was concerned. A favorite role was that of the young brother-hero of *The Brat*. Here my writer-brother takes in a young girl from the street to reform her—a rough rewrite of Shaw's *Pygmalion* (which was, of course, a rewrite of the Greek legend). The high spot of the play and my performance comes as the stuffed-shirt brother is about to throw the girl back into the street after exposing her to a better, more attractive life—and the young, attractively drunk playboy brother (me) comes to the rescue.

It was during this that I contracted a disease I have since learned to call "leadingladyitis." In this case it was aggravated by the

38

fact that the leading lady was a senior, and every boy has to have at least one experience of an older woman in his life. Actually, it is a theatrical phenomenon and comes about through the process of living a part to a certain extent. In this way you begin to see the other performer in the light of the role being played. In my case, it was short-lived because we had two weeks' rehearsal and one performance. Today, however, if I could give one bit of advice to youngsters starting out in theater or movies I'd say: don't marry your leading man or lady until you've done another role opposite someone else. Leadingladyitis is an infatuation that won't hold up, once the play is over and you each go back to playing yourselves.

CHAPTER

4
A way of life was ending and it was hard for me to
see it as also a beginning. The campus was so
beautiful it hurt that June afternoon when we,
as graduating seniors, stood in a circle holding a
long chain of woven ivy taken from the old brick
buildings. In keeping with tradition the chain
was cut, marking our separation from school and each other.

Fortunately I'd have a brief transition period, a sort of decompression chamber, to ease me out of one world and into the other. I was broke and in debt and I still didn't know what I wanted to do, so there would be one last summer of lifeguarding at Lowell Park, where I knew I could save the usual two hundred dollars.

Our family didn't exactly come from the wrong side of the tracks, but we were certainly always within sound of the train whistles. I remember my frustration many years later, walking through the darkness outside the old Hollywood Legion Stadium after a bitter Screen Actors Guild meeting at which I'd presided. There in the dark I heard an actress telling her friend that Ronald Reagan didn't understand their problems because he didn't know what it was like to work for only fifty-five dollars a day. My father never made more than fifty-five dollars *a week* in his whole life. I remember only one new car (a Chevrolet) in a lifetime of buying secondhand. My first long pants were my brother's hand-me-downs, a practice that went on until I outgrew him.

40

Dad's economic high-water mark had been reached in Dixon where he was a partner in the Fashion Boot Shop. Actually it was one of those work-capital partnerships in which he furnished the work and managerial skill and his former Tampico boss put up the capital. Jack was on a salary with some arrangement I never understood whereby, in a distant day, he would have earned a half interest in the business. The depression made sure that day would never dawn.

Nelle went to work in a dress shop, sales and alterations, for fourteen dollars a week. Jack took to the road as a shoe salesman, first at a salary, then on a drawing account against commissions. For a time he managed a small store for a cheap shoe chain outfit. This meant living in Springfield, Illinois, while Nelle held the fort in Dixon, two hundred miles to the north—with Moon and me at Eureka, halfway between. On one football trip we stayed overnight in Springfield. (It was quite a tussle convincing Mac that we wanted out to see our father, but we solved the problem by bringing him back to have dinner with the team.) Remembering the loving good taste of the store in Dixon, we at least had some conception of what he felt serving as manager and sole clerk of this hole-in-the-wall with its garish orange paper ads plastered over the windows and front and one cheap bench with iron armrests to separate the customers, if there was more than one at a time.

We were all home together for Christmas that last year of mine in college. On Christmas Eve, Moon and I were headed out on our dates when a special delivery arrived for Jack. I can still see the tiny apartment living room and Jack reading the single blue page the envelope contained. Without raising his head he quietly remarked, "Well, it's a hell of a Christmas present." The blue page was the traditional blue slip: he was fired. Before that year was out, I would send fifty dollars home from college, to apply on the grocery bill so credit could go on. Jack, I'm sure, never knew—but women are more practical and not bothered by un-

41

necessary pride, so Nelle had written me exactly what the situation was.

It was summer—the summer that would see FDR nominated. In our solid Republican country the Reagans were Democrats, and Jack had pinned his hopes on a reward for toiling in the political vineyard. He was busy, he believed in what he was doing, and he brought a lot of business sense to his volunter political chores. I was trying to reassure myself that I had prospects too. Over the years I had become a fixture among the families who regularly vacationed at the lodge. Most of them were from Chicago and many of them were second-generation lodge patrons—some had even met their mates and fallen in love on these year-after-year vacations. Their children were growing up, accepting Lowell Park as the normal way to spend a summer. Every morning they would descend on the beach for swimming lessons, and their grateful parents had made noises from time to time, like "when you are out of school, come see me."

However, the plain truth was—they weren't making those noises now. Again it was the mark of the depression with every man, no matter how high his station, worried about keeping his own job. The exception to this was the Altschuler family from Kansas City. Helen Altschuler, a former Dixon girl, arrived each summer, bringing two small daughters to visit their grandparents. Her husband, Sid, commuted for frequent long weekends and one vacation period. As usual, my friendship with them grew out of teaching the girls to swim.

Sid brought my future into the conversation one golden summer evening, sitting on the edge of the pier. He uttered what were not only hopeful words for me but what was literally the first note of optimism I'd heard about the state of the nation. He said, "This depression isn't going to last forever and smart businessmen are willing to take on young men who can learn their business in order to have trained manpower on hand when things start to roll." After a pause he asked, "What do you think you'd like to do?"

42

There it was—the question for which I had no answer. All I could do was say, "I don't know."

Fortunately he had no intention of letting it drop there. "That's the one thing I can't help you with," he said. "You'll have to come up with the answer to that one yourself. But," he continued, "I have connections in several lines. When you determine what line of work you want to get in, let me know—and if it's in one of those areas where I can help, I'll get you a job."

For the next several days and sleepless nights I truly faced my future with the realization that no good fairy would whisper in my ear and answer the question of what did I want to do. Out of the things that Sid had talked about came a new approach. No longer did I speculate about a paycheck and security. I really wrestled with the problem of what I would be happy doing for the next few decades.

In my junior year at Eureka our indefatigable Miss Ellen Marie Johnson had entered us in the annual one-act play contest at Northwestern University's School of Speech. This was the famous Eva le Gallienne Competition, and none of us really expected more than a polite rejection. Hundreds of colleges and universities from all over the United States entered and were weeded out, until finally an even dozen were invited to come to the university and stage their plays. Maybe it was Miss Johnson and her courageous selection of Edna St. Vincent Millay's fantasy, *Aria da Capo;* maybe it was just the free-swinging spirit our little school had—but we became one of the honored dozen, the only school not boasting a full drama department even to be selected. This was a contest more accustomed to competitors like Princeton's famous Triangle Club and the Yale Playhouse. Ours was really a home-grown effort, with Grecian costumes copied from our history books and sewed together by coeds in the various sororities. Quarterback Bud Cole and I played the Greek shepherd boys who carry the anti-war plot. My high spot was a death scene wherein I was strangled by Bud. No actor can ask for more. Dying is the way to live in the theater.

No Oscar show will ever be as thrilling to me as that final night when our little band of Greeks came in second on this first venture into the big time. But more was in store for me. We were still sitting in stunned ecstasy when my name was called. I stumbled down the aisle to join five other collegiate thespians and learned for the first time there were individual "Oscars" as well as rewards for team effort. The six of us had been selected for honors. Later the head of Northwestern's Drama Department sent for me and asked if I'd ever considered the stage as a career. I hadn't.

Preparing to face Sid Altschuler, I knew what my answer had to be: I wanted some form of show business. Actually I wanted show business, period, but the problem was how to go about it. Broadway and Hollywood were as inaccessible as outer space. I began to wrestle with the idea of some plan that would sound practical to a man like Sid. Remember, this was a time and place where announcing you wanted to be an actor could result in a sympathetic committee calling on your parents to suggest a suitable institution.

There was show business closer to home than Broadway and Hollywood—radio—and its big-time center was then Chicago. Quin Ryan had created a new profession by broadcasting play-by-play descriptions of football games. All over the country a little band of pioneers were as famous as the great teams and athletes they described: Graham MacNamee, Ted Husing, and Pat Flanagan. Once at a fraternity stunt show I had supplied the voice from backstage for a supposed football broadcast and, like my ice-cream scoop patter at the park, I could launch into a rapid-fire routine of "Here they come out of the huddle up to the line of scrimmage—a hike over to the left, the ball is snapped," as long as anyone would listen.

All of this was easier to say to Sid than, "I want to be an actor." When I had stated my case, he not unexpectedly said, "Well, you've picked a line in which I have no connections."

In a way, however, I'd come through on one of Sid's requests; I had told him what I wanted to do, so he still had something for

44

me. "You've picked a sound industry and one that should have hundreds of undreamed-of directions you can follow to a great future, once you are in. That's the important thing now—getting in, so start knocking on doors, tell anyone who'll listen that you believe you have a future in the business, and you'll take any kind of job, even sweeping floors, just to get in."

When the beach closed, I told Nelle my plan; I would go down to Eureka with Moon and hitchhike to Chicago from there, keeping her informed of my whereabouts. In Eureka some of my classmates returned to help in the pledging of a new crop of Tekes, and did a little ribbing about the grandiose nature of my ambition. In an effort to top them I made a confident boast, with the confidence all phony. "If I'm not making five thousand a year when I'm five years out of college," I said, "I'll consider these four years here were wasted." Well, at least I got a laugh. You must remember five thousand a year in those days was the novelist's way of describing a man as eminently successful. Actually I made good on that desperation shot and in exactly five years. But by then five thousand wasn't as big as it sounded on that autumn day in 1932.

Margaret's father was now the minister of the church in Eureka, so my trip down was far more than a farewell to Moon. How could we know it would truly be a farewell to the romance of youth? Margaret was to start teaching in a small high school and, as our lives traveled into diverging paths, we would find that it was true that before and after age twenty-one, people are often different. At any rate, our lovely and wholesome relationship did not survive growing up.

Thanks to an ex-Eurekan studying medicine in Chicago, I had a bed at his medical fraternity, but the sun was still high so NBC was first stop. A pretty receptionist informed me the program director only interviewed on Thursday. So already I'd learned something—on other stops I would ask for the program director. Of course, at the doctors' pad I related this first incident with slight alterations, so it came out, "I have an appointment Thursday

45

at NBC." Just hearing myself say it that way made me feel better.

The next few days took the bloom off the rose: CBS in the Wrigley Building, where I pushed my nose against the glass windows of the visitors' gallery to watch sleek, self-confident announcers step up to mikes and inform a listening world this was "The WBBM Air Theater, Wrrrrigley Building, Chicago." WGN, and then on down to stations I had to look up in the phone book. I couldn't afford cabs and I was afraid of the damn buses—as a matter of fact, the city itself scared the bejesus out of me. Everybody seemed to know where they were going and what they were doing, and I could get lost just looking for a men's room.

Thursday began to grow in my mind as really a definite appointment. So far I hadn't been in any station long enough to make my pitch about the industry's future and my willingness to sweep floors. But the girl had said, "They interview on Thursday." On Thursday I was there—back where I'd started at NBC. No one ushered me into an inner sanctuary. Instead, a nicely dressed and nice-appearing lady came out and led me to one of the divans in the reception room. Assistant, possibly, secretary. Probably she too was one of the anonymous benefactors in my saga and I wish I could meet her again to say thanks. She let me tell my story, she even asked enough questions to learn something about college and the play contest. Then she said, "Look, I think you've every right to try for a place in radio and to feel you have something to offer, but you are going at it the wrong way."

I was all ears. I'd been waiting for someone to throw me a bone all week, and she was at least offering a pat on the head. "This is the big time," she continued. "No one in the city wants to take a chance on inexperience. Go out in what we call the sticks—we shouldn't but we do—and try some of the smaller stations. They can't afford to compete with us for experienced talent, so they are often willing to give a newcomer a chance." As she rose to go back to her good fairy castle, she added, "I think you will make it —come back and see me after you have some experience."

Hitchhiking home the hundred miles from Chicago was a

frustrating experience (block number one). The rides were short with long waits in between. By late afternoon a drizzle had set in (block number two). Finally I did a thirty-mile stretch with a fellow who told me, somewhat unnecessarily, he'd been trapping skunks (block number three and you don't need blocks one and two). In case you don't know it, skunks are catching—at least, that part of their personality you can smell is. I think I acquired just the faintest whisper.

Over supper Jack heard the full story for the first time, including the part played by the lady at NBC. He asked a few questions about what radio stations there were in the sticks (everybody in Dixon listened to Chicago). I mentioned a few, being an old radio hand by this time. Then he made the suggestion that I should take the family Oldsmobile and map out a one-day tour of the nearest ones on the following Monday. My spirits bounced like a Yo-Yo. I still don't know whether Jack thought I had a chance at a radio job or whether he just wanted to ease my pain, but Monday was D-Day—D for another door to knock on.

There was a station in Davenport, Iowa, seventy-five miles away; another across the river in Rock Island, Illinois; and a couple more I could reach on a one-day circle. Davenport was to be the first stop: WOC—World of Chiropractic. Or didn't you know that many radio call letters stand for things, like WGN—World's Greatest Newspaper? WOC was no upstart in radio: it had been the first to pioneer in the idea that later became network, tying in with another pioneer, KDKA, to bring a Presidential inauguration to the Midwest for the first time in history. Founded by Colonel B. J. Palmer of the Palmer School of Chiropractic, it was located in the top floors of the school and shared time with WHO, Des Moines, which he had acquired. Half the programs came from WOC and half from WHO, but both stations broadcast all the programs simultaneously. If this sounds confusing, I didn't understand it myself for a long time—and certainly not then.

My total radio knowledge was still limited to knowing I should ask for the program director. All the hitchhiking, all the sore swollen feet from walking miles of Chicago sidewalks, all the reception room fast shuffles had brought me face to face with one of the most unforgettable characters I would ever know—Peter MacArthur. A saint, but a show business kind of saint with a vocabulary that could crackle and scorch. A veteran of vaudeville, he had come to America from Scotland with the original Harry Lauder troupe. Indeed, he was the only man Harry had ever granted permission to use any or all of his songs and material. Pete had stayed in vaudeville until, so cruelly crippled by arthritis, he could only get around by using two canes and strong language —and none of that of any use unless he was first lifted from his chair. He had found his way to the Palmer School seeking relief from his round-the-clock pain, and had stayed on—first as announcer, then as program director. Old-timers in the Midwest will still warm up when you remind them of that radio voice, rich with Highland burr, rolling out, "WOC, Davenport—where the West begins, in the state where the tall corn grows."

It was impossible to be a stranger with this man. I found myself spotlighted by a pair of twinkling eyes, and filled with a sure knowledge that he was personally interested in me—as he was in every human who crossed his path. "Where the hell have ye been?" he roared when he heard my mission. "Don't ye ever listen to the radio?" I didn't think it was politic to tell him we never tuned to WOC in our neighborhood, so I shrugged and waited to hear what it was I should have been hearing.

For one month they had been advertising an audition to hire an announcer, and just the week before one had been hired out of ninety-four applicants. It seems others aspired to radio careers. To come so close was infuriating and as I took my leave I asked, as sort of a get-off line, "How in hell does a guy ever get to be a sports announcer if he can't get inside a station?" This was the first time in all my door-thumping I'd mentioned sports or my hidden desire out loud.

48

The walls of the Palmer School were covered with mottoes and bits of philosophy. Waiting for the elevator, I was reading some of these, quite oblivious to the thumping and cursing in the hallway I'd just left. The door to the elevator opened and, as I started for it, the thumping and cursing caught up with me. (Pete would have made a great coach.) A cane rapped me in the shin. "Not so fast, ye big bastard, didn't ye hear me callin' ye?" He didn't wait for an answer. "Now what was it ye said about sports?" He pronounced sports as if it had twelve R's.

I told him my idea of someday progressing to the lofty status of sports announcer, if only I could get started serving whatever apprenticeship was required beforehand.

"Do ye perhaps know football?" he asked.

"I played for eight years," I answered, not feeling it was essential to break that down into scrubs, second string, and regular.

"Hmm!" I was getting those spotlight eyes again. "Do ye think ye could tell me about a game and make me see it?" he asked speculatively. "I mean, really see it, so as I'd know what was goin' on?"

I couldn't stop the excitement that was growing in me. "I think I could," I said.

"Come with me!" he barked.

Down another hall, through a door and into a studio all draped in heavy blue velvet (the custom of that pre-soundproof day). He pointed to a red light. "When that goes on, ye start talkin'. Tell us about a game and make me see it." He paused on his way out and said, "That's the mike in front of ye—ye won't be able to see me but I'll be listenin'. Good luck."

I was all alone in a half acre of blue velvet and I had several problems. First, nothing had been said about how long my imaginary game should go—and if it was to last any length of time, I would need names of players so there would be no stumbling or hesitation. Second, my dream game should get to some kind of climax to permit a little excitement to creep in. I came to a quick decision. The previous autumn we had played Western

49

State University down to the wire, trailing six to nothing. Then, with only twenty seconds left, Cole had called "fourteen to the right," an off-tackle play identical to the old Rockne special that saved so many games for Notre Dame. We were back on our own thirty-five-yard line and even our own team expected a pass, but we rolled out to the right, Bud cut in between end and tackle, reversed his field, and went sixty-five yards for the touchdown. His drop kick gave us the win.

By choosing the fourth quarter of this game, I'd have familiar names for both teams and a pretty fair country finish. Out of sheer gratitude to Eureka, I gave the college a stadium when the red light came on. "We are going into the fourth quarter now," I began. "A chill wind is blowing in through the end of the stadium and the long blue shadows are settling over the field. Western still leads, six to nothing, as Eureka—defending the south goal—puts the ball in play on their own twenty-yard line." I battled them back and forth, exchanged kicks, and kept watching the clock to make it come out long enough to pass for a quarter. When fifteen minutes had gone by, I figured it was safe to maneuver us Red Devils down to our own thirty-five and go for the old college-try finish. Incidentally, on that "fourteen" play, the right guard is a kind of essential guy in that he is supposed to take out the line backer ahead of Cole. In the actual game, I missed my assignment and never have figured how Cole managed to get loose. In this broadcast version, I murdered the line backer with a block that could be felt in the press box (Eureka didn't have one of those either). About twenty minutes had gone by when I reached this point, so I wound it up and even threw in that familiar line, "We return you now to our main studio."

When Pete came back in, I was wringing wet and hanging on the mike for support. He was chuckling and growling at the same time. "Ye did great, ye big S.O.B.! Now look," he always made it sound like *luke*), "we have a sponsor for four University of Iowa games. Ye be here a week from Saturday and I'll give ye five dollars and bus fare. If ye do all right on that one, ye'll do the other three."

The great day dawned, and dawn was when I departed from Dixon by bus. From Davenport I was told we'd go to Iowa City by car. Pete would go, of course, and climb to the top of that stadium, cursing every step. In addition, there would be two engineers, Paul Loyet, later president of the broadcasting company, and Roy Pratt. (The three of us would become virtually a team in the next few years.) Evidently Pete had done a little worrying too, because a staff announcer was going along and Pete told me he would share the broadcast. I was more than a little alarmed about what proportions that sharing would take, because everyone in Dixon was waiting to hear "little old hometown me."

We arrived at the stadium long before the crowd and made our way to the press box. From here on, everything was a new adventure to me except the hot dogs we had for lunch. (Mine stayed in a lump right in my middle.) I'd seen only a few games from a grandstand in my whole life, and I'd never been in a press box. Gradually the stadium filled up and an excitement caught me until I felt as if I were vibrating. It was to become a familiar feeling, it never deserted me on any game broadcast I ever did.

The other announcer did the pre-game stuff, including line-ups, then I heard him saying, "And now to begin the play-by-play, here is Ronald Reagan."

Before I knew it, Ronald Reagan was saying, "How do you do, ladies and gentlemen. We are speaking to you from high atop the Memorial Stadium of the University of Iowa, looking down from the west on the south forty-yard line." This too became part of the pattern: I've always believed in the "teller who" locating himself, so the audience can see the game through his eyes.

During that first quarter I played it straight, sticking to facts and making no conversational side excursions. I was content to be hopefully adequate. As prearranged, I turned the mike back to my companion (whom I now thought of as my competitor) at the quarter's end. This was to be my inspiration, as it turned out.

51

He was a capable radio man, he could ad-lib, but his knowledge of football was superficial. Suddenly hearing him pick his way through Big Ten football, with no appreciation for some of the highlights begging to be described, confidence began to fill me until I didn't think I could wait for the third quarter. My opposition began to run down during the between-halves fill and started reading clippings and publicity handouts. When I indicated I could lend a hand, he turned over the mike with obvious relief. I used the remainder of the intermission to describe the formations the two teams were using, so that listeners would have an understanding of the terms we were broadcasting. The third quarter started, and I was loving every minute of it until the gun reminded me it was time to relinquish the mike. As I turned to do so, a piece of yellow paper landed between us and Pete's scrawl was so big I couldn't help but read it. "Let the kid finish the game" was the message. The kid was overjoyed.

When the game was over, Pete didn't waste any time or give me that "we'll call you" routine. He just simply said, "Ye'll do the rest of the games." I could even boast a one-hundred-per cent increase in salary—now it was ten dollars a game and bus fare. It was only three more games and thirty dollars—but I was a sports announcer. After all, if one buck for playing the game makes you a pro, thirty-five for talking it should, too.

Of course, between Saturdays it was back to Dixon, but not to fret. I could actually feel occupied reading up on the teams I was to cover, familiarizing myself with names, records, and incidents shamelessly stolen from sports columns in the Chicago papers.

FDR was elected President and Jack went to work for the government. Dixon was really hard hit. Moon's old alma mater, the cement plant, closed its doors on twelve hours' notice, dumping another thousand unemployed into the already distressed town of ten thousand. Jack's job was handing out the foodstuffs the government bought and shipped in, as well as the scrip the government issued permitting the unemployed to go to the grocer and buy, the government in turn redeeming the scrip from the grocer for cash. There was no bureaucracy at Jack's level; he shared an office and secretary with the County Supervisor of Poor.

Every week the line would form—not bums or strangers but friends, fathers of kids I'd gone to school with. Most of them were first names to Jack and he was Jack to them. One thing sure, he didn't go by the rule book. It took him only a few weeks to start rounding up every odd job, every put-off chore from raking yards to thinning the woods at Lowell Park for the Park Board. He worked nights arranging a round-robin schedule so that every week a number of the men in the line got jobs for a few days or a week—and when they did, they skipped coming in that week for the handout. I've sat in that office and heard them as they reached the desk and asked, "When are you going to have another job for me, Jack?" He'd look at his list and tell them exactly how many others were in line before their next time up.

Jack would come home to dinner and quietly mention a name. Another friend, known to all of us, had newly joined the line on relief. The President said, "To dole out relief is to administer a narcotic, a subtle destroyer of the human spirit. The Federal government must, and shall, quit this business of relief." He said that, but it didn't work out that way. Wheels were turning in Washington and government was busy at the job it does best—growing. One day the welfare workers arrived with loads of furniture and, of course, the card files—enough to require a whole floor of offices in a downtown building. The letter P disappeared, and was replaced with C: people became cases. "Get me the file on the Smith case."—"Let me see the card on the Jones case." The day came when Jack, who'd kept right on in his regular routine, told a group he had a week's work for them and they said, "Jack, we can't take it." To his stunned surprise, he was told that the last time they took his jobs the new welfare staff had cut them off relief. Then their cases had to be reopened with interviews, applications, and new cards. The process took three weeks and in the meantime their families went hungry—all because they'd done a few days' honest work.

That night Jack didn't spit in the eye of the curse. He arrived home on foot, with a severe list to port. Knowing he had the car, I backtracked him and found it right where it had proved too much for him—sitting in the middle of the street with the door open and the motor running.

With the advent of Works Progress Administration, Jack found himself in charge locally, and thus officially opposed to the "welfare band." There were no boondoggles in Dixon to speak of under the WPA; parks were created out of brush and swamp riverbanks, bridges over the river, and even a hangar at the new airport. Jack, who was no engineer, figured a way to use the old streetcar rails, torn from our main street, as structural steel in the building. But his main battle was manpower. Practically all of the unemployed were able-bodied and capable, and they besieged him for chances at working for their keep, even calling on him at home. Using every pretext, including physical unfitness, those in charge of direct relief resisted releasing their charges to WPA.

Jack's life became one of almost permanent anger and frustration. However, his rage was directed only at his local tormentors. Being a loyal Democrat, he never criticized the administration or the government.

Just before Christmas a call came from Pete. It wasn't the looked-for job. Somehow this canny Scot knew I must be approaching the hopeless state, and his call was sort of a Christmas present to assure me I wasn't forgotten and to hang on a little longer. The call came shortly after the first of the year. One of the two staff announcers at the Davenport studio was leaving. I would be a staff announcer at a hundred dollars a month. My bag—and you can keep that singular—was packed, and I moved to Davenport. I was hired, I would be fired, I would be rehired, but I was out in the world at last.

CHAPTER

5

One hundred dollars a month doesn't sound like very much, but you have to remember the depression—also that I was used to nursing my summer earnings through an entire year. I have never been richer: I bought a meal ticket at the Palmer School cafeteria—it was good for three meals a day, six days a week, total cost $3.65! You could get a made-to-measure suit with two pair of pants for $18.50. Nelle had raised us to believe the Lord's share was a tenth. I still believe it. Nelle could even put it on an almost selfish basis by guaranteeing that the Lord would make your 90 per cent twice as big if you made sure He got His tenth. I checked with a local minister: would the Lord consider His share as being His, if I gave it to my brother to help him through school? The minister solemnly opined he thought the Lord would consider this full discharge of my obligation.

So Moon got ten dollars a month. Then, just to gild the lily, I pocketed a dime each morning and, as I walked along the street, from my room to the studio, I gave the dime to the first fellow who asked for a cup of coffee. The rest (and there were usually several) I had to pass by. In addition, I started repaying the Strong Foundation for my college loan. I suppose there are a few who skip out on these loans, but I'm equally sure most of us pay them back, knowing that by doing so we make it possible for someone else to get an education.

One part of my fresh life was pleasant, and I rolled up in it like in a blanket. This was the camaraderie, the informal life of radio, which even in a Midwestern town had the tang of show business. In spite of Jack's curse, I was not a teetotaler. Like almost every other young man, I had learned to drink—principally because it was against the law—and it was done out of a bottle that tasted like gasoline on the fraternity back porch or in a parked car. Now I was to discover the pleasure of more civilized drinking, in which just getting high was not the goal. Don't be misled: drinking has never been more than casual with me and, other than love for a good wine with dinner, I can and do leave it alone for long periods. Probably, down underneath, I think the world would be better off without it.

Not all of this new life was so pleasant. Being a staff announcer meant many hours of playing phonograph records, interspersed with the reading of commercials. Other hours were spent in lonely duty while the station carried network programs, and every half hour the local announcer would do the station break, read an ad, return the station to the network, and himself to a book. This was my downfall. The secret of announcing is to make reading sound like talking. I still am not good at a first reading of a script. At that time I was plain awful. I knew it, and so did the listeners. What was worse, so did the sponsors. I couldn't give it that easy conversational persuasive sell.

Once each week, late at night, we would present a program of romantic organ music from the Runge Mortuary. These programs were a sort of semi-commercial. We got the half hour of music free, and the mortuary got a discreet plug by way of mention that it was the source of the program. Unfortunately, no one informed me of this. My dramatic instinct rebelled at mentioning a mortuary in connection with "Drink to Me Only With Thine Eyes," so on this night we got the music and the mortuary got left. Check up one more infuriated sponsor.

I'm sure what happened next was inevitable. I was informed that I would be replaced. It was all very regretful, but it seemed that another fellow they had previously considered was now available, and if I was still around when they needed sports events, I'd be called. Actually, it was the end of the world.

Sitting in the announcer's booth with Hugh Hipple—whom I would meet many years later as Hugh Marlowe in Hollywood, a fine actor—I revealed my discouragement. Hugh said, "Ronnie, I've always believed the kindest thing a man can do in this business is tell someone when they should get another line of work." He continued, "I can tell in five minutes whether a fellow should be in show business or not."

I looked at him expectantly. "Well?" I said.

He just looked at me and shook his head sorrowfully. Looking back at my performance, I can understand and even agree.

The new replacement arrived. He was a schoolteacher and a fine fellow. Talk about inconsistency, they handed him to me for the showing-the-ropes phase. Then a miracle happened, and I was not about to kick a miracle in the face. He thought I was only temporary and had been hired with full knowledge of his arrival. When he learned this wasn't true, he demanded a contract as a guarantee of security. WOC was not in the habit of giving contracts, so he went back to teaching and the station was stuck. Someone else—not Pete, because Pete had never been a part of it—called me in and told me they would keep me on until they could find someone else. I blew my top, not to the extent of turning them down, but just to say that as long as they were stuck with me, why didn't someone tell me a little about the job, instead of turning me loose with a hot mike and a lack of instructions? Again, fate stepped in.

A friend, Glen Noonan—who later died serving his country in a far-off corner of Asia—dropped in to see me. I told him what had happened. He didn't commiserate; he proceeded to say exactly the right thing. He reminded me that I was nothing but ahead. He said, "You now have experience which you'd never had before. You can walk into another radio station and even introduce yourself as a sports announcer." A few weeks later he wrote me a letter and told me he had listened on his car radio

57

after he'd left me—he had heard my announcing—and knew I was going to be all right. It was true: our visit had taken place in the announcer's booth. He couldn't have been out of the building when time came for my next commercial. His words had cured my mental block with regard to reading. I was mad, didn't give a damn, and so I read that commercial freely, easily, and with a pretty good punch. There was no more talk of a replacement.

On a day in April I was called into Pete's office. He was on the phone and obviously selling something. Something turned out to be me. He was talking to his counterpart in our dual operation at WHO in Des Moines. Into the phone he shouted, "Wait a minute!" Then, to me, he said, "Do you know about track?" When I nodded yes, he turned to the phone again and said, "We've got a man." A week later I was in Des Moines to broadcast the Drake Relays.

As sports fans know, this event and the Penn Relays—traditionally taking place on the same weekend—are the two great amateur track events in our nation. I was awed by the WHO facilities. No blue velvet drapes here. The studios were new and modern, and once again I had to overcome that country-boy feeling. I didn't know at the time I was getting a preview of my future home.

So far Sid Altschuler's advice had proven faultless. Now I was to learn he had the gift of prophecy. He had told me the advantages of getting into a new industry and riding it to the top. Our broadcasting company was building one of the dozen fifty-kilowatt stations in the entire country. We dropped our hyphenated call letters and became WHO Des Moines, key station for NBC in the Midwest. I was a sports announcer in the solar plexus of the country. From five dollars for that first football game I would go to seventy-five dollars a week, and in those days this was big money—in addition to which there would be bonuses and extra money from touring the banquet circuit, writing a guest column, and hiring out to handle public-address system chores at events we weren't broadcasting. I did possibly forty-five football games from virtually every major press box in the Midwest. I covered

58

by telegraph more than six hundred big league baseball games, plus swimming meets, track meets, and even one swimming meet that didn't happen. The plums in local station work were those occasions where you fed a program to the network. My first such plum involved the nonexistent swimming meet.

The National AAU championships were held in Des Moines. Perched high on a diving tower, I was to broadcast a thirty-minute period during which would take place the top four or five events of the meet. Just as we went on the air coast to coast, an AAU official, Avery Brundage, a gentleman who was famous for his participation in a number of athletic debates, chose this moment to start another one. For thirty minutes I described the costumes of the arguing officials, identified the swimmers who were practicing dives and turns, and at the end of the thirty minutes returned the airwaves to the network without describing a single event. Five minutes later the first event took place. It established a new national swimming record.

Those were wonderful days. I was one of a profession just becoming popular and common—the visualizer for the armchair quarterback. During these five years my father Jack was to have the first of his heart attacks. I had the satisfaction of being able to send a monthly check that removed all his economic problems for the first time in his life. Now he was not only unemployed, he was physically unable to work, but, as Nelle confirmed later, it never entered his mind that he could apply for public assistance.

Through our city came the greats of the sports world, and all of them found their way to WHO to be interviewed. The colorful Doc Kearns, with his stories of the young Jack Dempsey. The one and only Ed Strangler Lewis; Max Baer came, as beautiful a piece of physical machinery as ever stepped into the fight ring. Standing in our hallway outside the studio door, he demonstrated a punch and accidently landed it in the midsection of an admiring mailroom clerk. Max was quite upset and stayed around the seven minutes it took to revive the clerk.

Not all of the memories are confined to sports personalities.

One night when we were doing a special broadcast raising money for flood victims in the Ohio Valley, a quiet, rather shy Englishman appeared, Leslie Howard. I was so stage-struck that I forgot his name as I stepped up to the microphone. Several years later he reminded me of this when we met, both under contract at Warners in Hollywood.

Once a very noted evangelist from Los Angeles came to Des Moines to hold a series of revival meetings. Why they should pick a sports announcer to interview the late Aimee Semple McPherson I'll never know, but interview her I did. She answered my questions graciously, then went into a fervent plea concerning the success of her meetings and I sat down—until suddenly I heard her say good night to our radio audience. There were four minutes to go by the radio clock. I didn't know enough about Aimee Semple McPherson—that is, that I could put on the air— to fill four minutes. I made a circular motion with my hand, the signal in those days for a phonograph record. A sleepy engineer in the control room reached out, pulled a record off a stack, put it on the turntable, and nodded to go ahead. In my most dulcet tones I said, "Ladies and gentlemen, we conclude this broadcast by the noted evangelist, Aimee Semple McPherson, with a brief interlude of transcribed music." I expected nothing less than the "Ave Maria." The Mills Brothers started singing "Minnie the Moocher's Wedding Day."

I have said radio was informal. On one crisp fall night, the evening before I was to broadcast a football game, I was on duty in the studio with thirty minutes to fill with records. In such cases the announcer picked his own records and ad-libbed his introductions. Imbued with the spirit of football, I picked all the college songs I could find in the library. There weren't enough to fill thirty minutes, so between records I read the schedule of football games for the following day and made my predictions on each game as to the winner.

When the half hour ended and we went to network, the phone

Young Ronald "Dutch" Reagan (right) with brother Neil.

The Reagan family (left to right): Jack, Neil, Ronald, and Nelle.

ABOVE LEFT: Summer job at Lowell Park. ABOVE RIGHT: The dedicated football player.

At WHO, Des Moines.

ABOVE: With Patricia Neal, visiting London Tower.
BELOW: Horseback riding in London's Hyde Park.

Photograph by George Konig, Keystone Press Agency Ltd.

ABOVE: Ronald Reagan, smiling at his wife, actress Nancy Davis, before receiving an honorary doctor's degree at Eureka College. BELOW: On a public relations tour for General Electric.

Hartford Times Photo

ABOVE: At a production banquet, with Eric Johnston. BELOW: Receiving award at United States Junior Chamber of Commerce banquet.

"Dick" Whittington Photograph

ABOVE: With Francis X. Bushman. BELOW: On Universal set for *The Killers,* Ronald Reagan and Angie Dickinson help John Cassavetes (center) celebrate his birthday.

Photograph made in connection with Universal Pictures' The Killers, courtesy of and copyrighted by Universal Pictures Company, Inc.

rang. It was Pete. The familiar Scotch growl questioned, "Where the hell did you get that idea?"

So I told him: it just seemed in keeping with the season. It became a regular Friday night feature. It also became a stepping-stone for someone else's career.

Moon, now graduated from Eureka and unemployed, was my house guest. I think Nelle had something to do with that. Realizing that disintegration could take place if he sat around Dixon, diploma in hand and unemployed, she urged a brotherly visit on him and backed her urging with bus fare. On one subsequent Friday night he was sitting in the studio, waiting for me to finish so we could journey together to Si's Moonlight Inn.

No one could talk of Des Moines in those days without mentioning this establishment. Its main commerce was a drink that even the repeal of prohibition couldn't outlaw—near beer spiked with alcohol. Si always claimed the drink was safe because he bought the alcohol from government agents. To stay open he had to advertise that he sold food. One veteran customer told me that he had once ordered a sandwich, taken a bite, and the sandwich bit him back. At any rate, it was the cherished pub and a must for all homegoing Iowans. Even the swankiest of parties, where attire was white tie and tails, was not officially over until the guests had stopped by Moonlight.

But to get back to Friday night and my brother. On a couple of my predictions, I noticed he was shaking his head in disagreement, so I turned on the mike in front of him and asked why he disagreed. We continued the program, debating each prediction, sometimes agreeing, sometimes disagreeing, and promising the audience we'd tell who had the best percentage on the following Friday night. It was as unplanned as that. It led to a fifteen-dollar-a-week job for Moon, doing the football scoreboard on Saturday nights because I was still out of town on my football broadcasts. That job led Moon to an announcing job at the reinstituted WOC in Davenport, to program directing, network producing, and his present position in Los Angeles as vice-president of an advertising agency. Sid Altschuler's advice was rubbing off on the rest of the family.

By this time Pete's arthritis was so bad he was on crutches, not canes. Each afternoon I lifted him from his chair and held him until he was balanced. Ed Reimer, Myrtle Williams, and one or two of the staff entertainers joined us. Myrtle was in charge of the music library and as bright and cheerful a personality as I'd ever known. Out to the car we went. Pete, growling and cursing, got lowered into the front seat; the rest piled in and in a daily ritual we took him home to his lovely—and very much in love—wife, Hup. At first these sessions were a cocktail hour, but then I think Hup decided this might not be the best thing for Pete, so cocktails became tea and, believe it or not, cream puffs.

Whatever the refreshments, Pete held court, and I've no way to measure the value of his teaching, his philosophy, or how much it still means to me. I know that this man, with troubles beyond our comprehension, was still the one person you went to when your own problems were too much to bear. Long after I was gone, and he was forced into retirement—unable to rise, with even his sight gone—in a new home in Florida, Hup told me that until his death the same thing held true: all who came in contact with him brought him their troubles, and he never failed to have an answer.

The best example of how he treated his own troubles can be told in an incident Myrtle related to me. She had found Pete daydreaming one afternoon and, intrigued by the look of joy on his face, had said, "Penny?"

Slowly he turned from the window. Like a little boy telling what he'd done at camp, he said, "I was just playing polo. Oh, I was riding like the wind, out ahead of everyone! I had a wonderful horse!" Myrtle came back to the studio, where I was on duty, to have a quiet cry.

Football remained my radio love. And, as I said earlier, Iowa was on the comeback trail. One day at the start of football season, two Negro boys walked out on the field and approached the Iowa coach, Ossie Solem, long-time friend of Knute Rockne. Rockne had credited him with upsetting some of his most successful seasons, with his hard-fighting Drake University teams. Now he was the head coach at Iowa, and so received his two visitors.

"Mr. Solem," one said, "my name is Don Simmons. I'm a good end. This is my brother, Ozzie, and he's the best halfback in Texas."

Solem was amused. He had the freshman coach give them uniforms and, fortunately, he tested Ozzie first. It was a simple test: he put him at halfback on the freshman team to carry the ball against the varsity. Five minutes and two touchdowns later, he sent the boys and the freshman coach to the registrar's office.

With the trouble going on today, and the bitter feelings engendered by extremists, both Negro and white, I can't help but point out my conviction that among the extremists you'll find no one who ever participated in athletics on a team that numbered among its personnel both Negroes and whites.

I was no stranger to the color problem. In college I played beside one of the finest men and, incidentally, one of the best centers I've ever known. Franklin Burkhardt came to Eureka in my junior year and automatically became first string center. He too was a sixty-minute man, and we bled together down there in the center of the line. I remember one day we met a team with no colored boys on its roster. This always made a difference. Soon, under the stress of combat, the muttered cracks started down in the line—all directed at Burky. What was worse, Burky had revealed by an involuntary groan that he had a bad knee. His opponent in the line went to work on that knee. Our huddle was seething; we all had plans for disposing of his tormentors. With quiet dignity Burky told us to play our own positions: this was his fight. As I've explained before, this was an era when you could use your hands on defense, and Burky used them. Completely within the rules, cleanly but with devastating effect,

63

you could hear the thud of flesh on headgear. In the fourth quarter the man who had been trying for his knee had to leave the game, literally beaten to his knees by Burky's hands. He started off the field, stopped for a moment halfway to the sideline, and stood there, head bowed. Then he turned and came back. He elbowed his way through the two teams until he came to Burkhardt. With tears running down his face, he stuck out his hand. He, who had used the term "black bastard" on almost every play, now said, "You're the whitest man I ever knew." When the game was over a few minutes later, we had to cut Burky's pants to get them over his swollen knee.

During my senior year I was filled with excitement when it developed that on one of our football trips the squad would stay overnight in my home town and work out on my old high school field. I took Mac into the hotel and introduced him to the owner. Then, in an agony of embarrassment, I heard my fellow townsman tell Mac that everyone could stay there but our two colored boys—Burky and a reserve tackle named Jim Rattan.

Mac said, "Then we'll go to another hotel."

The owner answered, "You might as well know no other hotel will take them either."

Remember, this was northern Illinois—not the Deep South. Mac was trembling with rage. He turned to me and said, "We'll sleep in the bus."

We both knew we couldn't do this. It would be worse because Burky and Jim would know they were the cause of everyone's discomfort. I said, "Mac, let's tell the fellows we have to break it up, that there aren't enough rooms for all of us. I'll take them home with me."

Mac looked at me and said, "Are you sure?"—and thank heaven I was sure. With no chance to call, the three of us arrived at home and Nelle and Jack didn't even blink or act as if anything had happened that was not a daily occurrence. Nothing was ever said, but I'm sure Burky wasn't fooled by the shortage of rooms in other hotels.

64

But baseball was the backbone of our sports program, and here my "think-out-loud" technique wouldn't work, or so it seemed. With our rise to big-time status, I found myself tagged to broadcast the home games of the Chicago Cubs and the Chicago White Sox. Then every American boy had a knowledge of baseball, but not big league ball. As a matter of fact, I had never seen a major league game. Football was different. I knew the game, how it felt to be on the field, and the smell of sweat and the taste of mud and blood don't change with the years. To make things even worse, our baseball games would be broadcast without my even being present at the ball park, thanks to a system known as telegraphic report. In Chicago, in the press box, a telegraph operator would tap out each play. Sitting on the opposite side of a glass window from me in our studios in Davenport, another telegraph operator, hearing this dot and dash, would type out the message, slide it through a slot in the window, and I would translate it into the audible sounds of baseball.

This was before the day of sportscast monopoly. There were as many as a dozen of us broadcasting the same game and at least half of these were available to our audience just for the turning of the dial. This meant that I would have to keep up with the play because these competitors were actually at the ball park, broadcasting on Chicago stations easily available to a large part of our audience. Therefore, my telegraphic messages would have to be very scanty, to lessen the time interval before I could get the play on the air. I might say that after we got under way and I fitted into the routine, a check revealed that I was only about a half a pitch behind the actual play.

Looking through the window I would see "Curly" (complete with headphones) start typing. This was my cue to start talking. It would go something like this: "The pitcher [whatever his name happened to be] has the sign, he's coming out of the windup, here's the pitch," and at that moment Curly would slip me the blank. It might contain the information S2C, and without a pause I would translate this into "It's a called strike breaking over the inside corner, making it two strikes on the batter." If the Cubs were in the field, I would continue while I waited for the next dot and dash, saying, "Hartnett returns the ball to Lon Warneke, Warneke is dusting his hands in the resin, steps back up on the mound, is getting the sign again from Hartnett, here's the windup and the pitch."

Of course, there had to be a bridge between this daily broadcast and my lack of familiarity with big league ball. The bridge was provided by Pat Flanagan. I believe I am correct in saying that he was the originator of the telegraphic report process. His brother wrote advertising copy at our station, so telephone arrangements were made and I went to Chicago where he generously instructed me in the technique and the problems. He also took me into the press box so that forever after I had engraved on my mind the picture of how it looked.

Pat was a good teacher and before too long I was spinning out games for all the world as if I were not four hundred miles from the ball park. On this summer's day the Cubs and the St. Louis Cards were locked in a scoreless tie: Dizzy Dean on the mound, Augie Galan at bat for the Cubs in the ninth inning. I saw Curly start to type so I finished the windup and had Dean send the ball on its way to the plate, took the slip from Curly, and found myself faced with the terse note: "The wire has gone dead."

I had a ball on the way to the plate and there was no way to call it back. At the same time, I was convinced that a ball game tied up in the ninth inning was no time to tell my audience we had lost contact with the game and they would have to listen to recorded music. I knew of only one thing that wouldn't get in the score column and betray me—a foul ball. So I had Augie foul this pitch down the left field foul line. I looked expectantly at Curly. He just shrugged helplessly, so I had Augie foul another one, and still another; then he fouled one back into the box seats. I described in detail the redheaded kid who had scrambled and gotten the souvenir ball. He fouled one into the upper deck that just missed being a home run. He fouled for six minutes and

66

forty-five seconds until I lost count. I began to be frightened that maybe I was establishing a new world record for a fellow staying at bat hitting fouls, and this could betray me. Yet I was into it so far I didn't dare reveal that the wire had gone dead. My voice was rising in pitch and threatening to crack—and then, bless him, Curly started typing. I clutched at the slip. It said: "Galan popped out on the first ball pitched." Not in my game he didn't—he popped out after practically making a career of foul balls.

During those years in Des Moines another facet of my life came into full fruition. I loved horses. I think the Irish are one of the lost tribes of the Arabs. Actually I had never been exposed to them, and I suppose, as a youngster, had only a yen to be like Tom Mix, but as I grew older the love grew stronger and wouldn't go away. I just plain wanted to ride a horse.

The 14th Cavalry Regiment was stationed in Des Moines. Ernie Saunders, one of our announcers, was a reserve officer. Through him I learned of the provisions of the Defense Act— namely, that you could sign up as a candidate for a commission and thus be eligible not only to ride cavalry mounts on the spacious reservation, but also to get the best cavalry training in horsemanship. I had no particular desire to be an officer. Like everyone else, I thought we had already fought the last war; still, doing correspondence courses and going to once-a-week classes wasn't too high a price to pay for getting astride a horse. One little inefficiency of the Army was to serve me in good stead. The physical examination did not come before you were accepted as a candidate, but took place only and finally when you were ready for a commission. It seems kind of silly, but that's the way it was—you could work and study for a few years and then find out you had flat feet or spavins.

However, it was great for me because the cavalry differs from other branches in that an officer must have good vision without the aid of glasses. For the next few years I would avoid ever completing the required courses which would bring me to the moment of commission. Of course, there was an eventual limit, and I reached it. If I wanted to continue riding, I had to go through the process of enlisting in the cavalry for twenty-four hours and at the same time file application for a commission.

Faced with the Army doctors, I said, "Fellows, you might as well save some time. Don't tell me to undress. I know I can pass all that bend-over stuff. You might as well take a look at my eyes and save time."

Well, of course, when they removed my glasses and said, "Read the letters on that card," I asked, "What card?"

Evidently these medics didn't think there would be a war either because, not having started to fill out a form, they didn't have to complete one. They couldn't cheat. Thereupon I went to a civilian doctor for an examination. This really wasn't too much help, because all doctors are an ethical breed and even civilians won't cheat. However, I did know a trick. Instead of holding a black card over one eye while I read with the other, I held my hand over my eye. I don't know how many of you know this, but a nearsighted person can punch a pinhole in a cardboard and that pinhole will have virtually the same effect as a corrective lens —so I managed to squeeze my fingers down to where I had the narrowest of slits, and which I was supposed to be reading with the uncovered eye, in reality I read with the covered eye, now corrected by virtue of squinting through this tiny slit between my fingers. I was practically eagle-eyed.

On the occasion of my final test for commission, having passed the physical and all of the written examinations, I was to experience some regret and even feel maybe the Lord was punishing me for cheating with eyes and fingers. That final test was to take command, on a big horse, of a platoon of regular Army cavalry. Two West Point graduates, also on horses, would ride beside me, alternating telling me maneuvers they wanted the platoon to execute, and asking questions regarding military science. With the platoon at a gallop, for example, I would be given a formation requiring several intermediate orders for proper execution. Con-

68

trolling the horse, trying to sort out the sequence of commands I must give, and remembering at the same time the arm signals for those commands, my other tormentor would ride up like Paul Revere and shout at me, "Explain the meaning of fire power and movement!"

I think I should tell you that on this particular Sunday morning it was also raining like crazy. I'd had some ridiculous thought that the whole deal might be called off. No such luck. The hours went by. I could almost feel the hatred of twenty-seven enlisted men, miserable and soaked to the skin, all for the purpose of creating one more second lieutenant. Finally, when I didn't think there was anything left to do, I looked up. We were still galloping, and there in front of me was a great big jump made out of telephone poles. The ground was swampy, the twenty-seven mounted men behind me were in a solid line, knee to knee. If my horse balked, ran out, or slipped, there was no way in the world we could escape being trampled. I thought surely a West Pointer was going to ride up beside me and tell me to right turn or left turn, or even stop—but my West Pointers were sitting under a tree, sheltered from some of the rain and well out of the path of the charging platoon. I closed my eyes, grabbed a handful of mane, and landed on the other side of the jump, a second lieutenant.

The Iowa winters that put us in the riding hall were beginning to give me a yen for warmth and sunshine and make me a collector of travel folders. A baseball announcer, of course, could have no summer vacations. I did some sharp figuring and talked the station into the idea that if they would put up the money, I would put up the time—and my vacation could be spent accompanying the Chicago Cubs on their training trip to Catalina Island. I made quite a pitch about what this would do for me in filling me with color and atmosphere for the coming baseball season. It worked.

I had never been west of Kansas City, so when I boarded the train for that first Catalina trip, I thought I was journeying to a winter resort. I had white buckskins, linen suits, white sports coat, and, of course, swimming trunks. California, as everyone knows, is the home of unusual weather. Joe Frisco, the great comic, always used to say California was the only place where you could fall asleep under a rosebush in full bloom and freeze to death. Everyone knew that except hick me.

The day I arrived was really unusual weather. It was a record-breaking eighty-two degrees in February. I, of course, assumed it was just standard. I wasn't in the hotel in Catalina ten minutes before, clad in trunks, I was running out to the end of the pier. I dived into the coldest water that was still liquid that I've ever known. Awe-struck natives watched me as if I were from outer space, and I rewarded them. I swear I didn't swim—I walked ashore on top of the waves.

Like any rookie, I was due for some hazing. Some of it was good-natured, some of it was unkind. I was the only radio man there and the newspapermen had an understandable resentment of sports announcers. Veteran sports writers are really a breed apart in their ability to coin pungent phrases. Once they had enjoyed the knowledge that the baseball public waited on the street corners to grab the first editions and read their descriptions of what had taken place in the ball park. Radio, of course, had changed this and, naturally, they were resentful.

The ball players, the fellows I really wanted to know, took no part in the hazing and, as a matter of fact, included me in their activities—I think mainly because they are wary of sports writers as actors are wary of critics. It was a case of any victim of the writers being automatically a friend.

In one thing I was completely normal. I returned to the Mid-west and, like everyone on their first California trip, decided it was a nice place to visit but—well . . . !

In this world of scores and sweatshirts, it had been a long time since the acting bug had stirred within me, but when it did it came out like a butterfly from a cocoon. Our station had developed a quite famous barn dance program, and one winter, just

70

prior to my annual Catalina trip, an act on that program known as the Oklahoma Outlaws was hired by Gene Autry to be featured in one of his Western movies. This suddenly made acting and movies seem very close. By a strange coincidence, at just about this time, a theater owner in Des Moines called me, and asked if I had ever thought of taking a screen test. I thought he must be a mind reader. It developed that one of the studios was sending a crew around the country, testing people in various towns. The theater owner was trying to line up a group in Des Moines. Now, of course, I know that this was in reality a favorite Hollywood publicity device, used to promote a picture, and no one ever really became an actor as the result of these tests. At that time, however, it just added to the restlessness and the sudden realization that sports might not be the only course my life would follow.

Arriving in Hollywood that year, I delayed going to Catalina by one day while I journeyed to the studio to visit the Oklahoma Outlaws. The WHO agent in charge of their Hollywood experience was my target. His appetite too had been whetted by the Hollywood glamour, so he gave sympathetic ear when I voiced my aspirations and introduced me to a casting director who was something less than enthusiastic. However, he did say that if I wanted to read for him I could do so when I returned from the island. Handing me two or three old scripts, he said, "Pick out a scene that you think fits you, and I'll listen to you read."

Some of Nelle's fey quality regarding hunches rubbed off on me. There have been a few moments in my life when I have known, or at least had a positive feeling, that something would happen. One day on Catalina, Charlie Grimm, the Cubs' manager, bawled me out for not even showing up at the practice field. How could I tell him that somewhere within myself was the knowledge I would no longer be a sports announcer? For the first time I was really having a vacation, riding horses, boating, and seeing the Catalina scenery.

The first night back on the mainland, I went down to the

Biltmore Bowl. Joy Hodges, an alumna of WHO, was singing there with Jimmy Grier's orchestra. Joy had had a number of parts in pictures, and it was my custom to look her up on each trip to California to bring her news of her old home town and, of course, to enjoy the pleasure of a glamorous and lovely young lady's company. I sent a note backstage and she came out between floor shows and joined me for dinner.

I told her the whole story of the Outlaws, the promised reading, even that sports announcing had actually been chosen years before as a steppingstone to acting.

Joy got right to the point. "Take off your glasses," she said. Her reaction was such that it implanted in me the desire to rid myself of glasses forevermore. I'm probably the world's number one pioneer in the use of corneal lenses.

Joy told me she didn't feel qualified to say whether I should forget my dream and continue sports announcing, but she said, "I know an agent who will be honest with you. If we're wrong, and you should forget this idea, he'll tell you. Will you see him if I make a date with him? But," she added, "for heaven's sake, don't see him with those glasses on!" That was really a funny line. Without the glasses I couldn't see him at all—but the important thing was, he'd see me.

At ten o'clock the next morning, I sat across the desk from Bill Meiklejohn. He asked me questions about my experience, and I decided a little lying in a good cause wouldn't hurt, so the Eureka Dramatic Club became a professional stock company. I doubled my salary and finally, unable to stand it, I said, "Look, Joy told me that you would level with me. Should I go back to Des Moines and forget this, or what do I do?"

He didn't answer. He just picked up the phone, dialed a number which turned out to be Warner Brothers studio, and asked for Max Arnow. Then, putting his hand over the phone, he said, "Max is the only casting director in town who has the power to say yes or no." He turned back to the phone and said, "Max, I have another Robert Taylor sitting in my office." I decided I didn't have a monopoly on little white lies: Bob, at that time, was the biggest sensation in pictures.

Bill's line was met with an answer even I could hear. Max's booming voice said, "God made only one Robert Taylor!"

Anyway, he gave Bill an appointment and we were on our way to Warner Brothers. I was welcomed like a piece of prize beef. "Stand up against the door. Are those your own shoulders? Let me hear you talk." Then, ignoring me, he said to Bill, "We'll shoot a test Wednesday."

I interrupted and said, "I can't Wednesday—I'll be with the ball club."

He called to an outer office, yelling to an unseen assistant, "We'll shoot a test Tuesday."

The assistant's voice answered, "We already have tests scheduled for Wednesday."

I think this actually tipped the scales in my favor. Max asserted his authority and said, "We'll shoot this one Tuesday."

When we got outside, Bill said, "Two tests are better than one—let's go to Paramount." I told him of my invitation to read. He said, "Forget it." His agent's instinct had told him he might have a sale cooking. At Paramount, we learned they were shooting a short in two days on Easter Sunday. It was a custom at that time, and at that studio, to put all their young contract people into a short and, on the basis of their performances, determine whose option would be dropped and who would be retained and, at the same time, get their money back by releasing the short. I was going to be stuck into this short.

Early Sunday morning I went through the business of make-up—and what a hell of a time they had with my crewcut hair. Crewcuts were about four inches shorter than Hollywood was wearing its actors' hair. All morning I sat ignored in the hustle and bustle. I was growing more restive. I had expected to be through and at Wrigley Field for the Cubs' exhibition game by noon. Finally, at one o'clock, I went up to the casting director—who seemed to be in charge—and asked him when he'd be finished

73

with me. He looked at me in pitying amazement, and said, "I might not get to you until eleven o'clock tonight."

This was a side of Hollywood I hadn't known. "You mean," I said, "that you got me here early this morning, and you might not use me until tonight?"

"Son," he said, "this is Hollywood"—and there I was, temper ready. I said, "Well, this is Des Moines, and you can shove Hollywood," and I went to the ball game.

I could afford to be brave: I had Tuesday coming up, and somehow I hadn't taken this Paramount thing seriously. Max had given me a scene from Philip Barry's play, *Holiday*. Tuesday morning, with the assistance of a starlet, and with the kindly help of a fine director and gentleman named MacDonald, I did the scene. Then they told me it would be several days before Mr. Warner could see this film and, of course, I would stick around, to which I said, "No, I will be on the train tomorrow—me and the Cubs are going home."

They were unbelieving, but I was adamant. It was only on the train that suddenly the horrified feeling came over me that maybe I had blown the whole thing. For the remainder of the trip, I consoled myself with the fact that at least I had a great story for the afternoon tea at Pete's. My firm hunch was unable to survive my foolishness in leaving town. (Actually I had done, through ignorance, the smartest thing it was possible to do. Hollywood just loves people who don't need Hollywood.)

I hadn't even had time to tell my story on that first day in Des Moines when a wire was delivered. It said: WARNER'S OFFER CONTRACT SEVEN YEARS, ONE YEAR'S OPTIONS, STARTING AT $200 A WEEK. WHAT SHALL I DO? It was signed Bill Meiklejohn.

I sent a reply: HAVE JUST DONE A CHILDISH TRICK. SIGN BEFORE THEY CHANGE THEIR MINDS—and then I yelled.

74

CHAPTER

6

In 1937 there was a Spanish Civil War going on, the Japanese were again fighting in China, and Hitler repudiated the Versailles Treaty—but I wasn't mad at anyone. I suppose history will not record that last fact, but my color could only be painted in a light rosy glow. I would don my shining armour and journey to Hollywood. I must check sometime and see if, when knighthood was in flower, armor included a reversed breastplate covering that part of the anatomy where kicks are delivered.

One of my happiest moments, of course, was calling home and telling Nelle and Jack what had happened. Like most Midwesterners, they had a lifelong dream of seeing California, but so far had never been west of Iowa. I told them we'd wait just long enough to find out if there would be some permanency in my Western living and then I would send for them.

With all my happiness, there were pains at leaving WHO and all the people who had come to mean so much to me. I might add this included a few million Iowa radio listeners. They had put up with my mistakes, lived through my learning, and demonstrated a loyalty that went beyond just being an audience.

The Warner contract had been dated to start June 1. I worked until the last few days of May, breaking in my replacement, and then early one morning—after a number of farewell toasts at Moonlight Inn—headed west in the pride of my life, my first convertible.

I crossed the burning desert, and sundown saw me driving that long stretch between the banked orange trees from San Bernardino to Los Angeles. Today the orange trees are gone, replaced by tract homes even closer together than the trees had been planted, and smog has replaced the fragrance of blossoms.

The next morning I called Bill Meiklejohn. His right-hand man—who would become a kindhearted guide in those first confusing days—George Ward, took me to Warner Brothers. On the drive out he warned me not to be upset if I didn't work for weeks and months, explaining this very often happened to new contract players. But we hadn't counted on Max Arnow. It would be some time later before I discovered that I was in Hollywood and at Warner Brothers because of a similarity in voice to that of a promising young actor, Ross Alexander, who—on the verge of stardom at Warner Brothers—was a tragic suicide. George was correct in that many young contract players do mark time for many months before ever facing a camera, but Max had other ideas.

Walking across the lot on our way to the make-up department, he said, "You're going to work. You'll have a chance to find out whether you can make it or not if you're willing to work."

Now this sounded like the normal thing one expected to hear from a new boss. I loved the poking and prodding that began, experiments in make-up and, particularly, the clinic that was held with regard to my hair. My crewcut and center part were on their way out, but not before the head of the hairdressing department had looked pityingly at my head and dubbed it "Bowl Number Seven."

There seemed to be an urgency in all of this experimenting. There was. I was slated to play the lead in a picture called *Love Is on the Air,* starting in about four days. I didn't know at the time that studios made two kinds of pictures: A's and B's. Needless to say, this was a B—but I didn't know it. All I knew was I was starring in my first movie, and that seemed to make a great deal of sense.

76

Let me explain: every studio had a production unit grinding out these B pictures for the second features on the double bills. Brynie Foy was Warner's executive producer of the B's. He was the eldest son of the great old vaudevillian, Eddie Foy, and one of the Seven Little Foys in that famous family act. I soon learned that I could go in to Brynie and tell him I had been laid off, but couldn't take it at the moment because of all my expenses. He would pick up the phone, call a couple of his henchmen, and actually get a picture going on four or five days' notice—just to put me back on salary.

In that first year of our getting acquainted, however, no such expedients were needed. I would do eight pictures in eleven months. This first starring vehicle was typical of Brynie's approach. I played a radio special events and news announcer, punished by the boss for brashness, and the punishment was assignment to the kiddies' program. Sound familiar? It was a rewrite of *Hi, Nellie,* the great Broadway newspaper stage success in which the star reporter was assigned to the lovelorn column. Brynie had made it about six times, but this was the first time in radio. Of course, like the original hero, I would outsmart the police and solve the crime. I've often described those first eight pictures, or most of them, as the kind in which you could count on me rushing into the room, hat on the back of my head, grabbing a phone, and yelling, "Give me the city desk—I've got a story that will crack this town wide open!"

A great many things in this three-week shooting schedule would make it plain I was in a new world. For one thing, looking at my four suits—with a script in hand that told me the part required twelve wardrobe changes—and faced with a contract that stipulated male actors furnish their own wardrobe, I would wonder how the miracle of the fish and loaves was performed. To this day, I stand in awe when I read of actors with wardrobes of thirty, forty, and fifty suits. Somehow the economies of my early life are too deeply ingrained. I have never had enough suits to go through a picture without doubling. Doubling means that toward the end of the picture you count on enough time having passed to dull the audience's memory, and you wear again the suits that you wore in earlier scenes.

Thanks to B. J. Frazer in high school and Miss Johnson at Eureka, I was fairly well grounded in the basic rules of acting. Now, however, I had to assimilate the tricks of the trade. A helpful cameraman, James Van Tree, would take me to his side of the camera and, while the stand-ins were in the actors' positions, show me how small the stage was in a close shot. Remember, the edge of the screen is the proscenium arch in pictures. When your head is up there in a closeup, that arch—meaning the limit of the stage—is right beside each ear. Thus I learned to reduce swaying and sudden head movements, as the camera moved closer. I learned about chalk marks, those footprints on the floor which marked where you were to come to a halt regardless of how fast you burst into a scene—and you can't look down to find them. It's part measuring your distance beforehand, like measuring your steps on a springboard in fancy diving, and part looking out of the bottom of your eyes. You learn also that if you come to those marks, hit them squarely and stop dead still, you look like a guard at Buckingham Palace coming to company halt. You have to shuffle your feet slightly, sort of a little aftermotion, and then it looks like a natural stop. Contrary to the stories of actors' jealousy, other performers are your greatest source of help. Little tips learned from their own experience, and the built-in desire of every performer to lend a hand, result in round-the-clock acting lessons for newcomers, if any newcomer is smart enough to listen.

Love Is on the Air got under way after a preliminary reading of the script. I didn't know this reading was not a regular thing, but only the result of the director's concern at being handed a brand-new actor for leading man. It almost resulted in losing the brand-new actor. There I was—faced with my nemesis, reading. It isn't that I flubbed the words, or stumbled and mispronounced; I even placed the emphasis on the right syllable. I just lack personality when I read. The words make sense, but the lines don't sound as if they are coming from a real live character. There must have been stark panic in cast and crew. A dialogue director named Joe Graham saved me: perhaps because of an intuitive sense regarding my weakness, and perhaps because he too was new in Hollywood from the stage and had a kind heart. He urged the director to wait until the next day and see how I did playing a scene without script in hand. All this, of course, I learned much later.

The next day, the first scene was a fast-talking, high-pitched argument between me and the radio manager. Everyone relaxed and my moment of danger was past. The second day I was introduced to the rushes. This is the custom of going at the end of each day's work and seeing on the screen what you shot the previous day. What a shock this was! It has taken me many years to get used to seeing myself as others see me, and also seeing myself instead of my mental picture of the character I'm playing. First of all, very few of us ever see ourselves except as we look directly at ourselves in a mirror. Thus we don't know how we look from behind, from the side, walking, standing, moving normally through a room. It's quite a jolt. Second is the fact that when you read a story you create a mental picture of each character. For the first few years this is true even in reading a script. You don't see yourself because you haven't had much experience in seeing yourself. Thus as you act the part, in your mind you envision your mental picture of the author's character. You go to the rushes and somebody has stolen that heroic figure, and there you are—just plain old everyday you—up on the screen. It's one hell of a letdown.

At least one familiar experience was mine in that first picture: leadingladyitis. June Travis was the love interest, and it was only natural that I should carry the plot into after-hours. June, a very nice and understanding person, was the daughter of a vice-president of the Chicago White Sox. We went down to the beach one night to ride the roller coaster and do all those amuse-

79

ment park things. At a shooting gallery, I carefully instructed her in the procedure in shooting a .22 rifle. She knocked off every clay pigeon in the place and then rang the bell with that 50-point shot that means sharpshooter—and she did it all without embarrassing me for my foot-in-mouth assumption that she couldn't shoot a rifle. She even managed to beat me throwing baseballs at milk bottles, and made me like it. Thus it was no chore at all to take care of my leadingladyitis and make me like it.

Before the cure, however, we reached one point in the script eagerly awaited by me. This was the scene where boy gets girl and you go into the clinch. The director said "Action" and that's just what he got. I moved in like there was no tomorrow, and the next thing the studio came undone like a wet cigar. I discovered that a kiss is only beautiful to the two people engaged in doing it. If you really kiss the girl, it shoves her face out of shape. Your lips should barely meet, thus leaving her as beautiful as you know she is—and yet you must give the impression of a fervent kiss. This is a lesson forgotten all too often today, and I cringe when I see the big two-head closeup on television or in pictures by a newer school who seem to be trying to push each other off camera instead of producing a romantic feeling with the audience. Someone should make every new performer and director look at the early love scenes of the Ernst Lubitsch pictures.

Anyway, this was not my only fault. My head was casting a shadow by getting in the path of her key light; my collar was pulled out of shape by the position of my arm; all in all, I had to draw back and start over with the realization that work is work, and fun is fun, and kissing was more fun at the high school picnic.

With hardly a pause between pictures, I was put to work in a thing called *Sergeant Murphy*. It had originally been bought for Jimmy Cagney. He was smart enough to turn it down, and it found its way to the B unit. Actually it wasn't too bad and was based on a true story of a cavalry horse, smuggled into England to become winner of the Grand National. This picture started shooting on location and thus introduced me to more of California than Hollywood.

We drove up to the beautiful Monterey Peninsula, to the 11th Cavalry, where all of the outdoor shooting would take place. This was a little more homelike and familiar to me than the sound stage at the studio. Playing a cavalryman, surrounded by regular Army personnel, was reminiscent of my last few years at Fort Des Moines. After all, I was second lieutenant now, Cavalry Reserve.

I was hardly out of one uniform when I was back in another, this time as a Navy flier. I was rushed to Coronado for an A picture—not as the lead, however. This picture, *Submarine D-1*, was already under way. It starred Pat O'Brien, George Brent, and Wayne Morris. Some place in the studio higher echelons it had been decided to provide a surprise ending to the picture, so that neither of the three stars would end up with the girl. I would come in as her fiancé in the last reel of the picture.

It was a pleasant week, exciting to be working in this higher-priced atmosphere and, as it developed, beginning a friendship with Pat O'Brien that would play an important part in all that has happened to me. As a sideline, I would also learn from this experience to take fan mail with a grain of salt, because all of the film I shot ended up on the cutting-room floor and they decided to let Wayne Morris get the girl. Fan magazines, however, printed pictures and stories of me, and plugged the picture—and I received a certain amount of mail from people who told me how much they loved me in *Submarine D-1*.

Before long, however, Brynie had me back at work. He had bought the experiences of a retired veteran of the Secret Service. I'm sure the Secret Service wasn't exciting enough for Brynie, and he threw away everything but the title. I became the Errol Flynn of the B's. I was as brave as Errol, but in a low-budget fashion. These were action pictures. I fought in prisons, where I was planted to obtain evidence; I fought in a dirigible down at sea, only because Brynie had available some wonderful stock footage of a dirigible down at sea. I fought in an airplane which was complete with a trap door that could drop the unwary to an awful death—if the villain could get his hands on the right lever. During all this, I made the firsthand acquaintance of most of the stuntmen in the business.

Once it was learned that I was still young enough and physically able to do my own fight scenes, the director could cut the schedule in half by putting in a double for the villain and shooting over the villain's shoulder on my face for most of the fight. One of my fights took only thirty seconds on the screen, but for three days I had been fighting Jack Woody, one of the better men at his trade. We went through tables, doors, back and forth, and across the room until, in spite of the faking, I was black and blue and stiff in every joint. On the third day, I was to deliver a knockout punch. Very simply, my fist was to go past his jaw; he himself would snap his head back, and in the sound room they would dub the sound of flesh meeting flesh. The director kept insisting that I was missing him too far. Perhaps he was anticipating getting a little better shot. He got it. Desperately, trying to obey orders, I caught Jack flush on the jaw. His eyes glazed, his knees went limp, and slowly he sank to the floor. I was filled with mingled emotions. Naturally I felt terrible about the accident. At the same time, it was the first time I had ever knocked anyone out, and it was kind of nice knowing I could do it.

A week later, in the same picture, I had to fight another villain. Enter Stuntman Number Two. In the course of routining our fight, I told him of what had happened and said, "I sure hope I never do that again." Quietly he informed me he knew it had happened: Jack was his roommate. On the third day of our fight there was another accident—only this time I had one eye closed, with a beautiful purple mouse that reminded me of that football game against Elmhurst many years before. He was properly apologetic—strangely enough, in almost the same words I had used to his roommate.

82

I did a lot of things I'm too smart to do now, but in those days I felt if the director asked you to do it, there must be a built-in guarantee that nothing could go wrong. I swam with the villains supposedly shooting at me from a railroad bridge; the bullets, hitting the water six inches from my face, were in reality metal slugs from a slingshot wielded by a prop man riding the camera dolly. I even let them shoot a bottle out of my hand with a slingshot.

No story of Hollywood should ever be told without due regard to that special breed I've already mentioned: the stuntmen. Their backgrounds are as varied as the things they do—former fighters, professional athletes, rodeo champions, race drivers and pilots. Doubling the stars is only a minor part of their daily work. They are the faceless men you see dying in battle, plunging from cliffs, dragged by horses, swept over waterfalls. They are independent bargainers. They have the respect of everyone in the business.

During all those action pictures, I would have one of two companions as comedy relief in each picture. They were great performers and have since proven their right to far better things than we were asked to do. They too were of the Seven Little Foys: Brynie's younger brothers, Charlie and Eddie.

Noel Smith was the director of most of these action epics, and the scripts were so rushed that he and Charlie or Eddie, and I, would rewrite most of them on the set and plug their more glaring holes. One, however, which came down to us was so bad we didn't think a repair job could help. The producer of this epic made the mistake of telling us we should shoot the scripts the way they were written—and with this one we did just that. Never has an egg of such dimensions been laid. In one scene the villain shot me, and after he walked away I took out of my pocket a Spanish language dictionary (the scene being laid in Mexico) now embedded with a bullet, kissed the book fervently, and said, "Boy, if you ever need an endorsement, call on me"—at which point I put the book in my hip pocket: I suppose in the event that next time he might shoot me in the fanny.

Brynie loved to get at the finished film with a pair of scissors and help in the cutting. He and Noel saw the first rough cut of this one. Noel told me that Brynie just got up and walked out of the projection room without a word. Two days later Noel's phone rang and, without any greeting whatsoever, Brynie's voice growled, "What the hell can we do with it?"

Noel was ready for him with some suggested retakes that would cost about thirty thousand dollars. Back into the projection room they went. Brynie watched it again, holding the suggestions which had been typed out. When the screen went blank he handed the typewritten pages to Noel, and said, "It isn't worth it."

If you think I exaggerate, let me tell you the studio promised this film would never be released in Hollywood, where it could destroy all of us. To this day, the promise has been kept. However, I was on a publicity junket in the Northwest, and walking back to the hotel one night I passed a small theater, where this turkey was on display. I stopped to look at the stills in front of the theater, and glanced up to find the ticket taker had recognized me. He was just standing there, shaking his head. I said, "Now wait a minute, I didn't even want to make this picture in the first place," and all he would say in reply was, "You should be ashamed."

About this time my first picture had been released and Bill Meiklejohn assured me it was safe to send for Nelle and Jack. Even though Jack's heart condition made him unemployable, I realized it wasn't doing him any good to just sit around feeling useless. Fan mail had started to arrive and was becoming a problem. I cooked up an idea that turned out to be not only good for him, but of great value to me. I turned this assignment over to him, and it became in reality a regular job in which he had a pass to the studio, working with the mail department. He took charge of ordering the necessary photos and stationery and, in short, set up a system for handling what would turn out to be thousands of letters.

Not all of my movies were in the B action epic class. Occasionally I descended from leads to bits and smaller supporting roles, but in so doing ascended to a better class of picture—the A's. Of course by this time, I learned that progress, careerwise, could be made only by getting into the A pictures. On one of these jaunts into higher-class atmosphere, I found myself playing a radio announcer in *Hollywood Hotel*. The star was one of the top box-office figures in Hollywood, Dick Powell, who couldn't have been nicer. Without realizing just how it happened, I found myself in one of the canvas director's chairs usually reserved for the stars and principals. Dick somehow, easily and smoothly, had drawn me into the inner circle as if I had more than two and a half lines.

I was one of thousands who were drawn to this very kind man, and who would think of him as a best friend. Sometimes our paths took us in different directions and months would pass without our seeing each other. Still in these later years, when we did meet again, it would be as if no interruption had occurred. I cannot recall Dick ever saying an unkind word about anyone. He always seemed to feel such genuine pleasure at seeing you, and he had a habit of greeting you with the line "God love you." It was quite a while before it really penetrated my consciousness that when Dick said it, it wasn't just an expression—he meant it.

There were other pictures with Dick, Humphrey Bogart, and Pat O'Brien—sometimes all in the same cast. One picture called *Cowboy From Brooklyn* saw me really do a nosedive and forget everything I thought I'd learned about the business. Dick was the cowboy; Pat O'Brien and I were to play two sharp Broadway hustlers out to parlay him into our meal ticket. Knowing Pat's great ability at fast talk, I decided my only chance was to do counterpoint and not try to match him in his specialty, but play against it by being soft and slow-spoken. Of course, it just didn't make any sense at all. Lloyd Bacon was the director, a fine director, but not really able to sit a greenhorn down and explain what he was doing wrong. Scene after scene I would discover had been rewritten after one or two of my drawling rehearsals, and

85

the rewrite would wind up with someone else being given most of my lines. I was miserable, too scared to ask the director what was going on, and really beginning to yearn for my good old Secret Service pictures where I was a big wheel.

A wonderful old character actress one day sat me down and laid it on the line. Dick and Pat had been too embarrassed to tell me, although both of them had gone to Bacon and begged him to tell me what I was doing wrong. He had shrugged them off, saying he just didn't know how to go about it. This old gal did. She said, "Pat builds the scene up and with your line you drop it right in the cellar—and he has to try and bring up the tempo all over again." With the ice broken, Pat felt free to join in giving me a lesson in acting.

The very next scene called for me to make an entrance in Grand Central Station, face a battery of the press, and, complete with straw hat and cane, do a carnival shill act introducing our cowboy discovery. Bacon must really have been dying, figuring how he would rewrite this scene to get rid of slowpoke me. Talk about history repeating itself: I was back in the announcer's booth at WOC, the day I got mad enough to read a commercial correctly. Bacon said, "Action," I came through the door like gangbusters, bounced the cane off the floor, caught it in mid-air, and launched into my pitch. There were no more rewrites.

Pictures with those pros were fun to see, but even more fun to make. Ann Sheridan was the love interest in this one. Neither of us knew that a few years later we would co-star in what would be the biggest break for both of us.

One of the accolades of which I was proudest during this period was my acceptance at a special table in the commissary. No formal invitation was issued; you just found that you were a member of a kind of club. Father Superior was a director, Brick Enright. With him would always be Mushy Callahan, studio physical ed instructor and former junior welterweight champion of the world. On any given day the rest of the chairs would be filled with Jimmy Cagney, Frank McHugh, Allan Jenkins, Pat, Dick, Bogart,

86

and a few others, with now and then guest appearances by those free-lance artists who were old stage veterans and buddies of the regulars, like Walter Catlett. The last one to sit down usually became target for that day.

Whoever was the victim fought alone. My cross was the horse cavalry. I actually used to study cavalry books at night in order to have answers the next day. In between ribbings, however, a still-worshiping movie fan like myself would sit back and listen to the stories, rich with the aroma of backstage and greasepaint. Cagney would reminisce about the time that he and Pat and Frank had Christmas dinner in a cheap hotel room, roasting wieners, which was all they could afford, in the gas jet, while the others watched through the transom to warn if the landlord was coming. There was the classic about the great John Barrymore, approached one day by an art-conscious lady who wanted to know if Mr. Barrymore thought that Romeo and Juliet had engaged in intimacies and advanced beyond the stage of innocence. Barrymore drew himself to his full height, arched his eyebrow, and said, "Madam, in the Chicago company, definitely."

Just about this time I was assigned a good part in what would turn out to be a top picture and a big money-maker. Warner's had bought the very successful play, *Brother Rat,* a military academy comedy about Virginia Military Institute. The story centered around three cadets always in trouble, played by Eddie Albert, star of the New York company, Wayne Morris, and me. My part was easily good enough to provide a steppingstone to stardom. Unhappily I learned another lesson. There is room for only one discovery in a picture. Eddie Albert stole all the honors, and deservedly so.

I was still a Midwest movie fan as far as the gay life of Hollywood was concerned. I had a feeling there must be an exotic night life going on into which I had not yet been initiated. I would be a long time finding out that the people of Hollywood are very much like the people next door. However, the publicity department saw that I dabbled a bit in café society to secure those

87

candid photographs needed for fan magazine publicity. One day on the set we were told of a big Warner premiere. Someone even newer than I asked, "Do we have to go?" and someone more experienced than I answered, "No, but you'll be around longer if you do." A publicity man asked me to escort a young girl under contract to the studio, who had recently done a great deal for sweaters in a Mervyn LeRoy picture. She was very young and very beautiful and we were both very scared—she in a gown borrowed from wardrobe, and I in a dinner jacket from the same place. Lana Turner and I went to the premiere in a taxi because I was afraid to drive my old convertible. I hadn't learned how easy it was to rent a limousine and play big shot.

The main part of my social life, however, was a tie with my Iowa background that served as a sort of decompression chamber. Several old friends from Drake University, companions of the Moonlight Inn days, had come to California seeking their fortunes. I turned out to be the only one employed for several months, and hence was the group's sole support. We explored California and did all the things that tourists do. I think our night life was really devoted to finding a substitute for Moonlight Inn, and we found our home away from home in a little emporium whose fame is greater than its size. It's still there on Santa Monica Boulevard, and I guess everyone who is anyone in Hollywood is familiar with Barney's Beanery. Barney is a kindly soul, who recognized our need for a pub we could call our own. He just smiled benevolently as we took over his piano player, a wonderful old ex-vaudevillian who knew all the harmonizing songs. Prosperous as I felt myself to be, I still didn't mind a little help now and then with my dependents, and Barney never interfered when we could find some drunk sentimental enough to buy us beers in return for some barbershop harmony. Only a few of our original group are left. One would die needlessly on a freeway; another would survive the Normandy campaign with the 3rd Engineers out in front of Patton's tanks, to die quietly at home of a coronary; and the rest of us are scattered. Only occasionally do our paths cross—those of us who are left—and we rediscover what a wonderful chapter it was in the life of each of us.

Of course Nelle and Jack had adopted the gang and it was mutual. They were in and out more than I was, and I think Nelle would have given someone an argument if he pointed out she hadn't really given birth to the whole gang. Jack was learning a little about Hollywood too. Every morning he would take the slow, careful walk the doctor had prescribed, and was soon well acquainted along his entire route. He never tired of shaking his head about this new land, insisting that Californians must be the hungriest people in the world. He said, "There's nothing, by God, but real estate offices and hot-dog stands."

CHAPTER

7

People come to Hollywood from many different places, and certainly are varied in their background and training, but all of them either bring one thing with them or acquire it upon arrival: the desire to see a certain story become a picture. I wanted to tell the story of Knute Rockne. I had no intention of playing Rockne. I had always seen Pat O'Brien as the logical star in the title role. I had something else in mind for myself—a fellow named George Gipp. No one could do the story of Rockne without devoting a portion of it to the great "Gipper."

It's hard to tell where legend ends and reality begins, but even the plainest, documented, factual story about Gipp still leaves him an extremely colorful character. In a day when college men observed the proprieties in dress, it is said that Gipp removed the cleats from a pair of football shoes which he wore daily, and his uniform in the classroom was usually a Notre Dame sweater worn over a sweatshirt with no shirt or tie. One night, filling time on a WHO broadcast, I had told the story of Gipp. As a freshman walking across the practice field, he had picked up a bouncing football and kicked it back toward the varsity players who were calling for it. He kicked it clear over the fence. Rockne persuaded this lackadaisical, easygoing stranger to don a football suit and then, irritated by Gipp's good humor, put him in the freshman backfield to carry the ball against the varsity—a varsity he had primed to murder the cocky freshman. Gipp went eighty yards for

90

a touchdown, tossed Rockne the ball, and said, "I guess the fellows are just tired." The rest of his story is sports history. One of the all-time great stars, he died two weeks after his last game. At the time of his death, as an indication of his versatility, he had a signed contract to play major league baseball.

Being brand-new in Hollywood, I explored my idea openly, questioning all who would hold still about whom to see, whether simply to do a treatment, or try to write a script, until I was sure everyone at Warner Brothers knew that I was an actor with pencil in hand. One day I stopped talking long enough to read in *Variety* the announcement that Warner Brothers were doing the life story of Rockne, starring Pat O'Brien. I rushed in to Brynie, clutching *Variety*, and sputtered that this was exactly what I had been trying to promote. He just grinned at me and said, "You talk too much." I suppose he thought I had some idea of charging plagiarism. The truth is, it had never occurred to me that one got money for story ideas: I just wanted them to make the picture so I could play Gipp.

When Brynie realized I was only excited about getting in the picture, he said, "Well, you'd better do something because they've already tested ten fellows for the part." I panicked. I knew I would hate whoever played this part. I went to see the producer. He was kind, but it was obvious he had no intention of even considering me for the part. Over and over again he kept saying, "Gipp was one of the greatest football players of all time." Finally it sank in: he was telling me I wasn't the type.

"But I played football for eight years," I protested. "I was able to go to college only because I played football."

Again came the answer: "But Gipp was the greatest player in the country."

My mind was beginning to function. "Wait a minute," I said. "You mean you think he has to weigh about two hundred pounds, and look like these fellows you see in the Coliseum?" He made a sort of shrugging gesture, and again repeated how great Gipp was. I was still too new in this business and too recent from the sports world to be polite. "You are producing the picture," I said, "and you don't know that Gipp weighed five pounds less than I weigh right now. He walked with a sort of slouch and a limp. He looked like a football player only when he was on the field." I wasn't getting any place. Then I remembered something a director had told me one day when we had been ordered to shoot a scene two different ways. I had thought it was a waste of time: we should decide in advance which version was correct and shoot only that one. The director had said, "You have to realize these fellows only believe what they see on film."

Without another word I left the producer's office, broke a few speed laws getting home, and dived for the bottom of my trunk. I came up with some photographs taken during my own college days (which weren't too many years back), and broke the same speed laws getting back to the studio. I barged into his office and slapped the pictures down on his desk. I must say the reaction was satisfying. Not very many fellows look like football players without the suit, and most do in the suit. I was smart enough to keep my mouth shut and let the photographs talk.

Holding them in his hand, he said, "Could I keep these for a while?"

I answered with one word, "Sure"—and headed home. I drove slower because it was hard to hold the wheel with all my fingers crossed.

I hadn't been in the house fifteen minutes when the phone rang. It was a call from casting: "Eight o'clock shooting—testing for the part of George Gipp."

Usually when a person is being tested for a role, some contract player is given the chore of playing the other part in the scene. You can imagine my gratitude when I arrived on the set and found that my assistant, complete with make-up, was Pat O'Brien, who already had signed for the Rockne part. It was a half a day's work he wasn't required to do, but he was there to give me all the tools possible to help me get the part he knew meant so much to me. I really didn't have to learn any lines; I had known Gipp's story

92

for years. My lines were straight from Rock's diary. Our test scene was where Gipp, ordered to carry the ball at that first practice, cocked an eyebrow and asked Rockne, "How far?"

I got the part. It occupied only one reel of the picture, but in that reel it was a nearly perfect part from an actor's standpoint. A great entrance, an action middle, and a death scene to finish up. By way of frosting on the cake, in the last reel of the picture Gipp is recalled to the audience when Rock asks the team to win one for the Gipper, and reveals for the first time that this was Gipp's dying request.

We shot most of the football stuff at Loyola. My first scene was, oddly enough, my entrance in the picture. (I had learned that Hollywood usually shoots the last scene first.) Pat handed me a football and then, as Rockne had done many years before, said, "Can you kick another one like that?" My line was, "I think so." However, in staging the scene, I had to kick the ball at a high enough angle to miss the camera which was in close for our two-shot. Instead of pointing my toe, I kept my foot in a normal position and caught the ball well up on my instep so as to get height. Pat and I started doing our lines. I could see the effort he was making to hold his face straight, and I was beginning to strangle a bit with the effort to choke down a laugh. I think we exchanged at least four lines of dialogue before the ball I had kicked came down right between us, almost hitting Pat on the head.

A few days later, we reached the scene wherein I was to run eighty yards for a touchdown. In typical location style (which means everything gets more and more confused until we reach complete chaos, then we film it), I was told, "Get into the football suit," then, "Get out of the football suit, we're going to shoot something else." It was early morning, so I sent to the lunch stand that usually follows location troops. I had a nice, big, greasy bacon-and-egg sandwich, a can of pineapple juice, and coffee—at which point I was told, "Get back in the football suit."

Well fortified with a heavy lump in my midsection, I did eighty

93

yards on a hot summer morning. Because it was a difficult dolly shot, I did the eighty yards all over again. Because the camera operator didn't like the way he had gotten the shot, I did eighty yards a third time. This time I didn't stop at the goal line: I just kept on going to the wooden fence where I was very sick. It's too bad I was several years ahead of my time. Today I could have gotten away with saying that throwing up was my own personal style of method acting.

The entire picture was a sentimental journey and a thrilling experience. Irish Pat—playing a Norwegian, coaching a team of all nations—chalked up an unforgettable performance. For inspiration Rockne's widow Bonnie was on the set every day as technical advisor. Between scenes most of our time was spent listening to reminiscences and stories of that great era when Notre Dame was the scourge of the football world. It was natural that Rock would one day use the story of Gipp's death to inspire a Notre Dame team. If the story had come out of his imagination, no one—including Bonnie—ever knew. To me the great significance was that Rock saved that story for eight years, and then didn't use it just to win a game, but used it to inspire a team that was losing mainly because of bickering and jealousy. For at least one half he gave this team, torn with dissension, the knowledge of what it was like to play together, and to sacrifice their individual quarrels for a common goal. As in every picture based on real life exploits, truth was stranger than fiction. There were scenes that couldn't be photographed because an audience wouldn't accept the truth, or it would appear too melodramatic. For instance, it is told that Jack Chevigny, who carried the last touchdown over the goal in that game and then was carried off the field himself with a broken leg, looked up from the stretcher and said, "That's the last one I can get for you, Gipper."

Filmed in early summer, the picture was rushed to completion for fall release. In a surprisingly short time a sneak preview was held in Pasadena, in keeping with the Hollywood custom of running a picture unannounced before a theater audience, to

94

get an "honest" reaction. Nervous as I was, I learned something unusual about watching myself. You can laugh at yourself on screen when you say something funny, but you can't make yourself cry. When I read Gipp's death scene I had a lump in my throat so big I couldn't talk. I can get the same lump just thinking about it, but suddenly there I was on the screen playing the scene, and I was as unmoved as if I had a cold in the nose. It was a terrible letdown and I went home thinking I was a failure. Actually, if I'd only been aware of it, the rest of the audience had the sniffles and I was unmoved simply because it is impossible to get worked up at your own death scene when you're sitting there well and healthy and very much alive.

Before I was out of bed the next morning, the phone rang. It was a studio call, to get into wardrobe for costume fittings right away: I was doing the second lead in an Errol Flynn picture, *Santa Fe Trail*. As a result of the preview the night before, a new door had been opened. Suddenly there were people on the lot greeting me who hadn't previously acknowledged my existence.

Arriving at the studio that morning, I was witness to something I hope I will remember as long as I'm in this business. On a rack in the fitting room were cavalry uniforms tagged with the name of the actor who, until that moment, had been assigned the part. Into the room rushed a wardrobe man, arms filled with uniforms hastily basted together for a first fitting. Without a word he gathered the completed uniforms in one arm, threw them in a corner, and hung the new ones in their place. It occurred to me then that it would be just as easy someday to throw my clothes in the corner and hang some other actor's in their place. It's a highly competitive business.

I discovered I would again be playing a biographical role, but with less attention to the truth this time. I was playing the young Lieutenant Custer and Flynn was playing J. E. B. Stuart, the great cavalry leader of the Confederacy, in a pre-Civil War epic that was in reality the story of John Brown. This, of course, was a stage of my career when I did the part assigned—gratefully, I might add—and didn't say, "Let me read the script first." Of course, I was aware that the stars read their scripts and decided whether or not they would do the picture. That is, most stars did. For about the first four days of shooting, neither Errol nor I had a call. At this point he flew into the studio in a rage. The fact that there could be four days' shooting without him had aroused his suspicion that perhaps this part wasn't important enough for him. He had sat down and read the script for the first time—and thus learned how important a part Raymond Massey had, in the role of John Brown.

Errol was a strange person, terribly unsure of himself and needlessly so. He was a beautiful piece of machinery, likable, with great charm, and yet convinced he lacked ability as an actor. As a result, he was conscious every minute of scenes favoring other actors and their position on the screen in relation to himself. He was apparently unaware of his own striking personality.

We worked all one night at the Warner ranch. At three o'clock in the morning we were shooting a scene around a campfire where, as cavalry officers, we were listening with amusement to the prophecies of an old Indian woman. Errol moved over to the director, had a whispered consultation, and a moment later my position in the group was changed, putting me behind a couple of other actors who had lesser roles but more height. This also removed me from the immediate vicinity of Flynn. During the rehearsal I realized that I wouldn't even be visible to the camera above the shoulders of the men in front of me. I figured that under the rules of the game I was entitled to protect myself, so as the rehearsal went on I kept quietly scraping a pile of loose earth together with my feet. I didn't make use of it in the rehearsal but when the cameras rolled, I quietly stepped up on my newly created gopher mound. When the time came for my one line in the scene it dropped like the gentle rain from heaven on the heads of the men in front.

I think I should mention Mike Curtiz was properly cast to direct the story of the madman John Brown. Our writer told me

96

that he had called the reference library at the studio, asking for a Brown biography under its title *God's Angry Man,* and a surprised voice on the other end of the phone had asked, "Is Mike missing again?"

We finally reached the end of the picture, and the hanging of John Brown. Mike was furious when he discovered he couldn't actually hang Massey but would have to use a dummy. When he was shooting a picture, Mike—who was normally a kind, good-natured soul—became a ruthless tyrant, as hard on himself as anyone else. It was a strange character quirk. In that hanging scene he was setting up his shot, looking through the viewfinder and motioning to a very elderly actor who played the minister, to move first to the left, then to the right; finally he kept motioning him to move back. The poor old fellow moved back one step too far, and fell twelve feet from the scaffold, breaking his leg. Mike walked across, looked down where he lay on the ground, turned to his assistant, and said, "Get me another minister."

With the completion of this picture, Rockne came back into my life. The picture was to be premiered at Notre Dame. There would be a big junket, including not only the cast of the picture but other stars as well. Bob Hope and all the regulars from his radio show made the trip. All in all, the party required two special cars to be added to the Super Chief.

I was building up such a head of steam over the trip that little else was on my mind. Certainly I was oblivious to what was going on in my immediate vicinity. Nelle cornered me one day and told me that someone else was excited. Jack would never let me see it, but the dream of his life was to make this trip. Here was an Irishman who had really worshiped from afar: he'd never seen a Notre Dame team play; he'd never even been to South Bend. He thought Pat O'Brien was the greatest man since Al Smith, and he sensed somehow his youngest son would pass a kind of milestone before the trip was over.

What a simple thing this would be for me to fix—still, I felt a chilling fear that made me hesitate. We had all lived too long in fear of the black curse. Nelle's optimism was in full tide—she'd tell Jack how important it was that he vote dry on the trip and she knew he could be trusted. Whatever happened, I'm glad she was so persuasive. It only took a phone call and the studio said yes before I got the question out of my mouth. This was characteristic of Warner's—you could battle about a lot of things but you traveled first cabin with them.

South Bend was something else again, with over a quarter of a million visitors crowded into that relatively small town. Rockne and Gipp are very much alive in the tradition that plays such an important role at Notre Dame, and everyone connected with the university was very willing to transfer their affection, for the moment at least, to Pat and myself as proxies. Saturday was the big day with lunch in the dining hall of St. Mary's followed by the game and at night the premiere.

First thing in the morning I called Jack's room, but there was no answer. All unsuspecting, I called the desk to ask if he had gone out. I was informed he and Pat had just come in. His weakness was prosperity, and this was prosperity in capital letters. The evening before at the university banquet he had sat with an old Dixon friend who was graduate manager of athletics at Notre Dame, and heard students, faculty, and distinguished alumni greet us with a thunderous ovation. Then while I peacefully slept, he had been taken into the inner circle, so to speak, by Pat who had adopted him in his warmhearted way. Some time later I was told of their early morning return to the hotel—it must have been quite a scene. Jack was sure the empty streets were a trap and that the quarter-million fans were lurking in an alley, just waiting to swoop down on Pat for autographs. At each intersection he would halt Pat while he tiptoed up to the corner, and peered cautiously around; then he would signal Pat to join him and they would scamper across the street to the shelter of the buildings. Pat loved every minute of it.

Unfortunately, I was in no frame of mind to enjoy a laugh. We were due at St. Mary's to lunch with hundreds of girl students, and the good sisters. It didn't ease my mind when I discovered

98

Jack was seated on the left of the Mother Superior. With little appetite I picked at my food, conscious that Jack was engaged in a lively non-stop conversation with his distinguished luncheon partner, not one word of which was audible to me. Fortunately I had underestimated him. On the way out of the dining hall, a beaming Mother Superior informed me my father was the most charming man she had ever met. I won't say I relaxed completely—we were still two thousand miles from home—but the homeward trek was as happy as the start and ended with Jack and Pat inseparable buddies.

Upon his return he told Nelle and Moon that he wouldn't mind now if his faulty heart did call it quits: he had had the most wonderful time of his life. Those words came to mean a great deal to us because, not too long after, his heart did give up the fight. I'm sure he knows that Pat and his new friends were there in the little church off Sunset Boulevard to say good-by.

MGM was sort of the Tiffany of Hollywood, so I was duly impressed when a loanout was arranged. The picture was the old Broadway play, *The Badman*, being refilmed for its umpteenth time. Only MGM would cast a fellow in the role of near-bankrupt rancher, and then wardrobe him in tailor-made Levi's. The effect of poverty was obtained by sandpapering and beating on the sidewalk the carefully tailored blue jeans, which went into the budget at seventy-five dollars a pair. If this sounds silly, it was, and thank heaven I had the good sense to think so at the time.

Wallace Beery was the "Badman," Lionel Barrymore my crotchety uncle, and the very nice Laraine Day the love interest. I was warned that Beery was an inveterate scene-stealer and would even get his face in the camera when it was a closeup on other players, with the camera shooting over his shoulder. The director briefed me on all that would happen, and assured me of closeups, to cover all stolen scenes. I gathered that I was not only being reassured but warned against protecting myself, lest it anger Mr. Beery who might just disappear in mid-picture.

If I had any ideas about protecting myself I forgot them when

99

I saw Wally operate. In one "two-shot" I thought I had him. He was standing beside his horse and I was at the horse's head. We were both profile to the camera, facing each other. With him anchored in place by a thousand pounds of horse, and me free to move around the horse's head, I didn't see how he could maneuver upstage and thus get the back of my head in the camera—but he was Wally Beery. He must have sprung that horse's ribs. By the scene's end he was full face to the camera, which was virtually shooting over my shoulder. Like the old adage about forced romance: when it's inevitable relax and enjoy it.

I'd been warned about Beery but no one had said anything about Barrymore. Let me make one thing plain—it was a great honor to work with him, and I'm glad I had the opportunity. Wally never rehearsed a line the way he would say it in the scene, so you were always on edge trying to anticipate a cue for your own line. Lionel was, of course, theater through and through, and you were made better by his great ability—providing you kept from being run over. He was confined to his wheelchair at the time and he could whip that contrivance around on a dime. It's hard to smile in a scene when your foot has been run over and your shin is bleeding from a hubcap blow.

Back in the meat and potatoes atmosphere of Warner's, I continued busy in some shaky-A pictures with now and then a lesser role in the class product. In *Million Dollar Baby*, with Priscilla Lane and wonderful old May Robson, I had another lesson in cinema make-believe, playing a concert pianist. For two weeks I went to the music department every day and spent hours at a dummy piano, following the hand movements of a pianist at a real piano playing Chopin, and all the music the picture called for. A lot of acting is imitation anyway, and I became pretty good as long as the piano remained silent. For a while there I almost convinced myself I could play.

I've always been glad that some of those pictures teamed me with Humphrey Bogart. Here too was a pro, but an affable, easy person, fond of gentle ribbing. At this time he was yet to reach his ultimate potential, which came about during the war years in *Casablanca*—a part he was given after George Raft turned it down.

By contrast I did a string of pictures with the Dead End Kids, which was an experience similar to going over Niagara Falls in a barrel the hard way—upstream. Counting noses and getting them all in one scene was a major chore, but sometimes it was a relief when they did take off and disappear for a few hours. You never knew when a canvas chair would go up in smoke, or be blown apart by the giant firecrackers they were never without. Having heard lurid tales from other actors, I approached my first picture with them in something of a sweat. Jimmy Cagney solved my problem one noon at the corner table. Having had his beginnings in the same New York Hell's Kitchen, he understood these kids as no one else could. "It's very simple," he said. "Just tell them you look forward to working with them but you'll slap hell out of them if they do one thing out of line." He was right— it was just that simple. I had the only unscorched chair on the set.

On one of my excursions into upper-crust picture-making I played in a truly fine movie, *Dark Victory*, with Bette Davis, George Brent, and Bogey. It wasn't, however, the rewarding experience it should have been. Most top directors let an actor interpret his role, and they go along on the course he has set, pulling a little more out of him and adding a touch here and there. But, now and then, even top directors cross a wire and get a short circuit. In this case the director had staked a claim on my role. I actually believe that he saw my part as a copy of his own earlier life. I was playing, he told me, the kind of young man who could dearly love Bette but at the same time the kind of fellow who could sit in the girls' dressing room dishing the dirt while they went on dressing in front of me. I had no trouble seeing him in that role, but for myself I want to think if I stroll through where the girls are short of clothes, there will be a great scurrying about and taking to cover.

I made a mistake I've promised myself will never be repeated. I tried to compromise and give him something of what he saw in the part. We came to our moment of truth near the end of the picture. In the scene George Brent comes to my apartment, desperate because of his failure to convince Bette that he loves her. She, in turn, thinks his love is pity because they both know she is dying. My part in the scene is to tell George she is on her way up to the apartment, and before I disappear I ask him to be kind to her because I love her too. It was a well-written scene, and a nice moment in the picture. I still insist there is only one way to play the scene and that is simply and with great sincerity. Our director hit the ceiling. He demanded, "Do you think you are playing the leading man? George has that part, you know." In the matter of studio standing, I was outweighed. He was a top director, doing only top pictures. I was up in that class on a raincheck. He didn't get what he wanted, whatever the hell that was, and I ended up not delivering the line the way my instinct told me it should be delivered. It was bad.

Brynie joined me in the shaky-A's with a timely production about the Battle of Britain. True to form, he reached down in the Warner grab bag, dusted off an old Cagney-O'Brien opus, *Ceiling Zero,* and we did it as *International Squadron.* The original had seen Cagney, a likable rascal, sacrifice himself to test out wing deicers. In our version I was a rascal who ferried Lockheed bombers to London, joined the R.A.F., and squared all my sins by taking a suicide mission. Those were strange times for a Hollywood that was used to getting battleships with just a phone call to Washington. Twin-engine Lockheed planes were rolling off the line a few blocks from the studio and being flown directly to England. If we needed one of those in our picture, we'd jolly well use it in a Lockheed hangar from 8 P.M. until 4 A.M. and then it was on its way to a real war. Our "Spitfire" fighter was a doctored-up Ryan monoplane that didn't even have retractable gear. It's funny, but people accepted our makeshift props with the same kindly understanding they gave to the local high school play.

This brought me finally to the picture that meant not only stardom, but still remains the finest picture I've ever been in: *King's Row*. There is no need to tell more than I have except to reiterate the debt I owe Sam Wood. If he were alive today, he could tell me on the phone he had a part for me and I'd say yes without waiting to hear the title of the script, let alone read it. It was a long, hard schedule and my first experience, I suppose, with an acting chore that got down inside and kind of wrung me out. Then with no more than a weekend off, Annie Sheridan and I joined a charming, talented gent from New York, Richard Whorf, in a Jerry Wald production called *Juke Girl*. This picture would have been a back-breaker if we'd had plenty of rest and a fresh start but, coming as it did, I discovered how nervous fatigue can creep up on you. On the night shift, going to work at 6 P.M., we shot night exteriors until sunup for thirty-eight nights. With all the misconceptions about pampered stars, none is so far afield as the belief that physical discomfort isn't tolerated.

Juke Girl was a serious story about the migrant crop-pickers in Florida. Night after freezing California night, we tried to act like sufferers from the humidity and heat of Florida, with glycerin sprayed on our goose bumps to simulate sweat. In every scene the background people smoked cigarettes to hide the fact that our breaths showed.

One big action scene involved a gang fight with goons smashing up a truckload of crated tomatoes. For three nights we wallowed around in those tomatoes—the same tomatoes. By the third night the prop men were scooping them up with shovels and slopping them back into the crates for the next shot. At midnight we called a halt for lunch, our clothes plastered with wet squashed tomatoes, so that no one felt like putting on a coat or sweater over the mess in spite of the cold night air. Suddenly there was a roar of anger from the first men in line, who happened to be stuntmen. The next thing we knew, a frightened caterer was sprinting out into the darkness across the tomato field with six burly stuntmen after him. The damn fool was serving stewed tomatoes.

Sneak previews are one way of learning you have a hit, but a sure method for measuring success is when a studio generously offers you a new contract while you are only halfway through the first one. Warner's had put a rough cut of *King's Row* together and wanted to talk new deal with me prior to the picture's release. My reaction was, "Let's wait until we've all seen the picture." I was outvoted by my own team. Lew Wasserman of MCA reminded me of a war that was going on, of Hollywood stars like Jimmy Stewart who had already been drafted, and of my own reserve officer status. He said, "We don't know how much time you have—let's get what we can while we can." I signed for a beginning salary three times as great as I'd been getting.

Juke Girl was finished (and I thought I was too), but Hal Wallis, in charge of all of Warner's productions, called and said he was sending out two scripts and I could take my choice. This was indeed heady wine—heretofore I had been *told* what I'd do.

One of the scripts was a so-so comedy, involving a boy and girl who worked at adjoining machines in an aircraft factory. The other was adventure and action: an R.A.F. crew shot down behind enemy lines and the saga of their escape and rescue. In the first I'd be *the* star; in the latter I'd co-star with Errol Flynn, and there was no denying his was the better part.

The next day I called and said, "Mr. Wallis, I can't decide between these two stories. You fellows have done all right by me so far, so I'll do whichever one you think is best for me to do."

If silence can register surprise, I heard it. I'm sure Hal hadn't taken many phone calls like this one. After a long, pregnant pause, he slowly answered, "All right—give me twenty-four hours and I'll call you."

Twenty-four hours later to the minute he called, and his choice was *Desperate Journey,* the Flynn picture. I said, "I must confess I lean toward that one, but I do have one concern. Having worked

104

with Errol before, will my part on the screen be as good as it is in the script? Of course," I added, "I'm in a little better position than I was the last time we worked together."

"Yes, you are," Hal replied. "But I promise you, the script will be shot as it is written."

That was good enough for me, so it was back to the R.A.F.

My high spot in the picture was a solo effort in which I knocked an arrogant Gestapo officer kicking, and calmly helped myself to his breakfast. It was one of those cocky bits that tickle audiences and Errol wanted to do the tickling. The day we moved onto the stage for that scene he became ill, and we had to stop shooting. All told, his illness recurred four times at quite an expense to the studio. Each illness saw a conference between director, producer, and Hal Wallis, and each conference ended with Hal ordering, "Shoot it as it's written." We did just that and I'm grateful to him: the scene got big laughs in the theater.

America was in the war by this time and I have no intention of doing a chapter on "Where Was I on December 7?" I was in bed asleep—how exciting can I make that? Many months before I had been ordered to March Field for a physical. Here my eyeball cheating back in Des Moines had caught up with me, and I was tagged "Limited service—eligible for corps area service command, or War Department overhead only." It was the opinion of the medicos at March that no such limited service officer would ever be called. All this, however, had taken place prior to Pearl Harbor. Now, with weeks of shooting on *Desperate Journey* still remaining, I received a letter that didn't even need opening: on the outside, stamped in red, were the words, "Immediate Action Active Duty." The inside informed me I would report to Fort Mason in San Fransico in fourteen days. Lew Wasserman had been right—I'd been collecting the new salary for exactly ten weeks and *King's Row* still hadn't been released.

The day we decided he was right we lunched in the Warner Green Room. Olivia de Havilland came in and joined us. In the course of conversation, Lew told us why Hollywood contracts are always seven years. It seems there is a California law that anything beyond seven becomes slavery. Lew hadn't dug this up just to play "Did you know that?" It was his opinion that the Hollywood custom of suspending actors and actresses—taking them off salary for refusal to play parts and then adding the suspension time to their contracts—was illegal. Fiery Olivia rose to this like a trout (a pretty trout) to a fly. She had taken so many suspensions she could grow old and still be on her original seven-year deal. What happened is history. With rare courage, she took on the whole picture industry and not only won her own freedom, but went all the way to the California Supreme Court in a $200,000 two-year battle that set the precedent for all actors.

I benefited from her courage while still in uniform. In spite of the newness of my contract, Warner's contacted Lew about tearing that one up and starting all over. One thing about the new contract puzzled me. All contracts are for forty weeks a year; mine was for forty-three. This particular demand of Lew's puzzled Jack Warner too. When all the commas were in place, J.L. said to Lew, "Now will you tell me why I've just given in to the only forty-three-week deal in the whole industry?"

Lew grinned like a kid with a hand in the cooky jar. "I knew you wouldn't go higher than three thousand five hundred dollars," he said, "and I've never written a million-dollar deal before—so three extra weeks for seven years makes this my first million-dollar sale."

Meanwhile, my fourteen days' grace had ended. I left for Fort Mason and as luck would have it, there, out of my *Sergeant Murphy* past, was an old friend from the Eleventh Cavalry—Bob Ferguson, now Colonel Ferguson. He'd learned through the grapevine that I was called up, and he just happened to be on hand: colonels can make things like that just happen. From him I learned I would be on the staff at Fort Mason as a liaison officer loading convoys.

CHAPTER

8

Colonel Ferguson turned me over to the adjutant at Fort Mason on that first day of my military service. I discovered that, even though I was in, another physical was required. I went through the same old business with the eyes, and one of the two examining doctors said, "If we sent you overseas, you'd shoot a general."

The other doctor looked up and said, "Yes, and you'd miss him."

Of course, I had to answer once again the question of how I got a commission in the first place. I figured enough years had gone by that no one would go to jail, so I explained my finger-squinting deception. Before my session with the medics ended, I was given my Army vaccinations. It didn't help any that I stood in line with the first batch to go through following the deaths of several men from inoculation with faulty vaccine. I wasn't alone in wondering if this vaccine was any different. I took the shots in my left arm, figuring I was going to need the right one for a lot of saluting. I wasn't long in waiting to deliver my first salute, to Colonel Phillip Booker.

The Colonel, a small, slim man with the wiry physique of a horseman, had been in the regular Army—specifically the field artillery—for thirty-four years. He was blunt, quiet, and all business. In a few moments I was turned over to the half-dozen lieutenants who would be my companions for the next few months.

Later in the afternoon, the Colonel came swinging through our outer office, paused in front of my desk, and in his Southern accent born of Virginia said, "Reagan, Mrs. Booker and I would be pleased if you'd have dinner with us tonight."

I must confess the invitation reassured me. Suddenly the world didn't look so new and strange. I thought, "Ah-*hah!* Even here, Hollywood does not go unnoticed." It was some time later before I learned Hollywood had nothing to do with my invitation. For thirty-four years the Colonel had done this with all newly commissioned officers as a kindly way of easing them into their new world—and all because of an unfortunate experience he himself had had when he first reported for duty.

Dinner was very pleasant that night, with not only the Colonel and his family, a lovely daughter and handsome son, but also a few other officers, both Navy and Army. All ranked higher than my second lieutenant bar.

Under the influence of a couple of pre-dinner martinis, and still confident that movies had given me an inside track, I relaxed enough to say, "Colonel Booker, you and I have something in common."

My remark caught everyone's attention, so we had a complete audience for the next few lines. "How's that, Reagan?" he said, and I said, "Well, I understand that you are a graduate of Virginia Military Institute, and I once played in a picture about V.M.I. called *Brother Rat*."

The Colonel looked me right in the eye. "Yes, Reagan," he answered, "I saw that picture—nothing ever made me so damned mad in my life."

Most of the time our half-dozen lieutenants, all cavalry, and fully conscious of the interservice rivalry between cavalry and the service of our commanding officer, the artillery, would hear the Colonel muttering to himself, "Never knew a cavalryman who knew a damned thing"—but we took no offense. We knew that with him loyalty was a two-way street and he would defend

108

us all the way to the Secretary of War if our mistakes were just that, simple mistakes.

Each one of us was equipped with a desk and the desks were equipped with glass tops. It's impossible to spend much time at a desk without using it as a footrest. Spurs were, of course, very hard on the glass tops. One day one of our lieutenants decided that, inasmuch as we weren't within shooting distance of a horse, he'd take off his spurs and slip them into a desk drawer to avoid the danger of cracking the glass. In this horseless era I'm sure many people, even in the military, have forgotten that spurs are a regulation part of the uniform for mounted troops. As Colonel Booker came swinging through our office, we popped up at attention. The Colonel didn't pause in his stride, and it didn't seem that he looked down as he passed the spurless lieutenant, but he uttered one line: "Aren't you afraid you'll catch cold, son?" He didn't wait for an answer. He didn't have to. He was hardly out the door before the lieutenant had the desk drawer open and his spurs back on.

I was having some trouble divorcing myself from the picture business. A San Francisco movie columnist arranged an interview through the post public relations office. When the Sunday paper featured this interview, along with several color photos of me in uniform, I had an instinctive feeling this was not the way to launch myself in the military. Actually there wasn't anything I could do about it. The request had come through an officer who outranked me. There followed requests for appearances at bond rallies and charity benefits. Then one night the post theater played *King's Row*. This was my first chance to see the picture that had brought me star status. Before a completely military audience, the officer in charge of the theater—and again one who outranked me—introduced me and made me say a few words. I was really beginning to squirm but didn't know any way to pull the string without looking hammy and as if I were being temperamental.

The payoff came when a request from higher headquarters

resulted in my being returned to Hollywood to appear at a giant rally of picture people for the purpose of launching the newly created USO program. Naturally I welcomed a trip home, but I couldn't escape the feeling that some of my associates were beginning to wonder just which business I was in. On Monday, following my Hollywood weekend, I arrived at the post at 8 A.M., ready to face the regular chores of tracking down supplies and lost equipment, and getting them stowed away on the proper ships. I had been in show business long enough to smell a scene—especially one featuring me. There was an atmosphere of hushed expectancy and I was told Colonel Booker was waiting to see me.

The atmosphere in his office was even more tense. The Colonel broke the news that I was wanted upstairs in the Commanding General's office. He made sure that I knew I was to stand at attention before the General, and address him in the third per son. That headquarters building was only a normal two stories, but it was the longest staircase I ever climbed. The General wasn't alone: two or three of his staff—all full colonels—were on hand for the execution, or maybe they just wanted a closeup view of that "odd ball" from Hollywood. The General was icy of eye and voice, even though he did permit me to sit down, and then he started a lecture which was to the effect that he understood I had a career to return to, and was justified in keeping that career alive, but that I was also an officer with a duty to perform. I don't know what he expected me to say beyond "Yes, sir," but my weeks of frustration and worry had built up a full head of steam. Instead of "Yes, sir," I told him I too was concerned about these inroads on my duty and that, while I realized my previous occupation could possibly be used to further the war effort—such as helping launch the USO program or selling bonds—I was also sure that some requests would be made simply because I was an actor, had uniform, and would travel. I confessed that I didn't feel qualified to decide which were useful and which weren't. I asked permission to refer all such requests to the General's office, so that I could serve where there was a

110

reason and a purpose, but that someone could refuse permission on military grounds for those appearances which were of no value and only interfered with my duties at the post.

Luck was with me. Out of honest concern I had spoken lines that couldn't have been improved by Shakespeare. Suddenly the General became fatherly and friendly, and promised me his office would do just what I had suggested. I exited with a feeling that, at least in spirit, he had taken me to the door with his arm around my shoulders. By the time I got downstairs, word had preceded me. One of the staff had slipped out before me and brought the word to Colonel Booker, who later quoted him as saying I "pulled the General's stinger before he even got warmed up."

A short time later every Army post received a Presidential directive that each post would observe I Am an American Day, with appropriate ceremonies. I received another call from the General—an order to prepare a program for his approval that would fill that part of the directive relating to appropriate ceremonies. Colonel Booker helped me work out the details of the military part, parade and all, but suggesting a well-known Hollywood personality to sing the National Anthem was my own idea and was, I figured, something that would give the General a little edge in his observance of the day that other generals couldn't boast. (I was learning fast.) In our next meeting the General approved the program and then, after clearing his throat a few times, questioned me about whom I had in mind for the National Anthem.

My newly acquired military instinct led me to hesitate and avoid a direct answer long enough for the General to express his own preference. It seems the General had always admired Jeanette MacDonald: indeed, he had never missed a MacDonald-Nelson Eddy picture. With a few quick phone calls I was able to report back in less than an hour that Miss MacDonald would be on hand.

In accepting our invitation, Jeanette had volunteered to do

more than just sing the National Anthem, and we had taken her up on her kind offer. All over San Francisco—in empty factory buildings, in the Cow Palace, and in the huge dog track—thousands of American men were housed, waiting to go overseas. Stripped of all organizational emblems, they weren't permitted to visit the city or set foot outside their quarters. They were bound by wartime secrecy.

We had arranged for Jeanette to do a concert for seventeen thousand of these anonymous soldiers gathered in the infield of the dog track. She sang to them from an improvised stage in the box seats. There may have been a few entertainers who thought soldiers wanted risqué material, but they were overlooking the fact that these were normal American boys, the ones a great general before the war's end would refer to as "the best damned kids in the world."

Jeanette's music was, of course, of somewhat classical tone and they loved it. She finally ran out of material, but they were whistling and cheering, and wanted more. In desperation she said, "I know only one more song that I can sing. It happens to be my favorite hymn." She started singing "The Battle Hymn of the Republic"—and then a strange and wonderful thing happened. All over the vast infield men started coming to their feet and, when she finished, seventeen thousand soldiers were standing, singing with her.

My days at Fort Mason were coming to an end. The Air Force had a priority on all manpower, particularly reserve officers, because it was the branch of service with the greatest need for expansion. Colonel Booker called me in one morning and showed me a letter from General George Kenny of the Air Force. In dry, military language it stated that the Air Force was creating a motion picture unit and that Fort Mason had a lieutenant with motion picture experience, and if he was not essential to the Command, and if the commanding officer was willing, and the lieutenant (a fellow named Reagan) was willing, could he be transferred to the Air Force and assigned to a base in Los Angeles?

The Colonel said, "Reagan, the General says if you are willing."
I thought I should at least bring to the Colonel's attention the fact that this assignment meant shipping me back home—something the Army does not normally do. Colonel Booker said he didn't think that was of any importance, and then he said, "To tell you the truth, whether you're willing or not, you're going—because in thirty-four years, this is the first time I've ever seen the Army make sense. This is putting a square peg in a square hole."

Now and then I have wished that the Colonel had described me as a round peg in a round hole but, at any rate, I was on my way home. I would regret one price I had to pay for this assignment: no more boots and breeches, not in the Air Force. There would be many times when the fly-boys would tease me about horse cavalry, and I would always answer, "I was physically unfit for the cavalry, but still plenty good enough for the Air Force."

My first duties in my new assignment involved interviewing and processing applicants for commissions. Naturally there were some who were looking for a way to escape a different kind of military service. For the most part, however, our volunteers were ineligible for regular military duty and simply and sincerely wanted to serve. My out in the former cases was the fact that we could not commission any man who was eligible for the draft. With me was a non-commissioned officer and former assistant director, interviewing men for enlisted status in the new unit. A great many people to this day harbor a feeling that the personnel of the motion picture unit were somehow draft dodgers avoiding danger. The Army doesn't play that way. There was a special job the Army wanted done and it was after men who could do that job. The overwhelming majority of men and officers serving at our post were limited service like myself, or men who by reason of family, age, or health were exempt from normal military duty. Nevertheless, some people can't resist looking for ulterior motives.

Of course, this new post—which later took over the Hal Roach

Studios—did have its wacky side. No one really believed it existed, and that included some of the men who belonged to it. From a motion picture standpoint, however, it added up to about two hundred million dollars' worth of talent on the hoof. We would turn out training films and documentaries, and conduct a training school for combat camera units. All of the newsreel material in the theaters, of bombings and strafings, was the product of these units. Happily I can point out that the Air Force had been pessimistic in its estimate of casualties, so the replacement need was less than had been anticipated. The result was that we were sending some of our combat trainees through the course three and four times while they waited for an assignment. I have yet to go out on a personal appearance without having at least several TV or news photographers tell me, after a press conference, they learned their trade in our combat camera school.

We were thirteen hundred men and officers, very few of whom had had any military training, and trapped by an Air Force regulation that said only flying officers could command a post. Our only flying officer was the stunt pilot, Paul Mantz. Paul had been commissioned to major because of his background as a great motion picture stunt pilot and his vast knowledge of aerial photography. With no more military training than any of the others, he found himself post commander. Being an old buddy of most of the Air Force top brass, he had a natural concern that we would be criticized for our lack of military know-how. I probably would have shared his worry except that at Fort Mason I had had a chance to see how the military operated when it had a specific non-combat function to perform. At Fort Mason we went to our desks like any civilians checking in for their daily stint. But not us. Every morning at the crack of dawn our men were rousted out to stand roll call. Now, roll call in the Army is usually for the purpose of assigning men their duties for the day. In a post such as ours, the men's duties were permanently assigned—for the most part the same jobs they'd done for years. They were film-cutters, wardrobe men, prop men, or engaged in some other type of work normally associated with the making of pictures.

At about three in the afternoon, picture production would stop while the whole outfit got into Class A uniforms and marched out in front for the ceremony attendant upon taking down the flag. One of our enlisted men was my old friend, Charlie Foy. Charlie had closed his nightclub for the duration and was doing his duty at what had become known in the industry as "Fort Roach." Charlie had ideas about the foolishness of a 6 A.M. roll call, so he had hired a soldier to stand there in the dark and yell "Present" when the name Foy was called. One day, thinking his stand-in was on leave, he hired an understudy, and thus his deception came to an unhappy end. When the name Foy was called by the squadron commander, two voices from opposite ends of the line yelled, "Present!"

I must say that whoever coined the phrase that war was a long period of boredom, punctuated by a few seconds of intense fear, was right—but someone must have gotten an overdose of fear because I got more than my share of boredom. We had inherited an officer who, oddly enough, had had a few months' training in the crash officer's training courses. He was filled with cadet spirit. He had the assignment each afternoon of marching our men out to the flagpole. I was standing at the corner of a studio street when they came swinging by, four abreast, our ex-cadet shouting orders like a true drillmaster. I shouldn't have done it, but on the other hand we should have been making pictures, not playing soldiers. When the column was just about halfway past me, so that my voice was audible to most of the men but not to their commander, I said, "Splendid body of men—with half this many I could conquer MGM." The ranks dissolved.

The very next day I saw the result of this chink in military decorum. They were practically at the same place when their commander bellowed, "Column right, march"—and Sonny Challif, down in the middle of the ranks, yelled, "Don't do it, fellows—

it's a people's army." For the second day in a row our column of troopers dissolved.

One friend of mine—a fine actor, Arthur Kennedy—was assigned to the wardrobe department. It was no secret to me that Arthur was smarting under the harassment of his sergeant, who just didn't like actors. One day the First Sergeant told me Private Kennedy requested permission to see me. His visit wasn't unexpected: we'd had dinner together the night before and I knew he was coming in to ask for a transfer. Still, with the Sergeant and the other non-com clerks watching from their desks, I had to go through the formality. Arthur, ramrod straight, stood before me and asked for a transfer in proper military fashion. I double-crossed him and said, "Don't you get along with your sergeant?"

He could have killed me, but he knew he had to answer. The non-com clerks were all ears. Art stood there, looking over my head, and then said, "Sir, I just feel he isn't exactly the type to stand on a blood-soaked beach and yell, "Onward, men!' "

He was rewarded with the assignment he wanted most of all—assistant to the post gardener. I'm not fooling: we were both farmers at heart. Like women exchanging recipes, we spent most of our social hours discussing fertilizers and crab grass. I was derelict in my duty to a certain extent. From my office window I could see the hedge that fronted the Roach property. Arthur dearly loved pruning that hedge. He manicured it every other day. He had discovered that when he got to the end of the hedge he was out of sight of the guard station, and he used to duck out and go home. I just couldn't believe the war effort would be helped by turning him in, and besides it wasn't my fault that I had the only window with a view of the hedge. There were a lot of days I'd have given a million bucks to have gone with him.

Through a strange twist that later was corrected, the very men who had prepared themselves for military service as reserve officers found that a kink in Army red tape prevented their promotions. When I finally became a first lieutenant, I had become so celebrated by lack of promotion that the enlisted men made a six-inch set of silver bars which I wore that whole first day. In due time I became a captain but, when I was proposed for major, I asked that the recommendation be canceled. I know the fortunes of war are distributed unevenly, but who was I to be a major for serving in California, without ever hearing a shot fired in anger?

Because some people can't respect a uniform unless it's on a dead soldier, I must speak of the serious side of Fort Roach. The military has need of many things, in wartime especially, so there will always be a need for specialized posts such as ours. None has ever been more successful in fulfilling its mission than was our wacky Hollywood stepchild. One of our thirty-minute training films cut the training period for aerial gunners by six weeks. Most of the millions of men who never experienced combat had an almost reverent feeling for the men who did face the enemy. Somehow there was a feeling that you understood better than a civilian what it was they were going through. In our post this was heightened by the millions of feet of raw film that came back to us from combat. We saw the shots that were edited out before the film could be viewed by the public. A fighter plane cracked up on landing, in flames, the pilot vainly trying to get out of the cockpit and dying before your eyes. His comrades rushing into the flames, vainly trying to save him, until they were pulled back with their own clothing on fire.

Two of our biggest jobs remained almost unknown. The first involved the destruction of the Nazi missile launching sites at Peenemunde. Had the Germans been able to launch these rockets at the English coast a year earlier than they did, there might not have been a Normandy invasion. From aerial reconnaissance and espionage, the Allied High Command had learned of the existence of these launching sites and knew full details of their construction. In Florida, the Air Force received hundreds of trainloads of concrete and steel, and built exact replicas of these massive launching sites. Then the bombers experimented in an effort to bring about their destruction. Our units made pictorial records of the experiments.

Day after day we sat in a projection room in Culver City and saw fantastic slow-motion films of huge bombs bouncing off these concrete buildings as if they were pebbles, until one day we saw on-screen armor-piercing bombs dropped from low altitudes, going through the huge concrete walls as if through cheese. Those films were flown directly to the 8th Air Force, and the launch sites were knocked out in time to postpone the V2 launchings long enough for D-Day to take place on schedule.

Possibly our most important job was also our most secret—in fact, it was one of the better-kept secrets of the war, ranking up with the atom bomb project. It was a pure Hollywood product. Everyone who has ever seen a picture based on World War II is familiar with the briefing which preceded a bombing attack: an officer, pointer in hand, using maps and photos to point out the target and give helpful clues so that the bomber crews could reach their objective.

All on their own, our special effects men—Hollywood geniuses in uniform—built a complete miniature of Tokyo. It covered most of the floor space of a sound stage. Above this they rigged a crane and camera mount and could photograph the miniature, giving an effect on the screen of movies taken from a plane traveling at any prescribed height and speed. Air Force headquarters was naturally skeptical, but an impressive group of generals arrived in Culver City to preview this Hollywood effort.

Our experts carefully intercut their movies of the model with real scenes taken from flights over Tokyo. Even though the generals were informed this had been done, they were unable to pick out those scenes that were actually Tokyo and tell them from the movies of the model. Skepticism turned to enthusiasm. Officers of all ranks began arriving at our post accompanied by huge cases of photos. The entire sound stage was put under twenty-four-hour guard and even our own personnel were denied admission—indeed, any knowledge of what was going on except for the few who would actually be engaged in the project. It was somewhat

118

reassuring to discover that Uncle Sam hadn't been quite as asleep as many of us had believed in the prewar years.

Some of the newly arrived officers were former missionaries, botanists, and travel agents. Their photographs had been accumulated over many years. Just by coincidence, a photograph of a butterfly would include in the background a factory or military installation. Additional models were built of other principal Japanese targets. By this time our experts could not only show the entire bomb run over a target, but could repeat the run as seen through the bombsight, and with the help of our animation department give a third view as the target would appear on radar if darkness or bad weather was encountered.

I got in on this project as narrator. It was enough to make all of us fearful of talking in our sleep, or taking an extra drink. We knew the bomb targets well in advance, including the proposed time of the bombing raid, because our geniuses—informed in advance of possible weather conditions—were even floating the right kind of clouds between the camera and the target. Bombing crews in the Pacific would sit in a theater and view a motion picture apparently taken from a plane traveling at, say, thirty thousand feet. Beneath them would be the Pacific, in the distance the hazy coastline. My voice, as briefing officer, would be heard above the sound of the plane motors. I would usually open with lines such as, "Gentlemen, you are approaching the coast of Honshu on a course of three hundred degrees. You are now twenty miles offshore. To your left, if you are on course, you should be able to see a narrow inlet. To your right—" Then I would mention some other visible landmark. In this way we would take the bombing crew right into the point where my voice said, "Bombs away." We kept these simulated bomb runs so authentic that, following each raid, recon planes would fly their film from Saipan direct to us so that we could burn out portions of our target scene and put in the scars of the bombing. Our film then would always look exactly the way the target would appear to the crews going in on the next run.

This effort was confined to Japan, because the war in Europe was drawing to a close and there was little of Hamburg or Berlin left to destroy. Only an outfit like ours could have accomplished this task. Here was the true magic of motion picture making, the climax of years of miracle-making that had made Hollywood the film capital of the world.

Of course old "Fort Wacky" had no trouble going from the sublime to the ridiculous. A special unit including some of our top talent was shipped to Europe to do a feature-length documentary in color film of the Thunderbolts, the fighter planes that dramatically broke through the fog and turned the tide in the Battle of the Bulge. One of the group was the top playwright, Norman Krasna. All of them had been given an intensive course in the combat camera school because all of them would double in brass as cameramen. At an advance air base in France, Norman found a lonely cross on the far side of the air strip. There was no name, no epitaph, just the date: December 24, 1944. All of his playwright's instinct was aroused by this lonely cross which evidently marked the final resting place of an unknown soldier who had died on Christmas Eve.

He knew that somehow it must be worked into the finished film. He photographed the cross against the blue sky, then waited hours to get it starkly silhouetted against the sunset. He even crept over to photograph it in the swirling mists of early dawn. He had hundreds of feet of color film, taken at every hour of the day and from every conceivable angle. Finally he needed more than film, so he revealed his secret in the officers' mess and demanded to know if there wasn't someone present who knew the history of this unnamed grave. He was met with blank surprise: no one had knowledge of any grave. They asked him just where this thing was located. He could tell them its exact whereabouts—he had practically worn a path across the airstrip leading to it. Suddenly, light dawned. The Army dates and marks buried latrines in this manner, so they won't be reopened before nature and quicklime have done their disease-preventive work. Norman possessed the most color footage of a latrine in Army history.

My own movie-making was not entirely confined to narrating training films. Irving Berlin wrote and produced a musical comedy called *This Is the Army*. It was Irving who had performed the same chore in World War I with his show, *Yip, Yip, Yap Hank*. All of the proceeds went to Army Emergency Relief. In World War II his production, following a worldwide stage run, was made into a movie. Warner Brothers made the picture, turning over every penny of the more than ten million dollars the picture grossed, including the profit from their own chain of theaters, to Army Relief.

A number of us were assigned temporary duty to take part in the film. I played the lead opposite Joan Leslie. Let me correct one false impression that has resulted from some typically erroneous fan magazine stories. None of us received picture pay. This was a military assignment and we drew our military pay. I was a first lieutenant at the time, so my gross was about $250 a month. In spite of the studio generosity and its sincere effort to see that every penny possible went to Army Relief, there were still some soreheads who complained that Warner's would profit because this big box-office show would result in audiences seeing the trailers advertising future Warner pictures whose receipts would not go to Army Relief. This was something of a new high in lint-picking.

It was a thrill for me to get away from the desk and feel once again that I was part of the picture business. There were old friends to work with: George Murphy played my father and I've never let him forget it—but in all honesty I must admit it took a cane, a lot of make-up, and a white dye job on his hair to prepare him for the role. Some of the cast of the picture went back in friendship to my earlier sports career. Joe Louis was sent on from the 1st Cavalry Division. Craig Stevens, later to become famous as Peter Gunn, also had a role in the picture.

A backstage story had been added to the stage musical. The

story tied our World War II epic to the World War I play, so a part had been written wherein Irving Berlin would sing his own World War I song, "Oh, How I Hate to Get Up in the Morning." For some reason known only to the gods of show business, song writers invariably have lousy voices. Irving was no exception. The day we filmed this number a husky grip standing beside me turned and whispered, "If the fellow who wrote this song could hear this guy sing it, he'd roll over in his grave."

The first week of shooting I was introduced to Irving five times, and each time he was glad to meet me. Then one day he sought me out. The night before he had seen the film we had shot those first few days. He said, "Young fellow, I just saw some of your work. You've got a few things to correct—for example, a huskiness of the voice—but you really should give this business some serious consideration when the war is over. It's very possible that you could have a career in show business." I thanked him very much and began to wonder if he just hadn't seen any movies, or if the war had been going on so long I'd been forgotten.

By the time the picture was finished, I knew one thing for sure. There was one outfit in the Army wackier than ours. The Army could never go so far afield from the rules as to have a show troupe and call it a show troupe. Obviously *This Is the Army* wasn't a regiment or a battalion, but it had to be something military—so it was officially designated a Task Force.

With the picture finished, I went back to my desk—only to be swept up in another frantic bit of picture-making. For many years Warner's had staged an annual party for all studio personnel. The big feature of the party was a film that was the talk of Hollywood. All during the year script clerks would quietly mark any take in which the performers had blown up or forgotten their lines—particularly if these lapses registered on film as profane or funny reactions by the performers. At the end of the year, all of the blowups were put together in a feature-length film, suitably scored by the music department. As a close personal friend of the Warners, General Arnold had seen one or two of these movies.

We received a call from the General at Fort Roach that he was entertaining a large number of generals and admirals, and wanted such a film from us. Knowing the General's favorite philosophy was "The difficult we do immediately, the impossible takes a little longer," no one at our post was going to tell the General that unless you plan in advance and save the blowups, they just don't exist—so we set out to produce the film the General wanted.

We wrote a script and filmed it just as we would any regular picture. I played a scene with a trick map that went rolling up, flapping like a runaway curtain, and one of our high spots was a scene of a pilot—apparently flying a fighter plane at thirty thousand feet when a grip, carrying a ladder, suddenly appeared off his wingtip, walking in thin air. Our show was pretty successful: it still turns up on television on the Late Late Show. To my knowledge, this is the first time it has ever been exposed as the fake it really was.

The war was drawing to a close. The Third Reich had collapsed, and somehow we all knew the Japanese phase would not take long. In addition to everything else I had experienced, I think the first crack in my staunch liberalism appeared in the last year and a half of my military career. Our post was classified as top sensitive, meaning that we were so involved with high-secret projects that we were subject to extra security measures. Because of this we had been denied civilian employees, in spite of a shortage of secretarial and clerical help. We were directly under the command of the Air Force General Staff, and we dealt directly with the Pentagon. In Washington, Congress charged the military with hoarding manpower in its vast civilian contingent while it raided defense plants and industry by way of the draft. The result was an Army order that every military installation would reduce its civilian employees by 35 percent over a six-month period. As far as I know, each installation carried out this order, but at the end of the six months the Defense Department had more civilian employees than when the reduction started. Neither Congress nor the military had figured on the ability of Civil Service to achieve eternal life here on earth. As fast as reductions took place, new positions were found for the displaced.

One day two men came into my office and introduced themselves as representing Civil Service headquarters. They informed me they were surveying our post for civilian personnel. I told them there must be some mistake, that we were denied civilian personnel because of our security status. They smiled and, somewhat superciliously, one of them said, "You'll have civilians." He was right: within two weeks we received an order that we would get 250 civilian employees. Our personnel section—responsible for the complete records of 1,300 men and officers—was only half the size of the contingent that moved in to man the personnel office keeping track of the 250 civilians. Their rules and regulations filled shelves from floor to ceiling, around virtually the four walls of a barrack-sized building. Every one of the employees we received was transferred in from another military installation in the area.

One day one of our writer officers stormed into my office, demanding a new secretary. He said his patience was exhausted and that the one he had couldn't spell cat. I called for the woman who was in charge of civilian personnel, and had the Captain tell her his story. Very pleasantly she replied, "All right—I'll draw up the papers and you sign the charges, Captain."

At this he grew suspicious and said, "What do you mean—charges?"

"Well, to remove this girl for lack of ability," she said, "we must have a trial similar to your military court-martial. You must take the stand in her presence, and establish her incompetence."

The Captain was horrified. He looked at me and said, "To hell with it. I don't care if we lose the war—I won't do it."

As adjutant, I had learned a little about Civil Service by this time, so I said, "Wait a minute." I turned to the woman and asked, "How can we solve the Captain's problem without a trial?"

She was all ready for us with what seemed to be normal Civil

Service procedure. There was a qualified secretary now doing clerical work who could be transferred to the Captain's office. Of course, this left a problem of what to do with the incompetent secretary, but this really wasn't such a difficult problem. She could be moved to another assignment, even though doing so meant an improved assignment. So the incompetent wound up with a promotion and a raise in pay. No one in the administrative hierarchy of Civil Service will ever interfere with this upgrading process because his own pay and rating are based on the number of employees beneath him and the grades of those employees. It's a built-in process for empire building.

A certain amount of trading took place with our sister service, the Signal Corps Motion Picture Unit, so one sunny afternoon I found myself in my car driving over to Disney Studios to narrate an animated short for the Signal Corps. On the way, listening to the car radio, I heard the announcement of a fantastic bomb that had just fallen on Hiroshima. It was the end, of course. It was also a beginning, but none of us knew that at the time.

CHAPTER

9

During World War II, the American Federation
of Labor—biggest grouping of autonomous unions
in the world—gave the United States a no-strike
pledge for the duration. The doubtful kudos for
breaking that fragile pledge went to the Hollywood unions.

As early as March, 1945—long before the dropping of the Hiroshima A-bomb—the first of a series of a half-dozen strikes was
called in the movie capital. The recurring rash of labor disputes
was to cost movie-makers approximately $150,000,000. About
8,000 workers lost 9,000,000 man-hours and $28,000,000 in wages.
The strikes contributed substantially—along with television and
the 1948 anti-trust federal action that split theater ownership
away from the major producers—to the final disintegration of
Hollywood as the key movie manufacturer of the world.

What made this acceleration of the decline and fall of a five-
billion-dollar business particularly ironic was the fact that the
strikes were unnecessary. They were almost entirely jurisdictional
squabbles between unions. Moreover, they created such a breach
between the units of Hollywood craftsmen (more than thirteen
hundred of them being arrested for violence in a single year)
that the Communists were able to infiltrate the movie business
with impunity. And let the truth be known they had a hand in
creating the mess in the first place.

When movies first loomed as potential runaway money-makers,
the pioneer producers hired labor from the then-flourishing local

stage companies. The stagehands, in those days, did everything from swinging a hammer and moving props to painting scenery and dismantling it. These men, organized into a union called the International Alliance of Theatrical Stage Employes (IATSE), were the traditional movie technicians. They were also a member of the gigantic AFL group. But their historical structure—cutting vertically up through many trades—was directly opposed to the way most other AFL unions were organized, on a horizontal plane. In other words, the majority of AFL unions were like layers in a cake; the IATSE almost alone, because of the traditional peculiarities of their work, cut down through the layers like a knife. Carpenters are carpenters, painters are painters, plumbers are plumbers, but stagehands are carpenters, painters, plumbers, and a dozen other things all at the same time.

The first Hollywood labor organizing came in 1916, just prior to the entrance of the United States into World War I. Previous to this the IATSE had been involved in numerous jurisdictional quarrels with their brethren in the AFL. They had won, for example, a fight with the International Brotherhood of Electrical Workers in 1914. The AFL awarded the stagehands jurisdiction over the motion picture projectionists. Encouraged by this, IATSE in 1918 launched a drive to form "one big union" of movie workers, which failed.

The simple disagreement (which later became hideously complicated) was that the IATSE considered such craftsmen as carpenters, painters, and electricians as true "stagehands" when it came to working in the Hollywood studios. The feeling of the building trades unions was that the only proper way to organize their unions was along craft lines. What really mixed it up was that the AFL recognized both points of view—and, in addition, the SAG, of which I was an officer, was also an AFL member in excellent standing.

This bickering actually preceded pictures, as witness the battle many years ago in New York between stagehands and carpenters. In that early day a theater owner would call on his stagehand employee to repair a broken seat out front or the lobby door or whatever required hammer, nail, and saw. Carpenters objected and peace came with a compromise that made a border of the footlights and proscenium arch. Behind this border, backstage as it were, the stagehands held forth; out front was the land of the craft unions. In 1920 or 1921 Big Bill Hutcheson, czar of the out-front carpenters, brought this dispute to Hollywood when he introduced a resolution in the AFL calling for a recognition of the picture studios as factories manufacturing film, and thus the province of the craft unions.

After years of jurisdictional set-tos, competing to supply manpower to the studios (a situation in which the producers were in the middle and of which they often took advantage), the IATSE signed a compromise agreement in 1925 with the carpenters. Later, in 1926, the same agreement was signed by the electrical workers. This, be it noted, was the famous 1926 Agreement. It formed the common core of contention twenty years after.

Its basic premise was that same "proscenium division." In this case, the proscenium was the entrance to the actual studio building normally referred to as the stage. All work in the stage was to be IATSE; all work on the lot outside was the job of the craft unions. It seemed fair enough. But, though the lid had been put on, the kettle still seethed underneath.

In August, 1933, an IATSE local struck to insure its control over sound-recording men. The International Brotherhood of Electrical Workers broke the truce by sending in its own technicians through the picket lines to the producers as strikebreakers. Their lead was followed by the United Brotherhood of Carpenters and Joiners and others. As a result of this strange unionized strikebreaking, the IATSE lost the battle to its own brother unions. In the years following it gradually pulled back into prominence and strength. In 1935 it demonstrated its power by closing the whole Paramount theater circuit in Chicago over a jurisdictional dispute with the IBEW.

The producers found that they could stay in business only a

128

very short time with their theaters closed. Because they had to, they yielded to the IATSE demands. This created the first closed shop in Hollywood. The other unions sullenly gave in for the moment—and bided their time.

Two years later, the fight again burst into the open. In 1937 a number of small craft groups (such as the make-up artists) banded together into the Federated Motion Picture Crafts. They had, up to this time, whimsically belonged to the Brotherhood of Painters, Decorators and Paper Hangers. They now found they could not share the IATSE Basic Studio Agreement and get a 10 per cent wage boost negotiated by IATSE, unless they joined that organization. Thus eleven FMPC unions, backed by the painters, struck the studios.

IATSE retaliated in exactly the same fashion as the painters and carpenters had done in 1933. They sent their members through the lines, into the studios, as strikebreakers. It chartered some of the FMPC members and got them favorable contracts. But the IATSE also withdrew its objections to the painters getting a contract as a craft union—the first instance of Hollywood producers extending recognition to a craft union local. It was a stagehand victory but one which was to cost them dear.

In 1939, this peace was disrupted by a clash between the IATSE and the ex-craft union members within its ranks. These agreed to form the United Studio Technicians Guild which developed enough strength to secure a National Labor Relations Board election. The alarmed IATSE then compromised some issues with the officials of the other craft unions, enough to win the election by a majority of more than two to one

Here it is pertinent to point out that the painters, headed by Herb Sorrell, were the only craft union which did not back the IATSE. The painters were later joined by some scenic artist rebels who joined the Screen Set Designers, Illustrators and Decorators, Local 1421. This group later became the spearhead of the series of 1945-47 strikes.

So much for the dry bones of the history of labor in Hollywood.

The IATSE was entrenched on one side; the craft unions sniped away, occasionally using big artillery; the AFL anxiously hovered over both sides. The producers spread out in no-man's land, shrewdly running from one side to the other, seeking what concessions they could get.

Such a recapitulation is useful to understand what was to come, the bloodiest and most destructive strike in movie history. The AFL Screen Actors Guild was to be the key agency in the strike negotiations and eventual settlement. It was a remarkably altruistic gesture, mixing in between two furious factions. The SAG got little credit from anyone except its own members. Its proper concern throughout was to prevent the closing of the studios. Such a closure would have thrown more than nine-tenths of its ten thousand SAG members out of work and twenty thousand other employees.

It should be pointed out that the SAG was as militant a labor organization—perhaps more so—as most of the older unions. It had a comparably rugged early history. In 1933, when it was organized, 90 per cent of the actors (contrary to the public impression) got less than five thousand dollars gross per year. About 50 per cent got less than two thousand dollars a year. All this before the deduction of taxes and the 10 per cent agents' fees. "Day players" were in the majority, getting possibly a day's work a week, if they were lucky—and being paid fifteen dollars for it.

It was standard usage for the studios to work the actors late every Saturday night, often into the early hours of Sunday. If a holiday intervened, the actor had to work all day the following Sunday to make it up. Meal periods were totally irregular. There was rarely as much as a twelve-hour rest between calls. There was no overtime or night pay—yet the work was far from continuous. A "nine-day picture" might mean that it would stretch out for as many weeks but the actor had to be on call and ready at any time for his nine days of work—being paid only for that specific time. He could be cut off the payroll at any moment and recalled later without reward for the intervening idleness. No travel time was allowed. Wardrobes and tests were generally without recompense. There was no arbitration machinery or any other way to redress a grievance except by falling to one's knees and weeping before the producer.

As for box-office returns, the public had been misinformed for years about the enormous salaries of the stars under the guise of sweet publicity. True, stars such as Douglas Fairbanks had at one time got thirty-seven thousand dollars a week (without income tax), but such days were long gone. Less than three cents out of each box-office dollar paid the entire cast of a picture from extras to stars.

Despite this, in March, 1933, the studios forced all actors under contract to take a 50 per cent pay cut. All free-lancers had to take a 20 per cent cut. Threats of an actors' union were heard but the producers made counterthreats of loss of jobs, if such a union were formed. Nevertheless, six actors met privately—including such men as Ralph Morgan and Grant Mitchell—and planned a self-governing guild. It was incorporated on June 30, 1933.

Most actors feared joining it. Actors Equity Association had tried earlier to organize such a group; it had failed miserably due to the use of the blacklist by the producers as a successful strikebreaker. Even after the SAG was a reality, detectives hired by the studios trailed such people as Robert Montgomery from place to place; meetings had to be clandestine; all details were hush-hush.

The first meeting in July turned up only twenty-one members. But they included people such as Alan Mowbray, Leon Ames, James Gleason, Ralph Morgan, Ken Thompson, Boris Karloff, and C. Aubrey Smith. Within a few months, the organization had most of the stars in movies. Its underlying strength came from these big names who could bargain as they pleased; they could put real power behind the man that Eddie Cantor described as "the little fellow who has never been protected and can't do anything for himself." The SAG motto became: "He best serves himself who serves others."

A four-year struggle for a union shop contract began. In 1935, the SAG became a member of the AFL. In 1937, in a meeting in the American Legion Stadium, by a 98 per cent majority, thousands of motion picture actors decided to strike. That evening broke the back of the studios. In a way the scene that night was more dramatic than many engineered for the screen. Actors made speeches to fellow actors about the "now or never" status of their position. It was well after midnight when a messenger arrived with a single sheet of paper. It read:

"We wish to express ourselves as being in favor of the Guild shop. We expect to have contracts drawn between the Screen Actors Guild and the studios before expiration of this week." It was signed by the two biggest producing moguls: Louis B. Mayer and Joseph M. Schenck.

In 1938, a novice in Hollywood, I suddenly found myself on the board of the SAG. The reason for it was not my fame nor fortune nor talents—but simply that the board had created a policy of a broad representation of all segments of the actors' world. They wanted day players, multiple-picture players, contract players, free-lancers, extras (we represented them at the time), and stars alike. After the election of the board, there were always some reluctant resignations. One of the vacancies happened to fit my classification: new, young contract player. I accepted with awe and pleasure.

Let me say here that I believe in the SAG with all my heart. It is a damned noble organization: I mean exactly that. It demonstrates in practical terms the instinctive brotherhood which exists in show business. The ones who made SAG work in the early days were the ones that didn't need it: Eddie Cantor, Edward Arnold, Ralph Morgan, Robert Montgomery, James Cagney, Walter Pidgeon, George Murphy, Harpo Marx, Cary Grant, Charles Boyer, Dick Powell—and a hundred other stars who could call their own tunes on screen salaries. They were willing to use their personal power in order to better the lot of their fellow actors. In contrast to the usual union custom where the minimum becomes the maximum, to this day they have kept 90 per cent of the membership with their own individual bargaining powers; only 10 per cent actually work for contract scale. This is a measure of their integrity: keeping the dignity of the artist intact with the benefits of the craftsman.

I must admit I was not sold on the idea right away. I was doing all right for myself; a union seemed unnecessary. It was Helen Broderick, that fine actress, who nailed me in a corner of the commissary one day at Warner's, after I'd made a crack about having to join a union, and gave me an hour's lecture on the facts of life. After that I turned really eager and I have considered myself a rabid union man ever since. My education was completed when I walked into the board room. I saw it crammed with the famous men of the business. I knew then I was beginning to find the rest of me.

My initiation into labor matters proceeded slowly but intensively over the next three years. I had to resign from the board when I was swept into the Army but I kept in touch. Almost as soon as I got out in 1945, I was reappointed to the board and found myself swept into a maelstrom of the most rugged decisions I have ever had to make.

The sperm of the 1945 strike appeared in June, 1937, shortly after SAG grew strong enough to make its own strike threat. A group of studio interior decorators formed the Society of Motion Picture Interior Decorators. Six months later, the SMPID (as it would be known in a world where initials have replaced titles) got a studio contract for five years. In 1942 it was renewed with a difference: if a majority wanted another bargaining representative or affiliated with another organization, the new contract said, it could insert the name of their new agent into the contract—or, at their option, the producers could call the whole thing off.

Meanwhile, in 1939, the stagehands had chartered their own

133

Local 44. It included jurisdiction over "set dressers," doing essentially the same job as the decorator members. Local 44 asked the studios for a contract; the producers refused, pointing to their agreement with the decorators. Richard Walsh, the stocky, spectacled, international president of the stagehands, agreed that 44 had not been certified as a bargaining agent and withdrew his request—with the proviso that the producers would take the same stand with any other uncertified union who claimed to represent this group of craftsmen. The producers agreed.

In October, 1943, the decorators voted to affiliate with Local 1421 of the painters' union—which also included set designers, illustrators, costume illustrators, sketch artists, and model builders. The next month the officers of 1421 asked for negotiations for a new contract, acting as the decorators' agents. The producers agreed. Negotiations went on until April, 1944, both in Hollywood and New York.

But the producers seemed to be unsure of their position in this area. The haggling stretched out to August. The studios asked the painters to get certification by the National Labor Board to quiet their doubts. At this point, the stagehands (IATSE 14) intervened with a claim for their own set decorators. The fracas hit the fan.

We can more than guess that tempers had been smoldering for a long time over the IATSE-craft unions dispute and that the protracted niggling and red tape finally blasted everything sky-high with an outside assist from those who didn't really want a solution—just a problem and trouble. At any rate, 1421 refused to ask for board certification but offered to prove it represented 100 per cent of the defunct decorators' union. The producers received these membership records and—possibly because of stagehand complaints—refused to honor them. A series of recriminatory letters, news stories, and column leaks followed; relations inevitably sank to name-calling on both sides. Conciliation meetings and hearings by the War Labor Board and the Department of Labor failed to settle the point. And to prove how easily a witch's brew can be concocted by determined cooks, remember the whole thing involved only seventy-eight decorators. William Green, president of the AFL, refused to touch it with a disinfected ten-foot pole. A highly confusing and non-binding arbitration was held which favored 1421 but was not attended by any stagehand representatives.

In January, 1945, a strike vote was overwhelmingly passed by 1421. The next month, the embattled producers filed a labor board petition requesting that an election be held to determine whether 1421 or stagehand 44 should be certified as bargainers with the studios. The storm built up as the NLRB hearings commenced in March.

Whether the patience of the craft unions was exhausted by the unconscionable delays or whether they expected defeat in the hearings is not material to what happened. March 12, 1945, the Conference of Studio Unions went on strike. Twelve thousand men hit the bricks.

At this juncture, it might be well be explain that the CSU (Conference of Studio Unions, since this introduces a new set of initials) was a rump group within the AFL in Hollywood. Its membership consisted of those unions who felt dissatisfied with the way that the local AFL Labor Council was aiding their interests. It included the painters, carpenters, electricians, and various other smaller unions. It had the support of non-AFL unions such as the International Association of Machinists, as well as the giant Congress of Industrial Organizations (CIO), then at loggerheads with the AFL, and independent groups, such as the Screen Writers Guild. From the beginning, the SAG held aloof from participation until the murky atmosphere of fact versus recrimination and rumor could be cleared up. At that time, it promised, it would take a vigorous and active part in whatever action deemed necessary.

Local 1421 established picket lines. Other AFL craft unions— including carpenters, electricians, and painters—honored them. So did the machinists, who had some time earlier read themselves

135

out of the AFL because of just such a jurisdictional strike. The next day Walsh wired the producers a warning. If they recognized 1421, the stagehands would not work. On the 14th, he also wired all studio and theater stagehand locals in the United States and Canada to stand by for a possible order to cease handling or exhibiting any motion picture made by Hollywood.

The situation amounted to a handsome deadlock. Two days later a wire came from William Green, president of the AFL, addressed to Sorrell:

I OFFICIALLY DISAVOW YOUR STRIKE AND CALL UPON YOU AND YOUR ASSOCIATES TO CEASE AND DESIST FROM USING THE NAME OF THE AMERICAN FEDERATION OF LABOR IN ANY WAY IN CONNECTION WITH YOUR STRIKE PARTICULARLY UPON BANNERS CARRIED BY PICKETS OR IN ADVERTISEMENTS OR IN PUBLIC STATEMENTS.

His telegram went on to demand that Sorrell and those on strike under his leadership "terminate immediately the unjustified strike in which you are engaged." It added that Green regarded it as "a violation of the no-strike pledge made by the AFL to the President of the United States for the duration of the war. It should never have occurred and ought to be terminated at once." Green concluded by pointing out that the "honor, integrity, standing and good name" of the AFL were at stake.

It was the strongest possible command to call off the strikers. It had no effect. The conclusion was obvious that other forces were encouraging Sorrell and his forces to continue their unauthorized walkout. I have indicated what these forces were: how powerful they were, I shall discuss later.

After March, the most fantastic confusion in the world—and Hollywood is normally a way-out town—ensued. I can only give the details that came to me through friends and the newspapers— remember, some of us were still engaged in a dispute called World War II. By the end of the first week in March, the 12,000-man strike had dwindled to 8,500 and the strikers had been denounced by L. P. Lindeloff, international head of the painters ...

136

Sorrell demanded that *all* jurisdictional questions be settled right away . . . and the Screen Officers and Employes Guild together with the Screen Publicists Guild went back to work. In April, all the studios closed and the picket lines vanished in mournful acknowledgment of the death of President Roosevelt . . . but the week before the producers had fired the striking set decorators. Two days before, the NLRB had ordered all the set decorators in motion pictures to vote as to whether they should be represented by 1421 or by IATSE 44 . . . both sides challenged all the votes—as a precautionary measure, I suppose—and the election was won handily by the stagehands.

At the end of six weeks of striking, both sides used the figures 95 per cent . . . the studio said they were working at 95 per cent capacity and Sorrell claimed his strike was 95 per cent effective. By the end of the next week, it was figured that about 1,200,000 man-hours had been lost together with about $1,500,000 in wages (Lindeloff switched his stand to support of the strike). Sorrell threatened a nationwide boycott of fifty-five "striker-made" pictures across the nation . . . and the state of California decided the strikers were not entitled to unemployment insurance. Some rebels in the stagehands supported Sorrell and the Screen Writers Guild, and two other small unions came out in support of Sorrell, together with the Screen Story Analysts Guild and the Screen Cartoonists Guild. The AFL Teamsters Union came out powerfully against it.

In July the office employees went back to work by secret vote . . . in August the publicists went back with them, which meant that at least there would be no shortage of cheesecake art for pin-ups in military lockers. In August, the Congress of Industrial Organizations—the CIO with which the AFL was then at dagger point—voted to support the strike and the Teamsters violently denounced the CIO, the SWG, and other strike-supporting unions.

The strike went on, undeterred by these developments. By tacit consent, on August 16, the AFL Executive Council in

137

Chicago upheld Green's telegram to Sorrell. They also told the stagehands to revoke four new charters issued to unions replacing those of the strikers and empowered Green to arrange conferences between the stagehands and the Conference of Studio Unions to bring about a settlement.

In October, the predicted violence broke out before Warner's . . . a thousand strikers turned up at 5:30 A.M. and overturned three autos . . . twenty were injured in the ensuing riots. There followed patrols of sheriffs and police officers . . . the strikers resorted to mass sitdowns after two days of fighting. The strike wound up at the end of October, with a reported 85 percent of the strikers going back to work or about four thousand men. They had lost an estimated $15,000,000 in pay.

As far as I was concerned, until the summer of 1945, the rumble of interior labor troubles was a faraway echo. I was the calm vacant center of the hurricane. By the time I got out of the Army Air Corps, all I wanted to do—in common with several million other veterans—was to rest up awhile, make love to my wife, and come up refreshed to a better job in an ideal world. (As it came out, I was disappointed in all these postwar ambitions.)

I had heard about the strikes from the start but I was relatively unconcerned. I was still in the Army. It would be six months from January before I would get my discharge—though I didn't know it then—and Hollywood, in spite of my being stationed in Culver City, seemed as far away as another planet. I like to pay attention to one thing at a time. At the moment, finishing off the war in Europe and the Pacific seemed all-important.

Moreover, what I heard and read in the papers placed me on the side of the strikers. I was then and continue to be a strong believer in the rights of unions, as well as in the rights of individuals. I think we have the right as free men to refuse to work for just grievances: the strike is an inalienable weapon of any citizen. I knew little and cared less about the rumors about

138

Communists. I was truly so naïve I thought the nearest Communists were fighting in Stalingrad.

Finally, I was a near-hopeless hemophilic liberal. I bled for "causes"; I had voted Democratic, following my father, in every election. I had followed FDR blindly, though with some misgivings. I was to continue voting Democratic through the 1948 election—Harry S. Truman can credit me with at least one assist—but never thereafter. The story of my disillusionment with big government is linked fundamentally with the ideals that suddenly sprouted and put forth in the war years.

Like most of the soldiers who came back, I expected a world suddenly reformed. I hoped and believed that the blood and death and confusion of World War II would result in a regeneration of mankind, that the whole struggle was simply the immolation of the phoenix of human liberties and that the bird of happiness would rise out of the ashes and fly everywhere at once. It seemed impossible that anyone would be blind to the possibilities of the future, or that business could go on as usual. If men could cooperate in war, how much better they could work together in peace!

I was wrong. I learned that a thousand bucks under the table was the formula for buying a new car. I learned that the real estate squeeze was on for the serviceman. I discovered that the rich had got just a little richer and a lot of the poor had done a pretty good job of grabbing a quick buck. I discovered that the world was almost the same and perhaps a little worse.

My first reaction was to take a vacation at Lake Arrowhead. There I could laze around and take time to figure things out. One of the first impulses was to rent a speedboat twenty-four hours a day. The rental proprietor thought I was crazy. "It's all right," I assured him, "I just want to know that the boat is there at the dock any time I want to take a drive on the water. I can't walk on it any more." In the end, the rental cost more than the total cost of the boat. It was worth it.

The results of my weeks of freedom crystallized a determination in my mind. I would work with the tools I had: my thoughts, my speaking abilities, my reputation as an actor. I would try to bring about the regeneration of the world I believed should have automatically appeared.

This introduced me to the world of reality as opposed to make-believe. To this day, I am trying to assess what the slow awakening of my faculties cost me. Perhaps I will never be able to add it up. But it came. When it did, it was hard-hitting enough to rid me of all illusion. If Hollywood was an island, no man could live in it.

The proper post-World War II school tie in the United States seemed to be either a violent red or black with inconspicuous swastikas. Those of us who didn't share either of these political tastes felt a little bashful about wearing ties with a red-white-and-blue pinstripe: it seemed almost boastful, seeing as how we'd won. Most of us preferred an inconspicuous, neutral gray.

About this time I had the uncomfortable consciousness of being unusually naïve. Something seemed wrong—and I wasn't exactly sure what it was. But one of the few advantages of naïveté lies in the fact that you don't have too much mental rubbish. You can approach a fresh notion with the delight of a child snatching up a bright new dime. Preconceived ideas and pear-shaped prejudices appear crystal clear to the ingenuous.

Coming out of the cage of the Army back into the free-for-all civilian life, I was well fixed. My $3,500-a-week contract was running; Warner's were casting about for a movie script that would pay them off. I was ware and healthy but I didn't have a practical thought in my head. I hoped it would be a long time before I got one.

So what did I do with my newfound freedom? I built two model boats—the U.S.S. *America* and a freighter. They were about two feet long, took two months to construct, and cost me a total of $105.75. I drove people like Dick Powell nuts, trying to convince them life wasn't complete until you built a model boat.

I suppose this was proper therapy. My timetable of emancipation had run from discharge in August, 1945, to Lake Arrowhead for a few weeks, then back to Hollywood (where I was finally to go to work for Warner's in March of 1946). In between: the model boats. I had never built any such things before nor have I since, but then it seemed exactly the right thing to do. I still have them preserved in glass cases as a symbol to recall what I felt. Incidentally, they are pretty good.

Meanwhile I was blindly and busily joining every organization I could find that would guarantee to save the world. I was not sharp about Communism: the Russians still seemed to be our allies. There were as yet no rumbles of the spying that the USSR pros had been doing in the United States during the war; nor any rumor of the plans the Russians had for the capitalism which had saved their hides on every front. In that era, the American Communists were high on the Hollywood hog, but only by reason of deception. Most of us called them liberals and, being liberal ourselves, bedded down with them with no thought for the safety of our wallets.

Thus my first evangelism came in the form of being hell-bent on saving the world from neo-Fascism. At that time there were visible dangers of this. I myself observed more than forty veterans' organizations arise; most of them seemed to be highly intolerant of color, creed, and common sense. I joined the American Veterans Committee because of their feeling that the members should be citizens first and veterans afterward—and, as it worked out, I became a large wheel in their operations.

But in the meantime I became an easy mark for speechmaking on the rubber-chicken and glass-tinkling circuits. It fed my ego, since I had been so long away from the screen. I loved it. But, though I did not realize it then, both my material and my audiences were hand-picked, or at least I was being spoon-fed and steered more than a little bit. I considered myself quite a success until one evening in the spring of 1946. I had made my usual energetic pitch to howls of applause, but afterward a rather diffident local minister approached me.

"I agree with most of what you said," he murmured, "but don't you think, while you're denouncing Fascism, it would be fair to speak out equally strongly against the tyranny of Communism?"

I agreed it was fair. I wrote a new last paragraph to my speech, doing just that. As it happened, my next address was as a substitute speaker for Jimmy Roosevelt. I took the rostrum. In a forty-minute talk, I got riotous applause more than twenty times. Then I denounced Communism.

The silence was ghastly. I stumbled off the stage into the clasp of a friend whose face reflected my own amazement. "Did you hear that?" he whispered.

"I didn't hear anything," I muttered.

"That's what I heard," he said.

Two days later, I received a letter from a woman who had attended the meeting. "I'm sure you were aware of the reaction to your last paragraph," she wrote. "I hope you recognize what it means." At the moment, I didn't; but from that time on, I commenced to back off from speaking engagements. I had been shooting off my mouth without knowing my real target. I determined to do my own research, find out my own facts. A series of hard-nosed happenings began to change my whole view on the American dangers. Most of them tied in directly with events in my own bailiwick of acting.

Largely because the AFL executive council in Cincinnati that October had ordered it terminated, the strike had simmered down. At the same time that the AFL ordered all back to work, it allowed thirty days for the unions involved to settle their dispute. The month of grace produced nothing but local squabbles. Thus three AFL vice-presidents—W. C. Doherty, head of the mail-carriers, Felix Knight, head of the railway car-men, and W. C. Birthright, head of the barbers—came into the scene. Deliberately chosen as unfamiliar with Hollywood to give a neutral decision, they interviewed all parties to the dispute within a whirlwind four days. They sat down in their hotel room, reviewed the evidence, and on December 26 published a unanimous decision.

It gave the seventy-two set decorators to the painters. But on the larger question, the split between the IATSE and the carpenters, it went back to traditional guidelines. It said that an old agreement (February, 1925), known as the "1926 Agreement" on just such a jurisdictional dispute, should be "put into full force and effect immediately." The "Three Wise Men"—as they were known contemptuously by some, admiringly by others—spelled out the lines of demarcation. The carpenters got all work in the shops, all mill and carpentry, and all permanent construction. The IATSE got the building of props and miniature sets and, except for the mill and trim work, the "erection of sets on stages." This was the moot point; it appeared to be at least a partial IATSE victory.

But the squeamish labor situation persisted into January, 1946. The arbitration decision had also made clear such points as the fact that the office employees belonged with the AFL employees' union (SEG), not with Sorrell's SOEG in the CSU-painters. Maybe I should interject here the fact that Sorrell had once been questioned by his own "international head man," Lindeloff of the painters, as to how he could justify taking publicity men into a painters' union, and Herb replied, "Well, they paint word pictures."

In mid-January, the office workers at Republic and Universal studios were ordered by Sorrell to join the CSU; a fifteen-minute work stoppage emphasized the demand . . . two office unions asked for charters in Sorrell's outfit, which in turn demanded strike action because five studios had recognized SEG. The CSU denounced the original arbitration award and the painters refused to work on IATSE-erected sets. The AFL central labor council in Hollywood started to debate a motion to oust Sorrell.

In February, the AFL went along with giving five hundred set erectors to IATSE, authorizing a charter for a new AFL-IAM union to replace the expelled IAM . . . Sorrell demanded forty-eight hours' pay for thirty-six hours' work and issued a strike call for the 16th unless the CSU got a new 50 per cent pay raise . . .

the producers offered to negotiate if the CSU accepted the arbitration award. Sorrell refused but the strike was never called.

In March the publicists who had stayed at work got an IATSE charter . . . Sorrell was put on trial by the Los Angeles courts as a result of certain activities. He got an even break—convicted on one count, acquitted on another. Late that month he charged the producers with stalling on a contract, but it was clear that his own court appearances were responsible for the delay. He called a mass meeting of "all unions." Only the CSU members responded.

Meanwhile, the SAG had its own hands full to iron out an international reciprocal treaty which discriminated against actors —forcing them to pay double income tax if they worked in foreign countries. Looking back, I realize now that some of these Guild problems contributed to my present beliefs. Few people realize the extent to which show people have been relegated to second-class citizenship. This treaty (and there were three more like it later on which all had to be fought) contained a clause that simply stated the protections of the treaty applied to *"all citizens of both countries* EXCEPT *entertainers."*

Right about this time, Eric Johnston, the supposed czar of the movies, inspired his office to censor Howard Hughes's picture, *The Outlaw*. It added a humorous note in the whole proceeding. In the improbable plot, the sheriff had found Billy the Kid with his girl. "O.K.," said Billy, as the mammacious figure of Jane Russell stood sideways between them. "You stole my horse, I stole your girl." The sheriff nodded. "Sure," he replied. "Tit for tat." It was kind of a shame to lose such dialogue. A scene like that could become as immortal as Shakespeare's "Alas, poor Yorick . . ."

Most of us were at our wits' end to guess just what nipple would satisfy Sorrell and his dozen CSU unions (out of the forty-three existing in Hollywood). It was clear the argument was solely over jurisdiction and Sorrell had admitted it; but at other times he claimed it was solely wages and hours, a legitimate beef. The seesaw went violently up and down. *Time* magazine hailed Sorrell as a new "dictator" on the labor scene. The NLRB charged ten movie studios with various misdemeanors.

None of us yet believed that what a few anonymous people wanted was exactly what was happening in Hollywood—a state of chaos where it was rapidly becoming impossible to produce any movies at all. By June, Pat Casey, the producers' labor negotiator, said the situation was "explosive." The first sign came when AFL cameramen refused to use cameras serviced by the ex-AFL machinists. In reply Sorrell said painters would refuse to work on sets where this boycott continued. A work stoppage of seven hundred men commenced.

The pattern was becoming clear, if only we had taken time to see it. A violent strike triggered by a dispute over seventy-two set designers and which union they belonged to; when that was settled without the industry shutting down, the same group of unions repeated the performance in support of the machinists' union.

The Guild had never been happy about its position in the first strike, feeling it had ducked the problem and never really advised its members on a definite course of action. Now the same situation erupted, with our phones jangling and spouting questions—and we had no answers.

The Guild board met in a hastily called afternoon session. I sat near a window, more intent on the seven-story view than the discussion. My prewar Guild experience conditioned me to place all evil at the so-called "stagehand's" door. But I became aware that something had shifted and that prewar villains might be postwar good guys. Both sides were making claims; one had to be lying. Up went my arm and President Bob Montgomery recognized me. "Find out who's lying," I said, "and then we can advise our fellow members. In a jurisdictional strike there is no neutrality: work and you help one side, stay home and you help the other."

My motion born of naïveté turned out to be effective. We simply invited both factions to sit down with management—and the Guild as a neutral party—and find a peaceful solution. A meeting was arranged in July at the Beverly Hills Hotel. We managed to keep the issues disentangled and total agreement was reached in what came to be known as the Treaty of Beverly Hills. The two-day strike ended. Everyone got a 25 per cent raise (except the actors). Sorrell claimed it was his idea. No one complained when he took the credit; too much was at stake to reopen old wounds with that kind of provocative discussion.

Then came the famous "clarification" of the Three Wise Men. It was a curious document. It came purportedly from the arbitration trio, mimeoed and unsigned. It came from the HQ of the Hutcheson's carpenters' union. It repeated what had been said before—with the addition of some confusing phraseology which indicated there was a carpenter in the woodpile.

"Pursuant to instructions handed down by the executive council at its session held on August 15, 1946," the committee reviewed its original work and "reaffirmed its original decision." An oddly poignant paragraph declared that the IATSE had "jurisdiction over the erection of sets on stages" exclusive of mill and trim work but that "the word erection is construed to mean assemblage of such sets on stages or locations." It added that "it is to be clearly understood that the committee recognizes the jurisdiction over construction work on such sets as coming within the purview of the United Brotherhood of Carpenters and Joiners"—and then, amazingly enough, went on to direct all to "strictly adhere to the provisions of the directive handed down on December 26, 1945."

It was a puzzler. It meant everything to everyone. The CSU took it as victory; the IATSE, at first, as confirmation. At our SAG board meeting that month, we looked tiredly at each other. "All right," I said, trying to work up hope, "it worked before, this group conference thing. Let's try it again."

We called the producers. We said the CSU again claimed it was solely a wage-and-hour matter. Would they consent to sit down at a bargaining table? "All right," they replied dubiously, "as long as we are protected from someone making impossible demands." "Right," we said, "we'll watch for that."

146

Next, we approached Brewer. We pointed out that the AFL convention was only three weeks away. We asked him why he could not yield to the "clarification," then protest it at the convention.

"If it were only a case of jobs," Brewer said, "I might go along with you. But we're a little union of about thirty thousand; Hutcheson has nearly a million carpenters. This is an attempt to destroy our union."

Perhaps we heard an echo of the famous pronouncement of Hutcheson: "God made the trees but the wood belongs to the carpenters." Not really believing Brewer's analysis, we rushed over to the carpenter representative, Joe Cambiano. "Joe," we said, "this thing can be settled if you just give us the guarantee that all you want is the set erectors and that you have no designs on anyone else."

To our astonishment, Cambiano sat silent. We repeated our request. "It's true that you'll go along, isn't it?" we insisted. "You don't want to muscle into what the stagehands have been doing for fifty years."

Cambiano pulled a chair to him. "A chair is a chair," he said. "It doesn't become a prop just because it's on a stage. Anything that's wood or wood substitute belongs to the carpenters."

We sat aghast. Brewer had been right. But we had to be sure. Again we asked Cambiano if he really meant what he said; he repeated it like an automaton. "We can't go back to Brewer and tell him that," we expostulated. "It means you're out to raid him, to ruin him." Cambiano sat silent.

Our committee of depressed actors made one last try. We rang Sorrell. We asked him if he would sit down to discuss matters, wages and hours alone being the issue. "Not by a goddamned sight," he rumbled. "The strike call is out for tomorrow morning. If the producers don't do what we ask, that's that." The strike began Thursday, September 12, with mass picketing at Warner's and MGM.

The only possible next step was to get to the AFL convention and plead our cause for labor peace there. The SAG board shot off a resolution for submission on the convention floor, imploring that permanent machinery of this sort be set up—and we went to Chicago. I was doing a picture based on Philip Wylie's book, *Night unto Night,* but Warner's closed it down and let me go.

On arrival we were told that our resolution for arbitration procedures had arrived too late for consideration. But it was admitted by unanimous vote and passed unanimously by the convention. I might add that since that day in October, 1946, up to the present—eighteen years later—not a single thing has been done by the AFL to set up arbitration proceedings for such disputes in Hollywood. The resolution simply had no teeth.

Our group—Walter Pidgeon, Dick Powell, Jane Wyman, Alexis Smith, Gene Kelly, Robert Taylor, George Murphy, and myself—were the SAG men in Chicago. Bob Montgomery, then producing a play in New York, flew out for one day because Hutcheson said he would talk to no one else. We decided to talk as soon as possible to the three arbitrators themselves—to discover what they meant by their original decision and the later "clarification."

We wangled a meeting with them—three distinguished, sincere, and, I am positive, thoroughly honest men. We were to find out later that they had courage of a high order. The scene is still clear in my memory of our gathering around a long table in one of the Morrison Hotel conference rooms. They informed us that they were individuals only. They had ceased to exist as an official arbitration body the instant they had handed down their binding directive in December, 1945. However, they were willing to tell us whatever they could.

We wanted to know the history of how they had arrived at their award. They said they saw three possible courses of action: (1) to draw the line between craft unions—impossible because of the nature of the IATSE, which cut across such lines; (2) to throw out all unions and create one big new union—no, because it would be a violation of the long industrial history and tradition of the unions; and (3) to review all awards and compromises before

148

and to renew the best elements. This last was the one they selected as the fairest.

"What about the August clarification?" we asked.

"It was a mistake," they said. "And a third clarification would be another mistake."

"Why did you make it?"

"We wrote it," they said, "as a result of eight months of ceaseless pressure on the part of Hutcheson. He wanted a basket of words, something over which he could haggle. We've made the one mistake; we won't make it again nor do we want any further pressure."

"What do you mean, pressure?"

"To go into that, we'd have to explain the whole picture of the internal politics of the AFL."

"We were under the impression that there was a misunderstanding as to what the December award meant," we said.

"There was never any doubt, not even on Hutcheson's part. With the exception of mill and trim work, we intended to give jurisdiction over set erection to the IATSE."

We were determined to pin the issues down so no one could challenge "misunderstanding" when we got back to Hollywood. "Do you understand," we demanded, "that a set is sometimes built like a house, from the ground up, on a stage?"

"Yes."

"You intend this work to be done by the IATSE?"

"Yes, exactly."

"Why not?" Doherty added. "That is an entertainment industry and, historically, the IATSE has been an entertainment union. Why shouldn't it work in entertainment business? The members certainly can't go out and compete with the building trades."

"You mean the construction, erection, building of a set?" The questions were coming chiefly from Gene Kelly, a good friend of Sorrell's. Gene was also a man of remarkable integrity. He merely wanted to make sure of his ground.

"Yes," the arbitrators said.

"Do you mean that the first vice-president of the AFL is deliberately and willfully flouting the principles of arbitration by blocking the award?" I asked incredulously.

They nodded their heads. "That's it," they said.

We were beginning to get wiser, if a little sadder. But we still had a job to do. We went directly to the quarters of William Green, president of the AFL. We told him what we had learned. We said that if something was not done about this one-man block in the AFL, the Screen Actors Guild was prepared to fly stars to every key city in the United States to make personal appearances and show films of the violence outside the studio gates, and to tell the people that one man—the first vice-president of the AFL, Bill Hutcheson—was responsible. To our consternation, Green burst into tears. With his cheeks still wet, he said brokenly, "What can I do? We are a federation of independent unions. I have no power to do anything!"

"Can you get Hutcheson and Walsh together?"

"Hutcheson has said he wouldn't enter the same room with Walsh."

"All right," we said grimly. "But just tell Hutcheson what we're going to do. Will you?"

"Yes."

"Immediately?"

"Immediately."

We asked one last question to make sure of ourselves. "Is it your understanding that the arbitrators awarded the jurisdiction over set construction to the IATSE?"

Green nodded. "That is my understanding," he said.

We went back to our hotel. Up until now Hutcheson had flatly refused to see us. Within ten minutes, he called and invited us over at ten that night. We got ready and went to his hotel and were ushered into his jolly, Santa-like presence.

"Never been on a motion picture set in my life," he rumbled, shaking hands. "But I know construction. I know that construction and erection are the same. You tell Dick Walsh to obey that directive and your troubles are over."

"Your interpretation of it or what the three who wrote it meant?" I asked.

"What do you mean?"

"We've talked to them. They intended to give jurisdiction to the IATSE."

"Erection, maybe, but not construction."

"That's your interpretation, not theirs," I said. "Which do you want Walsh to accept?" It was a question I was to repeat, by actual count, seven times that evening. The last time, well past midnight, Hutcheson dropped his good-fellowship and became angry. This was his undoing because he blurted out the admission of his violation of the pledge to accept arbitration.

"Those three stupid blockheads of arbitrators don't know anything about construction," he cried. "They said they based what they did on the 1926 Agreement. Well, I refused to sign that twenty years ago and I refuse to sign it now!"

Nevertheless the discussions continued, with lawyers darting in and out like beagles on leashes. "How are you going to police your arbitration?" asked Hutcheson contemptuously.

"In this country," I said, "if you decide to play ball and use an umpire, you obey his decisions."

"Look," Hutcheson said in exasperation, "thirty years ago the AFL ruled against my men in a dispute with the machinists. I haven't obeyed that for thirty years. Because of that the IAM got out of the AFL and I've kept them out."

"You've got men on the street who should be working in the studios," we said.

"They can get other jobs."

"It's specialized work," we protested.

"It's all construction," Hutcheson said, gesturing, "it's all construction."

"You have fifteen hundred men out," I said.

151

Hutcheson cocked his head roguishly. "Oh, no," he said, "I figure it's more like twenty-five hundred."

"That's worse," I said.

"Look," Hutcheson said heavily, "I've got 850,000 carpenters. I only pay head tax to the AFL on 600,000. I've got enough back of me to afford to keep those twenty-five hundred men on the street for the next ten years!"

"Can the twenty-five hundred afford it?" I asked.

There was no answer.

It was apparent we were getting nowhere. This was a road-block in labor consisting of one arrogant man completely wrapped in the cloak of his own power. No one, he was convinced, could tell him what to do. So finally, at three in the morning, we gave up. And in parting, Hutcheson gave us a farewell that had an ominous new note.

"Tell Walsh," he boomed after us, "that if he'll give in on the August directive, I'll run Sorrell out of Hollywood and break up the CSU in five minutes. I'll do the same to the Commies." This too was an admission because up to now he had charged there were no Communists involved in any way.

We were still thinking that one over when we went down in the elevator and out into the lobby.

It was as silent as a grave at that hour. Only one man was there: Herb Sorrell.

Just to keep everything straight, we went over to see him and report what Hutcheson had said. Sorrell listened intently and then replied, "It doesn't matter a damn what Hutcheson says. This thing is going on, no matter what he does! When it ends up, there'll be only one man running labor in Hollywood and that man will be me!"

With triple delusions of grandeur ringing in our ears, we passed wearily from the lobby of the hotel to our rest. But one of us (old liberal me) was so wide-eyed by this time it seemed my eyes could never close again.

152

CHAPTER

10

That marathon five-hour session in the dead of night at Hutcheson's hotel told us about all we wanted to know. We were ready to go home. We had to tell the membership of SAG what we had found out: the strike of Sorrell and the CSU was a jurisdictional affair.

But there were still some threads to be tied up and some vain hopes to be exploded. We told Sorrell, the wandering painter, what the Three Wise Men had told us. He said that wasn't his understanding. We told him to talk to them himself. He said he would. Hutcheson relented and met with Walsh—but both stood firm. Joe Keenan—an AFL official who enters into the plot a little later as mediator—came to us. He said Dave Dubinsky, president of the garment workers, had been approached by Sorrell. Sorrell offered to swing all the movie costumers into Dubinsky's union, away from the IATSE, if the ILGWU would charter them.

Thus we returned from Chicago—with little done and the strike still raging but with full knowledge of what our report to the membership must be. But first we called a meeting of all the representatives of Hollywood labor at a conference on October 24 in the Hollywood Knickerbocker Hotel. We outlined what had happened, chronologically and factually. We told them of such things as the unsolicited visit from Morrissey, head of the Hod Carriers and Sandhogs, who volunteered his backing in our fight for permanent arbitration against such disputes. I watched the faces of the audience. I think there were some pretty astounded

153

men there when they heard of Sorrell's various plans to juggle his union membership.

It put Sorrell on the spot. He rose to the occasion. "Hell," he said, "what they tell you isn't what the arbitrators told me!"

Gene Kelly shook his head. "That's what they said to us," he said. "I'm sorry you weren't there, Herb. But you have an airplane." (I forgot to mention that Sorrell had been given an airplane by his union and flew it himself.) "We'll go back to Chicago together and talk to them tomorrow."

Sorrell shook his head and I got up. "There's an easier and better and faster way," I said. "Let's have a conference telephone call at the SAG headquarters. Anyone interested can come and listen in. Will you agree to abide by what they say on the other end, Herb?"

"Damn right!" shouted Sorrell.

Next day the green and beige offices of the SAG bulged with excitement. At last, we felt, we would find out who was lying to whom—and nail down the strike. We had no idea of the real truth that was to come out. Our feeling of neutrality, which had worn pretty thin during the Chicago outing, was again high. Perhaps Sorrell had talked to the arbitrators; perhaps mistakes had been made; perhaps the strike was not a jurisdictional raid after all. What we wanted was everyone back to work, the industry functioning as a whole on an equitable basis.

The SAG staff started to round up agreements. There was considerable doubt if the call could be arranged. But W. C. Birthright (in Kansas City, Missouri) and Felix Knight (in Indianapolis) agreed to it immediately. (Doherty was on his way to Europe.) The time was set for 3 P.M. on the coast, 5 P.M. Central Time.

Other principals were called. Sorrell agreed to sit in; so did Roy Tinsdale and Jim Skelton. I was contacted by semaphore on the Warner ranch where I was finishing up a picture. Gene Kelly was hauled in from MGM. George Murphy was wakened from sweet dreams and agreed to come. Others, such as Eddie Arnold, were summoned. Seven trunk lines and twelve telephones were set up, situated in various offices. Sorrell, evidently suspicious of the whole affair, phoned in and asked if he could hook up a loudspeaker to his telephone. Agreed. He called back and asked if he could bring a court reporter. Agreed.

Finally the deadline arrived. The conversation began at 3:10 and lasted until 3:38 P.M. After it was over, there was nothing anyone could say. It was clear, conclusive—and amazing.

In the first place, they made plain that Sorrell's story of having met with them was all in his imagination; they had never discussed the arbitration award with him. But this item was nothing compared to the next bombshell.

Roy Tinsdale was trying to get an answer about the wording of a particular paragraph in the August clarification. Both Birthright and Knight seemed to have trouble understanding his questions. Gripping my phone, I suddenly realized I was squeezing the receiver so hard that my ear hurt. A wild idea came to me and the next moment it was confirmed. Birthright told Tinsdale that the document that had turned Hollywood upside down over his and the other names of the arbitrators had never been written by them. It was a clear phony, evidently invented by someone in Hutcheson's office.

What the four hundred dollar telephone call meant, in simple terms, was that the "clarification" which had set off labor rivalry in Hollywood was a deliberate fraud: a lie, and a hoax. We did not know—or care—who had done it. We only knew it had been issued by the authority of someone who wanted the strike settled his way, regardless of how many people were thrown out of work.

We figured that at long last, to anyone of goodwill, the strike was over. We were wrong.

In late September, a thousand strikers had massed at Warner's. Three autos had been overturned, clubs, chains, bottles, bricks, and two-by-fours were used freely. Now various homes of the IATSE members were bombed by night; other workers were ambushed and slugged. Violence began to reappear on the picket lines. One of our committee asked if the violence could be halted. "We don't advocate violence," Sorrell replied blandly.

"Advocate!" we cried.

"I mean," Sorrell amended himself hastily, "that we don't allow it but we can no more control our members than you can keep your actors from committing rape."

It was a peculiarly infelicitous remark. But we asked for a final meeting to see what could be done. Instead of coming to it —as he agreed—Sorrell went back and held a press conference. He declared that the IATSE had broken off all negotiations because of the "phony issue" of the bombings. By that time we were used to such statements.

By this time, the ground under the SAG board had been firmed up. Our members had expressed overwhelming agreement with the course we had taken.

The SAG position remained that the CSU struck because it imagined that the AFL arbitrators gave jurisdiction over set erection to the carpenters. The CSU had discovered this was a false premise. The CSU called the strike in the face of warnings that their men could be replaced—and in the face of CSU agreement that there would be no work stoppage because of jurisdictional quarrels.

By January, 1947, it was estimated that the wages lost amounted to $28,000,000. It had affected ten major studios and fifteen film laboratories. Over $500,000 from mysterious sources had been spent by the CSU in its vain efforts.

A letter in February, 1947, signed by the heads of twenty-five unions, representing twenty-five thousand workers and 75 per cent of the workers in Hollywood, put the situation plainly. It declared the industry had been "cursed by ever-recurring strikes called by a small group of unions." It went on to detail the facts: "Of the approximately 30,000 AFL union workers in the motion picture industry, less than 7,000 are represented by the disruptive leadership of a few unions which call themselves the Conference of Studio Unions. The CSU is a rump organization, conflicting with our duly constituted AFL central labor council of Los Angeles. For some years now, the CSU leadership has been attempting to capture or destroy other AFL unions in the industry. The existing strike is strictly jurisdictional and has been so labelled by the AFL. Any support given to the current CSU strike is support for a program of the destruction of AFL unions in the studios."

By February, the word was out to the CSU unions that the strike was lost; that its members should try to get their jobs back by whatever means they could, as individuals. The CSU dissolved like sugar in hot water.

The last note was struck three years later. A charge brought by the carpenters' union against the studios and the IATSE, alleging unfair labor practices, was thrown out by the United States Supreme Court.

Now came the revelation of the Communist putsch for control of motion pictures. As the tenth report of the Senate Fact-Finding Committee on Un-American Activities in California (1959) put it: "The Communist Party working in Hollywood wanted control over everything that moved on wheels—sound trucks, camera platforms, transportation of equipment and personnel to and from locations, and even the tray-dollies in the cafeterias. They soon moved Communist units into those unions having jurisdiction over carpenters, painters, musicians, grips, and electricians. To control these trade unions was to control the motion picture industry." Where did they get the money? To quote once more: "In 1934 a considerable sum of money was sent by the Soviet Commissar for Heavy Industry, who was then registered at the Claremont Hotel in Berkeley, to a Communist contact in Hollywood. This money was to be used for the purpose of creating an entering wedge . . ."

The report went on: "In November, 1950, the National Executive Board of the AFL Painters' Union announced the results of its searching investigation into the affair (the strike) and declared that Sorrell had 'willfully and knowingly associated with groups subservient to the Communist Party line' and ordered him not to

157

hold any union office for five years and not to attend any union meetings during that period. In February, 1952, Sorrell's local union was dissolved and he dropped out of all union activities."

Long before it became so irrefutably documented, the influence of the Communists on the 1945-47 strike was clear. While others had been dodging the question, the SAG—prompted by the strike —had taken the strongest possible position on the question. A statement of policy by the board of directors in 1946 declared that the SAG "has in the past, does now, and will in the future rigorously oppose by every power which is within its legal rights, any Fascist or Communist influence in the motion picture industry." Afterward, in 1951, the board said: "All participants in the international Communist Party conspiracy against our nation should be exposed for what they are—enemies of our country and of our form of government." Two years later, the membership resoundingly endorsed this position. By a majority exceeding 96 per cent, it adopted a new bylaw which says in part: "No person who is a member of the Communist Party or of any other organization seeking to overthrow the government of the United States by force and violence shall be eligible for membership in the Screen Actors Guild." And SAG went further. It asserted it would fight any secret blacklist set up by any group of employers but— "if any actor by his own actions outside union activities has so offended American public opinion that he has made himself unsaleable at the boxoffice, the Guild cannot and would not want to force any employer to hire him." It pointed out that such an attitude is the "individual actor's personal responsibility and it cannot be shifted to his union."

In all the battles over the weary months the Screen Actors Guild never used the word Communist except in general terms, nor did we point a finger at any individual. We fought on the issues and proved that if you keep the people informed on those issues, they won't make a mistake. Some of the people against us were Communists, some were knowing fellow travelers, and many were innocent dupes sincerely supporting a cause they believed was

158

just. We did not attempt to separate them into those categories by name, nor will I in this account. To the best of my ability I'll relate their words and deeds, but not whether they were of the party, the fellow-traveler, or the sucker group.

But I will say of the Communists—they were the cause of the labor strife, they used minor jurisdictional disputes as excuses for their scheme. Their aim was to gain economic control of the motion picture industry in order to finance their activities and subvert the screen for their propaganda.

The actors got in the act because we were the one single group which could automatically shut down the studios just by not appearing before the cameras. Roy Brewer was one labor leader who talked as much about labor's responsibility as he did about its privilege. The class warfare boys would try to exploit this as a pro-boss attitude and, of course, they would run a rumor mill exhuming the ghost of all the Browne-Bioff evil. They wouldn't be lacking in gangland ectoplasm for this ghost. It was actually the most sordid kind of extortion of the most repulsive labor racketeers but also involved some of the biggest Hollywood names.

In that World War II period, the movie business had become a power vacuum. It sucked into itself all sorts of scum, arriving for the sake of both politics and profit. The great men in the business had been accustomed to using money to solve all their troubles, especially to avoid any bad publicity—a fear-inspired technique which exists to this day. Samuel Bioff, a bland pudgy man, had insinuated himself and a collection of ex-Capone thugs into the IATSE in the late 1930's. He and his co-extortionist, George E. Browne, then head of the IATSE, mulcted the union of more than $1,000,000 in dues (assessing the union members 2 percent of their annual salaries). They blackmailed the producers out of more than $100,000 a year. Under oath, Bioff confessed to a five-year plan to take 20 per cent of all Hollywood profits. Eventually, he proposed a 50 per cent ownership of all studios.

The power behind his threats lay in his ability to strike the projectionists of the theaters across the country. Such a move would cut off the basic source of Hollywood cash. Some of the producers panicked. They yielded to this pressure, apparently not having guts enough to go either to the newspapers or the police. One of the threats used was that "anyone who resigns from this operation resigns feet first." Sorrell later made strike capital out of this sick operation. He claimed to have refused a $55,000 personal bribe from Bioff.

In 1941 both Bioff and Browne were convicted of extortion. They got jail sentences of ten years apiece. Bioff, two years later, testified against his former associates. In 1955, living in Phoenix under the name of "William Nelson," Bioff was blown to bits by a bomb concealed in his car.

Those responsible for breaking open the B&B scheme were Westbrook Pegler with his anti-racketeering columns and a continuing campaign in the trade paper *Variety*. Both were vitally aided by information gathered and transmitted by investigators hired by the SAG. One of our first tip-offs on the plot, by the way, came when Ken Thompson, now a member of the SAG office staff, glimpsed a .45 automatic in Bioff's open desk drawer. He wondered how it was going to be used in labor negotiations.

When SAG was pressured to contribute to the boodle-kit, we flatly refused. Not only that, we were directly responsible for the ousting of Bioff and Browne from the AFL fold. The hierarchy was very reluctant to fire them, despite the heap of evidence. So Bob Montgomery and an SAG committee paid a visit to the annual AFL convention in Atlantic City. Bob used the only weapon he had: he told the officials that although SAG was a new, relatively small union, it could get a lot of publicity. He threatened that, if the AFL did not toss out B&B, the SAG would send actors across the country to inform the public of secret labor corruption. It was this explosive technique which finally blew Bioff and Browne out of their entrenched graft. It also was where I got the idea for my threat later to President Green.

160

The foulness of this scandal was certainly partially responsible for the forming of the CSU in 1942. There was a good deal of dissatisfaction with the AFL brass. No one could understand how they had allowed such criminal conditions to fester in their organization. The CSU came in with the good wishes of a lot of us. What we didn't know was that the House Un-American Activities Committee in 1947 had received testimony that the signature of Herb Sorrell—according to two qualified handwriting experts—exactly matched the signature of "Herb Stewart" on a Communist party document.

Says the 1959 Senate report: "The left-wing control of the conference (of Studio Unions) was openly headed by one Herb Sorrell, a large and muscular man with a most aggressive attitude. He has appeared before us and we have heretofore published his record of subversive connections," adding that his signature had been authenticated on a Communist membership book.

For a decade there had been mysterious, well-heeled persons floating around Hollywood. One of these was Jeff Kibre, an emaciated, curly-headed, voluble CIO organizer. He came to Hollywood in the 1930's to collect the dissatisfied AFL unions—then the bitter rival of the CIO—into one big group. The CSU—a dozen out of the forty-three unions—was the ultimate result. Kibre later turned up farther north on the West Coast, in the CIO fishery and cannery unions. His claim to fame was to be fined two thousand dollars by a court for his role in illegal price fixing. The last notice I had of him was that he popped up on the New York waterfront as an activist for Harry Bridges, head of the Western longshoremen—often accused but never convicted of Communist membership.

A much less shadowy figure was that of John Howard Lawson. A competent playwright, he was very much in evidence organizing meetings and on picket lines. He had frankly admitted that it was his aim "to present the Communist position and to do so in the most specific manner." The fog closed in again around the chunky, bespectacled figure of one who called himself "V. J. Jerome." He appeared to be next in the chain of command above Lawson. The direct link to the international Communist organization was evident when it became known that the commander-in-chief of Operation Hollywood for the Communists was Gerhard Eisler. Eisler, who at one time took personal charge of the Hollywood strike maneuvers, was afterward proved to be the top Communist agent in the United States. Exposed, he fled to East Germany. There he commenced a violent radio campaign of vituperation against this country which went on for years.

It is instructive at this point to quote again from the report of the California Senate Fact-Finding Committee: "During the late thirties and early forties V. J. Jerome made several trips to California from New York in his capacity as chief of the (Communist) party's Cultural Commission. Copies of telegrams that passed between Communist officials immediately before and after his visits show how each was followed by a rash of new activity in the process of subverting Hollywood. As the writer, John Howard Lawson, was moved into position as Jerome's California representative, the boss made fewer trips. Lawson's Communist record has been thoroughly covered in previous reports following his appearance before us several years ago."

The Communist plan for Hollywood was remarkably simple. It was merely to take over the motion picture business. Not only for its profit, as the hoodlums had tried—but also for a grand world-wide propaganda base. In those days before television and massive foreign film production, American films dominated 95 per cent of the world's movie screens. We had a weekly audience of about 500,000,000 souls. Takeover of this enormous plant and its gradual transformation into a Communist gristmill was a grandiose idea. It would have been a magnificent coup for our enemies.

Using the CSU as a vehicle for Communist aims was a first step of admirable directness. It meant the unscrupulous manipulation of what might have been a legitimate dispute. The genuine rights of the movie workers were used to cover up the Communist

162

spoor. Cries of "anti-labor" or "union-busting" or "pro-Fascists" were used to deafen innocent adherents. Part of the giveaway to us lay in the timing: bits fitted together, once we in the SAG collected, collated, and confirmed our evidence and suspicions. The early outbreaks in 1945—including laud and praise of Bridges—coincided with the switch in the US-USSR relations. The war was almost surely being won by the Allies. The no-strike pledge in Hollywood could no longer be of real help to the Communists. Free now of the Nazi wolf at their throat, they in turn gathered themselves to turn against the United States as the citadel of capitalism.

One version, pieced together at SAG, went in three steps: (1) to create paralyzing strikes on whatever pretext possible; (2) at the height of the paralysis, to put through a plan to blanket the workers in the studios under one huge union—which was to be adopted by Bridges's longshoremen group; (3) to gradually work into the movies the requisite propaganda attitudes (while siphoning off the money) to soften the American public's hardening attitude toward Communism.

Other versions of the master scheme by different individuals varied only slightly. According to the testimony given under oath to the House Un-American Activities Committee by Edward Dmytryk, a self-confessed Communist (at a time when he was earning six thousand dollars a week as a director), the plan was as follows: (1) to line up big-name dupes to collect money and create prestige; (2) to infiltrate the talent guilds and craft unions and take over; (3) to revise the content of the movies into a propaganda handle. In this respect the "sophisticated" unions—such as the Screen Writers Guild—were less cautious than the lowly craft unions, who reacted with instinctive abhorrence. Let me interject here that Eddie Dmytryk is an example of how a person motivated by idealism can find himself walking the Commie treadmill until his own intelligence brings disillusionment. Once he saw through the "humanitarian" trappings to the ugly reality that lay underneath, Eddie did an heroic job in bringing other disillusioned but

163

frightened ex-Communists to the House Committee and the FBI. Between them, they added much to what we know about the Commie takeover plot. Of course, his former comrades then did their best to destroy him.

It can be seen how readily these accounts dovetail. The only item which was unclear to me—then and now—was how longshoremen could make movies. But Bridges and his men may have had talents of which I was unaware.

These days, when the duplicity of the Communists is known at home and abroad—after Korea and Cuba—it is easy to say they can be detected and despised. But in the 1940's it was quite different. There were Communists in positions of influence, actively working with Hollywood films, with the ultimate objective of propaganda in mind. Even today the Communists have succeeded in convincing many that their bitter beliefs were mere boyish peccadilloes, sort of avant-garde thinking, like abstract art and coffee-house poetry. In 1961, the *Saturday Evening Post*—in all pompous sincerity, I suppose—gave Ring Lardner, Jr., the privilege of telling millions how he had "suffered" in Hollywood by being quizzed about his Communist connections. In 1962, Alger Hiss, convicted of perjury when he denied that he had passed secrets to the Russians, was able to get a television audience of more millions to criticize a man who had been for eight years the Vice-President of the United States—an event equivalent to Benedict Arnold being given time to denounce Vice-President John Adams.

Perhaps Communism may become fashionable in the Hollywood intellectual sets again. I don't know. Perhaps, like the measles, it will always be with us. We can only be wary and informed about tyranny—and remember that measles may be deadly without an antitoxin. It may be that each American generation must be re-educated to the precariousness of liberty.

For my part, I owe it to that period that I managed to sort out a lot of items in my personal life. From being an active (though unconscious) partisan in what now and then turned out to be Communist causes, I little by little became disillusioned or perhaps, in my case, I should say awakened. One of the first examples I had was the Communist infiltration into the original American Veterans Committee.

This came hard. I expected great things of the AVC. As evidence of my expectations I had taken the lead in assuming a number of obligations. One of these was securing for the group the free use of the 750-seat auditorium of radio station KFWB. Things worked out fine—except for those who thought the AVC was ripe for infiltration and takeover. Thus when I came back after a few weeks' shooting on location, I found that the meeting place had been transferred to a hall owned by the Screen Cartoonists Guild. This spot could seat only seventy-five. The night I arrived, hundreds of AVC boys were milling about outside, unable to get in. The KFWB hall was still available and gratis—but someone preferred a hall which could hold only a "small, working majority." It was an old Communist trick but new to me.

Still, I didn't believe it had been done on purpose. Not until the day I got the AVC call to report in full Air Corps uniform, to picket a studio. Astounded, I investigated. I found that the action had been taken by a vote of seventy-three members out of a total of thirteen hundred. I called back and said that if this was done as purporting to represent the AVC membership, I would take full-page ads in the papers denouncing it. In less than an hour, it was called off.

I resigned shortly thereafter from the AVC board and membership. It had become a hotbed of Communists in Hollywood according to the activities which were reported on by the California Senate Fact-Finding Committee on Un-American Activities in some detail in 1947, in 1949, and 1951. Its reputation suffered so much that it had to be taken over in its entirety and cleansed by the national organization. I still mourn it as one of the potential platforms that the citizen-serviceman could have used to help make a better world. (Today it seems unduly concerned with all and only those issues which will contribute a Big Brother type of government.)

Life became fuller and fuller of curiouser and curiouser incidents in those post-World War II days, many of them overlapping. For example, my disillusionment also came full circle with a noble-spoken organization, the Hollywood Independent Citizens Committee of Arts, Sciences, and Professions. HICCASP, as it was known—pronounced like the cough of a dying man—was a prominent organization. It was studded with more jewel-like names than a crown tiara. When I got a call to fill a vacancy on its board, I felt honored. I went to that first meeting determined to do no more than keep my mouth shut. It was held in the home of a Hollywood celebrity. When I entered, to my surprise, I discovered there were perhaps seventy people in the room, some of them characters I hadn't expected to encounter. All of them were board members. Because of the overlap of other events, such as the strike, I now knew Communists were for real. Dore Schary, then head of MGM, was present. I slipped into a seat beside him.

"Lots of people here I didn't think I'd see," I whispered.

He looked at me rather strangely, I thought. "Stick around," he advised grimly.

The meeting went on in all harmony until Jimmy Roosevelt got to his feet. With urbane suavity, he said that some of the members of HICCASP had become concerned with the fact that it was being accused of being a Communist front organization. It was, he said, a good time to issue a statement to reassure the public. In short, he asked the board to sign a declaration of principles which would repudiate Communism.

It sounded good to me, sort of like that last paragraph I had inserted in my speech. I was amazed at the reaction. A well-known musician sprang to his feet. He offered to recite the USSR constitution from memory, yelling that it was a lot more democratic than that of the United States. A prominent movie writer leaped upward. He said that if there was ever a war between the United States and Russia, he would volunteer for Russia—a declaration

166

somewhat watered down since he had been nowhere, even when we were fighting with the USSR against Hitler. A couple of friends took him out and calmed him down.

After this hubbub of dismay had continued for a while, I decided that an Irishman couldn't stay out. I thought besides that Jimmy needed someone to stand up for him. I took the floor and endorsed what he said. Well, sir, I found myself waist-high in epithets such as "Fascist" and "capitalist scum" and "enemy of the proletariat" and "witch-hunter" and "Red-baiter" before I could say boo. Linus Pauling, the scientist, who was there, was very quiet. Dalton Trumbo, the writer, was very vociferous. Most vehement of all, however, was John Howard Lawson. He persisted in waving a long finger under my nose and telling me off. One woman of liberal leanings actually had a heart attack and had to be taken home, the emotional atmosphere was so strong.

You can imagine what this did to my naïveté. Here was a HICCASP that I had admired and honored. Suddenly it was broken up into a Kilkenny brawl by a simple statement which I thought any American would be proud to subscribe to. The lines were sharply divided. John Cromwell, who was presiding, finally settled it by appointing a committee of both sides to look into the matter of a statement. We broke up in dudgeon. As I left, Dore maneuvered next to me. Out of the side of his mouth, he muttered, "Come up to Olivia de Havilland's apartment."

Needless to say, I raced over there. I found a solid group of about a dozen gathering in glee. They consisted of citizens like Johnny Green, the composer, Don Hartman and Eddie Knopf, the writers, and, of course, Jimmy and Dore and Olivia and a few others. They were pleased because the whole thing had been a preconceived plot to smoke out the "others." Olivia had suspected that perhaps HICCASP was being infiltrated when she had been given a Trumbo-written speech to deliver in Seattle. She read it first, luckily. She found it so full of Communist-oriented tidbits that she refused to deliver it. She talked to Jimmy and they concocted the disinfecting resolution. I remember that I kept grinning at Olivia until she asked me what was so funny. "Nothing," I said, "except that I thought you were one." She grinned right back. "I thought *you* were one," she murmured. "Until tonight, that is."

The problem now was to write a statement of policy. I started—Lincoln and I—to scribble one on the back of an envelope. It was amended and reworked and finally accepted. It was deliberately a very innocuous document (for purposes of entrapment) until the last phrases. These read: "We reaffirm our belief in free enterprise and the democratic system and repudiate Communism as desirable for the United States."

These days that seems eminently mild and reasonable. But in HICCASP as constituted—except for our little group of plotters—it was dynamite. It proved strong enough, that little sentence, to blow the whole organization sky-high.

A few nights later we met at Jimmy's. It was a joint committee meeting, to hack out the resolution. We got the floor and read what we had composed. Again, the howls and denunciations; again the finger of Lawson under my nose. "This organization," he shouted, "will never adopt a statement which endorses free enterprise and repudiates Communism! And, for your information, I may add that a two-party system is in no way necessary or even desirable for democracy!" Then he hastily assured me he was not personally a Communist.

"Let's let the whole membership decide by secret ballot," I said amiably. "This really shouldn't be left to the board of directors."

"The membership isn't politically sophisticated enough to make this decision," I was blandly informed by Lawson. It was the first time I had ever heard the phrase. It was a goodie. I still hear it used and like Pavlov's dog I react, particularly when innocents use it defending the idea of government by an intellectual elite.

We didn't get to the membership—we didn't even get back to the board. It seems HICCASP had an even more exclusive intel-

168

lectual elite—an executive committee—and somehow it was decided to settle the issue in this rarefied atmosphere. Olivia was our only representative on this group. She presented our resolution and dutifully phoned each one of us that she was the only "aye" vote.

I resigned from the board by telegram that night. So did some others. Very shortly HICCASP gave its last groan and expired as an organization.

Light was dawning in some obscure region in my head. I was beginning to see the seamy side of liberalism. Too many of the patches on the progressive coat were of a color I didn't personally care for. Something the liberal will have to explain and stand trial for is his inability to see the Communist as he truly is and not as some kind of Peck's Bad Boy of liberalism who is basically all right but just a bit overboard and rough-edged. This ideological myopia is even true of some who have met the Reds in philosophical combat and who should have learned something from crossing swords. Jimmy Roosevelt, who has led the fight for abolition of the House Committee on Un-American Activities, was one of our embattled little group who saw the destruction of HICCASP.

In 1948, the California Senate Fact-Finding Committee reported that HICCASP was a "Communist front" and that "the individuals now involved (in HICCASP) have a long record of duplicity and betrayal of the interests of labor, minority and liberal groups, whom they attempt to speak for with typical Stalinist effrontery. Particularly callous was their betrayal of Jewish victims of Nazi persecution during the Hitler-Stalin pact."

The next item on my oops-sorry agenda came later when I was deep in the strike. It was a visit from three men from a well-known government agency. Their names and connections—though amply proved to me—will have to remain anonymous.

My visitors rang the bell and identified themselves thoroughly. I invited them in. We had some coffee. One said, "We have some information which might be useful to you; we thought you might have some information helpful to us."

Instinctively my old liberal reaction popped up before I could think and almost by rote I found myself saying, "Now look, I don't go in for Red-baiting."

"We don't either," said the second one. "It isn't a question of that. It's a question of national security. You served with the Air Corps. You know what spies and saboteurs are."

"We thought someone the Communists hated as much as they hate you might be willing to help us," added the third.

That got me. It's always a jolt to discover others have been talking you over. "What do you mean?" I asked.

"Well," he said, "they held a meeting last night." He described the house, gave the address, told me who was there, and what they said. I broke in. "What did they say about *me?*" I demanded.

"The exact quotation," he replied, "was: 'What are we going to do about that sonofabitching bastard Reagan?' Will that do for openers?"

It was enough. We got to talking. I must confess they opened my eyes to a good many things. I came to admire these men: they never accused anyone of being a Communist unless they had every last bit of evidence which would stand up against the most vicious court assault. They were extremely careful never to smear anyone or guess even on good but less than complete evidence. They were very thorough, very patient, and very accurate. We exchanged information for a few hours. At last, they stood up and made their farewells.

As they moved toward the door, one turned and said quizzically, "What were you doing at this address one night several months ago, by the way?"

Astonished, I replied, "That's Jimmy Roosevelt's house!"

They nodded. "We know," one said.

"I've already told you about that," I said. "That's where we held that HICCASP committee meeting. Why?"

He named one of the group's best-known members.

170

"What's he got to do with it?" I inquired.

"For a long time," one said over his shoulder, "we've known exactly where he has been and who he has been with."

The whole interview was an eye-opener. My next encounter was even more revealing. It came via a phone call from Bill Holden. He seemed excited. I was a little annoyed because I was busy memorizing facts and figures for our report on the strike situation to the big SAG meeting.

"I've found out that there is a meeting at Ida Lupino's," he told me.

"But Ida isn't one of Them," I expostulated.

"I know," Bill said impatiently. "They are just borrowing her patio." As Bill explained it, a half-dozen innocents, Ida among them, had been invited to a meeting supposedly to hear about the labor dispute and decide what actors should do about it. Of course, the whole thing was a brainwash job to hook the half-dozen big names for a cover-up. Bill said, "Let's go."

It sounded like fun. Bill picked me up and we wandered over to Ida's. We were warmly welcomed by Ida, but things were different when we reached the patio. It was a big crowd, chaired by Sterling Hayden—about seventy-five people, all of them astonished and miffed by the appearance of Holden and me. We sat down in a corner and prepared to listen to what we knew we would hear. There were a few huddles and some scurrying around before they finally gave in and started the meeting.

Sure enough, the CSU was lauded to the skies, the IATSE was damned, and the SAG drew faint praise indeed for trying to be blessed with the peacemakers. I writhed in my seat but Bill held me back, like a jockey going into the stretch. At last, as the denunciations—in pretty familiar language by this time—had run down, Bill patted me. He said, "Now!"

I bounced to my feet and asked for the floor. Hayden gave it to me. I confronted one of the most hostile audiences I could ever hope to address. "The SAG has been investigating this thing," I said cheerfully, "and we're happy to see groups like this so interested. But I thought there might be some facts you didn't know." Thereupon I launched into a dress rehearsal of the same report I was to give to the mass SAG meeting two nights later. It was giving the opposition ammunition but it was also a chance to spike their guns with regard to brainwashing their hand-picked names.

I spoke for about forty minutes. Then I asked for questions. I got them—from every angle. Few were asking for information. Most of them were of the so-you-stopped-beating-your-wife variety. I managed to keep my temper in spite of interruptions and boos and the customary name-calling.

Finally, in the rear, John Garfield—a fellow Guild board member—stood up. "Why don't you listen to him?" he asked. "He does have information you don't have."

As I've indicated before, this was a jolting surprise. John had seemed too close to the other camp to be on his feet defending me. From my position facing the rows of rented folding chairs, I saw a well-known character actor take John to the back of the garden. Over the heads of the group who were all facing me I could see him back John up against a tree and, with one hand holding him by the shirt front, he read an angry riot act, punctuated by a jabbing finger. While I could hear nothing of what was said, I was so fascinated by the tableau I almost forgot to parry the hostile shots coming my own way. John stayed back there, leaning against the tree, hands deep in his pockets, after the actor left him, and finally he edged his way to a back gate and left.

I told Bill what I'd seen when the meeting finally ended and we even talked of calling John and seeing what we could do over a few beers. What a different world it might have become for John if we had. A few years later he died of a heart attack and after his death, like a voice from the grave, the press carried the story of his last forty-eight hours. He had gone to the FBI and the House Committee and poured out a story of fourteen years in which the Communist party had turned him on and off like a hot-water faucet. He had never been a member because he was more useful to them the other way. He told of trying to break away once and how they talked him back into line: it was that night at the patio meeting.

At a later point in the strike some of us from the board would meet with a committee drawn from this patio group who had demanded a membership meeting so they could try once again to sway the Guild members into supporting the strike. We were scared to death of their ability to do just this, but we'd agreed to the meeting when Jack Dales (as scared as any of us) said, "We have to give them the meeting. If we are afraid that our members can't be trusted to make the right decision, then the Commies have already won and our system doesn't work." It was a pretty good lesson and a pretty good example of why the Guild operates on a level I call noble.

One of their committee was again Sterling Hayden. It bothered me a great deal to see him on that side. Here was a man with a magnificent war record. Dropped by parachute behind enemy lines, he had fought beside the Yugoslav partisans and seen men die fighting the Nazis, dedicated men who professed Communism as the only alternative to Hitler. At war's end, disillusioned by what seemed to him a greedy postwar reversion to grab and get, he had sought out the Communists.

This night I couldn't help but be aware that he listened and never spoke. I caught him several times eying his companions with a speculative look, particularly when they would arrogantly ignore the facts we were laying before them regarding our meetings with Sorrell and the phone call to the Three Wise Men.

I might say, once again we were doing what we had done that night in the patio, telling them exactly what we were going to say to the members at the coming meeting. It wasn't as foolish as you might think—the truth is pretty hard to lick or rebut, even when you have advance warning.

Not too much later Sterling Hayden made his decision. He had been on the wrong side: he would right that wrong. He too went before the House Committee of Congress and told his story, exposing the Communist plot to take over the motion picture industry. It was a brave thing to do but a brave man was doing it. Testifying under oath on the Communist maneuvers to take over Hollywood, Sterling Hayden was asked what tripped them up. His reply: "We ran into a one-man battalion named Ronnie Reagan."

But all of this was much later. The meeting at Ida's in the patio was just a few nights before our first membership meeting at which I would make the report I'd already exposed, and the board would ask the membership to vote approval of crossing the picket lines. The next day I was back at work on *Night unto Night,* doing location shots at the beach. I was called to a phone at an oil station nearby.

"There's a group being formed to deal with you," the unidentified voice said. "They're going to fix you so you won't ever act again."

I took it as a joke. I told it with chuckles to the gang; I was surprised that they took it seriously. When I got back to Warner's, I found they took it very seriously. The police were waiting with a license to carry a gun. I was fitted with a shoulder holster and a loaded .32 Smith & Wesson. To me it was still ten-cent melodrama and I couldn't believe it enough to put on the harness. What got me to slip it on was the arrival that night of a policeman to guard our house. Somehow I didn't think the department tossed policemen around as part of a practical joke.

The clincher to the whole business, in my estimation, came when the grapevine informed me that the group was openly scoffing at this very secret operation: "This is all cooked-up nonsense. If we had wanted to throw acid in Reagan's face, we would have done it, not talked about it." I thought that was strange. No one had mentioned acid-throwing—up to that revealing moment.

Thereafter, I mounted the holstered gun religiously every morning and took it off the last thing at night. I learned how much a person gets to lean on hardware like that. After months of wearing it took a real effort of will to discard it. I kept thinking: "The very night you take it off may be the night when you need it most."

One thing I do know the Communists hate. If only those liberals who can still say, "Oh, I suppose so-and-so is a Communist but we just don't talk about it—after all, he's my friend," if only they could find themselves taking a stand just once on an issue wherein they stood in the way of a "party" maneuver, they'd learn their friendship was a one-way street. Communists are not neutral: they'll tolerate you while you are neutral because at the moment you aren't in their way. Eddie Arnold and I were crossing an intersection one night on our way to a board meeting, just after I'd taken my first stand on the strike issue. Coming toward us were two actors we both knew. My smile was already forming and I had just started to greet them when one of the two thrust his face close to mine, his eyes burning with hatred. "Fascist!" he hissed, literally spitting the word at me.

It was an interesting period in my life. Nor was it without rewards and sacrifices. By the time it was over, I was president of the Screen Actors Guild—and I had lost my wife.

CHAPTER

11

By March 15, 1947, Hutcheson and Sorrell had aired their split, and defections from the ranks of the CSU were increasing. These were not, however, harbingers of peace. If anything, these cracks in the enemy front only meant more violence and a stepping up of offensive measures. There were forty-one pictures in production against forty-five the previous year, indicating the strike had failed to close down the studios.

From the beginning of the strike the Guild had adopted a policy of telling the complete factual story to any group requesting it and, since I had made the first report to the membership, I sort of inherited this narrator's job in all subsequent tellings.

I had been elected president to fill out the unexpired term of Bob Montgomery. Bob had spiked an expected attack—that a number of the board and officers were actually producers, incapable of truly representing rank-and-file actors—by resigning. All three vice-presidents, having similar producer-percentage deals, followed suit. This was one of the greatest blows ever dealt the Screen Actors Guild. Not because of my election—someone had to be president—but because of the why of my election.

The Communists benefited the most from this policy, even though it seemed that we had nipped their propaganda blossom in the bud. A tradition was born as every officer and several board members resigned. I myself would step down from my sixth term as president more than ten years later because I was successful in acquiring an ownership interest in a TV program. But with the Guild still deeply involved in a fight literally for the life of the industry, we saw our top combat forces deprived of such veterans as Bob, Jimmy Cagney, Cary Grant, Dick Powell, Harpo Marx, Pat O'Brien, and Charles Boyer. Others would follow until the tradition became so firmly established that today the Guild is denied the service of the overwhelming majority of actors and actresses who achieve stardom.

The Guild was, and is, unique—and part of its record is due to the fact that people started it who didn't need it themselves but were willing to lend their individual bargaining power as stars to get benefits for players who needed collective strength. I not only believe the Guild has an almost 100 percent record of "right decisions"—I think it has been statesmanlike in every important crisis. At the same time it has never been stuffy. It couldn't be with a membership roster that is a Who's Who of the big league in the entertainment world.

There is no way to picture the atmosphere of a typical board meeting. I'm sure our own industry could never photograph it as a movie scene and capture the flavor. Into the room drift thirty-odd people, all with faces as familiar as your next of kin. For three or four hours they dispose of mundane workaday problems and there isn't a remote whiff of glamour. I have seen them debate an issue with great heat—finally a vote sees the motion carried, 19 to 17. Obviously the debate changed no one's mind. Then you really see the secret of the Guild's success: one of the nineteen, with victory in hand, says, "Wait a minute—if it's that close there must be something wrong. Let's table it and think about it until the next meeting." Congress should be so smart.

Of course, being entertainers, they can't resist a cue, so even the most heated discussion can erupt when someone comes up with a funny line. One night I watched dignified Paul Harvey (who played so many bankers and senators), George Murphy, and Gene Kelly, as we waited for the elevator. They were already

177

seriously discussing a matter that would face them in the board meeting upstairs. Someone opened the door to the drugstore off the lobby, and a catchy jukebox tune was audible. Gene's foot began to tap and he did an intricate little dance step. Murph (a pretty fair country dancer himself) topped him with a tap routine ending with a kick away from the marble wall, at which Paul—with great dignity—went into a very passable time-step. The elevator door opened and they stepped in, and none of them had changed expression or paused for a second in their heated discussion.

Bob Montgomery, probably more than any single individual, was responsible for the SAG being in a position to stand firm against the Communist attempt at takeover. Long before most of us were even conscious such a threat existed, he had proposed —and the membership had overwhelmingly approved—a change in the bylaws that stymied the Comrades in their favorite practice, namely, "Come to the meeting early and stay late." Under the changed bylaws, nothing affecting Guild policy can be passed by a vote of the membership at a meeting. It must be submitted to the entire membership for a secret mail ballot. Adopt this in every union and see how many faults of labor would disappear. The rank-and-file working man is as honest and fair as any citizen: give him a chance to vote in the privacy of his home, and you'll find out. A certain element of the Guild continually tries to cancel this bylaw change, sneering that we are a mail order union. Our cheerful answer is always a question, "What's wrong with letting everybody vote?"

There was no question but that the Writers Guild, and to a certain extent the Directors Guild, went through a period in those postwar years when a number of their members were motivated by rather exotic political beliefs. They came to us with a grandiose scheme for forming a tri-guild alliance, so that in certain matters the actors, writers, and directors could face the industry as a single force. It listened good: so good that Bob might have had trouble making any warning register—so he let us find out

178

for ourselves. I was one of those who happened to discuss this informally with some members of the other two guilds. Bob suggested that we should all first agree to a statement of purpose and principle; then he tried a rough copy for size. It specified some of the matters we should jointly handle and it wound up with a seemingly innocuous bow to patriotism in that we pledge to combat the influence of any "ism" in the industry, such as Nazism, Fascism, or Communism. Bob knew his men very well; I was floored that they could be so unsubtle. They agreed to the entire statement except for one word—they wouldn't hold still for being opposed to that third "ism," the one that begins with C. We held firm and so there never was a tri-guild alliance.

George Murphy was a worthy successor to Bob Montgomery, and equally aware of the strange creatures crawling from under the make-believe rocks in our make-believe town. I owe a great deal to this cool, dapper guy who had to deal with me in my early white-eyed liberal daze. There were some of our associates, I'm sure, who believed I was red as Moscow, but Murph never wavered in his defense of me even though I ranted and railed at him as an arch-reactionary (which he isn't).

The late Edward Arnold was another tower of strength in those dark days. As a matter of fact, the CSO picket line paper, a mimeographed blast with a heavy load of invective, made a package deal of us by always giving us vaudeville booking: "Ronnie, George, and Eddie." Sometimes when an uproar hits the board room, it seems as if you can still hear that famous rolling laugh of Eddie's.

I don't know whether the Guild was contagious, or if we were just lucky in the people we hired as permanent staff. Whatever it was, we had the best. Jack Dales, who used to collect gold medals running the quarter mile at Stanford, should have a king-size medal for running our establishment as executive secretary. There is no limit to his loyalty; indeed, he is more SAG than any member I've ever known.

Ken Thompson, Jack's assistant, was a prime movie type. He

had played many suave screen villians and played them so smoothly a lot of people couldn't believe he was a hero in negotiations. He was even accused of carrying a "little black pay-off bag" to pass money to Bioff and Browne. What he had in the bag was a portable typewriter, to take down an account of the meeting in which he told those characters—on behalf of the Guild—to go to hell. He did his typing with the knowledge that Willy had opened his center desk drawer and a Colt .45 was just under his folded hands.

Pat Somerset, the blond affable Englishman who was in charge of labor relations and therefore eyebrow-deep in the strike, must have wondered why he quit acting. He related a conversation to us that he had with one of the labor leaders, and he was still a little wide-eyed in the telling. The man had been in a reminiscent mood and he was telling anecdotes of a painters' strike. "You know," he said in his heavy voice, "we used to catch those scab painters being sent home in trucks. I didn't have any trouble getting guys to stop the trucks, or even to hold those scabs down, but when it came to breaking their arms I was the only one with guts enough to do it." He went on: "They'd hold one of 'em down for me and I'd put his arm over my knee and break it, so he couldn't paint any more. It made a goddamned satisfying noise when it broke, too." Then he laughed and added, "I've often wondered how many of 'em might have been left-handed, and there I was always breaking the right arm."

Pat wasn't the only labor expert to get a jolt. When Joe Keenan was considering our invitation to serve as labor czar, this experienced negotiator came out of a meeting with the CSU strike committee, shaking his head. "I just heard the damnedest thing I've ever heard," he said. "One of those CSU fellows turned to Sorrell right in front of me and said, 'When do we get this strike back in our own hands? The Communists have been running it for the last six months.'" Then, said Joe, "Herb told him, 'Just give me time, I'll get it back in our hands yet.'" That was enough for Joe Keenan—he went to Germany to represent the United States occupation forces in labor matters.

But to get back to our own people, there was Buck Harris, in charge of SAG public relations. Spectacled, nervous, but with the right touch for the right words, he is one of those rare people who can be a stalwart liberal but at the same time a knowledgeable, effective anti-Communist.

If we ever erect a statue called the "Spirit of SAG," I'm afraid it won't be of an actress but of Jack Dales's secretary, Midge. The Guild comes ahead of the world in her book, and small though she is physically, she's ten feet tall when the going gets tough.

Unfortunately there were individuals other than CSU members who didn't quite see the splendid virtue of the Guild. There was a "Citizens Fact Finding Committee." It credited the information from one side only and hurried up the publicity trail, hellbent for investigating something. The "Hollywood Interfaith Council" got into the picture, offering to meet with the warring factions to help them find a "just and lasting peace." We didn't want to claim a monopoly on this middleman stuff, but we had a real fear that a new, inexperienced group could give the strikers a second breath. We called these good people and offered to give them all our records and transcripts of the endless meetings and, incidentally, told them we were hard put to see what they could do that hadn't already been tried. With some surprise they told us they had "only volunteered in answer to a request from the Screen Actors Guild." That made the surprise unanimous until they told us an actor and actress had come to them claiming to represent the Guild, and had asked their help. It took only one session with our documentation, and they decided labor relations they could do without.

A particularly upsetting incident involved a Roman Catholic priest, a teacher of political science at Loyola University, Father Dunne. He took to the air waves and blasted the SAG and all opponents of the CSU eloquently and with vigor. The papers reported also that he appeared on the platform at CSU rallies. George Murphy and I decided he must be the victim of a snow job. We knew he had never been exposed to the Guild side of the controversy, and he was saying some pretty harsh things about us. We called and asked if we could see him, and then went down to the university one evening, armed with our records. We were a little taken aback when he introduced us to his lawyer, and coldly informed us he had asked the lawyer to sit in on our meeting. It was a short meeting. The next night he was back on radio kicking our brains out. But not for long: someone else began to teach political science and he was on the other side of the country.

I've referred earlier to the petition demanding a membership meeting, and the committee that called on us to set up procedure for the meeting, but I overlooked one curious aspect of that get-together. Jack Carson came to me on the set the day before we were to meet. "Maybe this is crazy," he said, "but I was at a dinner party the other night and they were all talking about some meeting you are going to have." I confirmed that we were indeed having a meeting (when weren't we having a meeting?). "Well," he went on, "I heard them say they'd have to make you lose your temper and that they could put something over if they could get you mad."

The next night we met. For insurance, I'd told Jack Dales what Carson had heard; now we waited to see which of the delegation would light the fuse. But we were living in a cockeyed world: when the riding started it came from one of our own committee—John Garfield. I have already told of John and what amounted to practically his deathbed confession. This was another page in his strange story of torment. Of course, having been forewarned, he could have stabbed me and I wouldn't have lost my temper. Besides, a glance at Jack Dales was enough to shut down any excess flow of adrenalin.

Came the night of the membership meeting and we were treated to further examples of their very deep bag of tricks. They had

182

prevailed upon a number of people to say a few words, and I don't doubt some of these spoke from a sincere desire to be helpful in ending the whole bitter, miserable mess. Katie Hepburn read a speech which I recognized as a word-for-word copy of a CSU strike bulletin several weeks old. She surely was unaware that her script had already had a first run on the picket line and she was speaking in sincerity only to end the mess.

We had tried to be patient so far. Now I wondered if we hadn't failed our members in not really laying it on the line so they wouldn't be suckered into taking part by appeals to their emotions. My conscience really played this tune when Eddie G. Robinson got up and appealed for peace. Eddie is one of the warmest-hearted, truly kind people in the world; he sees no evil in anyone. He believed then, as he believes now, that all the hatred will go away if we'll just talk to each other.

However, people like Katie and Eddie were prologue. I had already made my speech, which was a chronological report of our meetings with the "Wise Men," and our conference phone call. None of this was a surprise to the steering committee who had called the meeting because we had told them in the earlier joint committee meeting exactly what I was going to do. Then Alexander Knox got up with a very witty, well-delivered but bitter satire of all I had said. Our meeting was held in the old Legion Fight Stadium and the speakers' platform was the ring. No fighter ever bled in that ring as I did. Alex was getting laughs, and that meant they were laughing at me. But suddenly a change occurred: the laughs stopped and slowly an audible murmur could be heard. Then the murmur erupted into angry cries of "Sit down"—"What would you have done?"—"Shut up." He never got to finish his concoction of ridicule—he was literally booed off the platform. Jack Dales had been right: "Tell the people the truth—all of it—and they'll recognize it." The SAG membership know the script and they had decided who were the good guys and who were the bad.

The strike really began to vanish like a Cheshire cat when

the police picked up five suspects accused of the IATSE bombings. Three of them were longshoremen from Bridges' union! The courts thought enough of the preliminary evidence to put them under fifty thousand dollars' bail each. Then the secretary of the Screen Writers Guild, William Pomerantz, resigned. To "work with the CSU," he said. The roused writers commenced to clean their own house. The CSU made an international appeal for a boycott of all pictures in which certain stars appeared—and guess whose name led all the rest. Not because I really deserved top billing but just because I was becoming notorious, I presume.

Then, finally, thirty-four of the original set decorators applied for membership in the IATSE. Sorrell denied there was violence at a meeting of the painters caused by a thirty-two-member petition asking the international officers to take over. However, the police records put it down as "quelling a riot."

In February, 1947, the IBEW members had withdrawn from the CSU. Their local was taken over by the international officers. The NLRB ruled that workers who had violated their no-strike pledge were not entitled to be hired back. Magazine articles appeared, exposing Communist methods in infiltrating unions in exact, affidavited detail.

The picket lines that spring dropped to almost nothing. But four thousand men were still out, and the bulk of them were guys we knew and had worked with. They weren't involved in the plotting and scheming. They were cannon fodder in this war and had obeyed their unions' orders to strike in good faith that their cause was just.

One rainy Sunday afternoon, I answered the doorbell to see a small shrunken man, who identified himself as one of the strikers. I thought: "Here it is at last, and me without that gun." He asked to come in and told me he'd heard I was telling a story different than the one he was getting from his union, and he'd like to hear my version. It took hours, but I gave him a factual account of every move we'd made and resisted any temptation to editorialize. He got straight reporting. When I finished, he said, "I've sus-

184

pected this for some time. Now I'm going downtown and circulate this petition." He showed me a petition addressed to the governor of California, asking him to intervene and force the unions to let the strikers go back to work.

I was horrified. "You know you will probably get the hell beaten out of you, or even killed, if you do that," I said.

He turned around in the doorway with an indescribable look. "Mr. Reagan," he said, "ask the finance company who owns my car and my home now." I watched him walk down the driveway in the soaking rain, and I was mad enough to get that gun and start a war of my own. Here were the real casualties, the human beings who gave up savings and homes and cars, out of loyalty to the Herb Sorrells and the Big Bill Hutchesons who, if they thought of them at all, thought of them as ammunition—easily expendable.

Now I understood what John Emerich Edward Dalberg, First Baron Acton, had meant when he said: "Power tends to corrupt; absolute power corrupts absolutely"—whether it was union leadership, management, gangsters, or politicians. We had had examples of all of them crammed into a single period.

Even in memory it seems impossible that my workaday world was continuing through all this—meaning that I was making pictures. In fact, one picture opened the door to finding another part of me, a part which has today become a major facet of my life.

Hollywood has a way of talking to itself and believing everything it says. For example, someone can become a star on the Bel Air circuit (this is my name for the picture hierarchy who show movies to each other in their home projection rooms) but be relatively unknown out where the box office grows. Still, such a star will go on collecting parts for quite a while because he or she is locally fashionable.

As a result of *King's Row* I was a star, but I had a sneaking suspicion that a lot of people across America hadn't stayed in a breathless state of palpitation for three and a half years, waiting for my return. In the first place, my Air Force chores had exposed me to the Monday morning conversation of a lot of Civil Service stenographers, average age eighteen, and they weren't "oohing and aahing" over Robert Taylor, Jimmy Stewart, or Tyrone Power, let alone me. Their age group was about sixty per cent of the movie audience and they had come to ticket-buying age while all of us were off-screen. They had a new set of heroes.

Jack Warner thought I was a star and I liked the idea of his continuing to think that. It seemed to me that R.R. should do his "first out" in company with someone who hadn't been away—sort of insurance, like a ball carrier picking up a down field blocker. After several months of waiting it out, what seemed to be the perfect answer came along. The studio paged me for a part in Stephen Longstreet's book, *Stallion Road*, a story of two men, a woman, and a whole herd of beautiful horses. They had me hooked on the horses alone, but the real clincher was the male co-star, Humphrey Bogart, who sold tickets like they were going out of production any minute.

One week before shooting started, Bogey checked out of the cast and was replaced by Zachary Scott. Don't get me wrong: "Zack" is a fine actor and was a pleasure to work with, but Bogey was practically number one box office, and I was looking for a free ride. Then, after long debate, the studio decided on black and white instead of color. This too was a blow, because a picture like this depends to a certain extent on visual beauty, and there is nothing more beautiful than California in the spring, especially when it's all covered with horses. Speaking of beauty, our feminine partner was as well cast as ever an actress could be: Alexis Smith loved everything about the show, and we all loved her. Actually it was a happy company and going to work was like going to a party every day for 109 days. Yes, this was a new world to me—only pictures like *Ben Hur* should take 109 days.

Prior to the war I had achieved that status symbol of all contract players: I could get away with saying, "I quit at six o'clock." Now, freshly back, I decided I'd better re-establish this right from the start. The first day of shooting, I sought out the first assistant. "Fellows," I began, all palsy-walsy, "I think we should get one thing straight. You know I quit at six o'clock."

"You're going to be pretty lonesome that last hour," he said. "We quit at five."

It seems that during the war, with revenues flowing in like water and the government milking off most of the profit through an excess profits tax, a certain looseness in production standards had crept in. Everyone figured production costs were 90 per cent government money, so why not share the wealth?

I'd been a long time away from horses and I desperately wanted to do my own riding and jumping in this one. Like a golfer after a long layoff, I needed professional coaching and mentioned this at a party one night. Dan Dailey and Oleg Cassini, who had seen service in the cavalry (I've often wondered how Oleg got from cinching horses to designing flounces for females), recommended a former Italian cavalry officer and count: Nino Pepitone. They didn't have to say any more—the Italian cavalry fathered the modern forward seat in riding and has influenced the cavalry of every country in the world.

I met small, dark-mustached Nino and his American wife, Ruth, and we wound up in a four-year partnership that ended when their love of horses took them to the track and mine to the farm.

The studio was searching for a black thoroughbred-type mare who could jump, to play the part of Tarbaby in the picture. Nino introduced me to his pride and joy, a three-year-old black thoroughbred filly he called Baby. She was a jumper, and would be my mount during our instruction periods. It was love at first sight—"leadingladyitis" without reservation. I called the studio and told them I'd found the girl we were looking for. They hired her at thirty-five dollars a day and before the picture was over I'd bought her from Nino in two installments. First I owned a half interest, and then I had to have her all for my own. There is an old horseman's saying, "Never marry a horse," but nearly everyone does—at least their first one. Baby is now an old, retired *grande dame* who mothered my present mount, a dapple gray named Nancy D. and her successor-to-be, an almost black colt named High Shine.

The four-year partnership with Nino opened up a way of life I'd longed for but been afraid to try. In my limited cavalry experience, all the emphasis had been on military and riding. They'd never gotten around to any teaching with regard to care of the animal or even saddling and grooming. To me the thought of being responsible for horses on a farm presented so much that was new and mysterious I never got beyond the yearning stage. Now, however, with Ruth and Nino as the residents in charge, it all became possible.

First I acquired an eight-acre plot, complete with stables and living quarters over in Northridge. Nino was amazed to discover that my idea of fun was to do what needed to be done, myself. This included building paddock fences—even a quarter-mile track with the inner rail posts slanted at the proper angle and every post hole dug by hand, by me. Our little rectangle became a model horse nursery (oh yes, the business end of our partnership was breeding race horses for the market). Soon civilization began to surround us as Los Angeles started its building boom, and we decided to get out before the newcomers started circulating those "we don't like manure" petitions. To tell the truth, I'd run out of things to do and wanted to really farm.

Our move was to three hundred acres-plus of beautiful scenery in the Malibu hills, where I can never finish all that has to be done if dreams are to materialize completely. We raise our own hay and there is no way to make anyone but a farmer understand the thrill of looking back at a furrow you've plowed in your own ground. In odd moments I build jumps out of timber and stones—paneling all the fences with jumps so that Nancy D. and I can ride the whole ranch without using a gate. We've added cattle to the operation and, all in all, my greatest problem is remembering that show business comes first or there won't be a farm. My every instinct is to turn down an acting job if it interferes with getting the plowing done.

During all this fence building on the eight acres, however, I was interrupted for my second postwar picture, a dramatization of Philip Wylie's book, *Night unto Night*. It was an unusual story, as most of his are, and I'm not sure we got the most out of his book. A new Scandinavian import was leading lady Viveca Lindfors, an intense and very talented actress. I played a scientist who had discovered he had an incurable ailment. Viveca played a young widow whose husband, a naval officer, had been killed in action. She had discovered his body washed ashore with some wreckage, practically in front of their Florida beach home, and her problem was one of almost believing in ghosts as a result of this psychic shock.

If you are thinking this was a hard story to bring to life on the screen, you are right. We were doing pretty well, however, except for the key scene, where for the first time I learn the reason for her disturbance—namely, the finding of her husband's body. We photographed this scene four times, and rejected it each time when it was shown in the rushes: it just didn't come off. The producer had fallen in love with a pictorial shot of two riders on horseback far in the distance at sundown on the lonely beach. His justification was that seeing them triggered Viveca into telling me that her husband had been asleep on the beach, waiting for her (she was late), when two riders had stepped on him and killed him. It seemed the producer had decided that, Wylie or no Wylie, we weren't going to mention war or the Navy. We did this scene the fifth time, and I knew—as we all did—it was no better than the other four. Thus happened my first foray into script doctoring. I asked Don Siegal, the director, if he'd shoot one more version with a slight change of lines and keep it on hand. I'd figured a way to keep the producer's sunset horse shot in.

I told Don that, number one, a horse wouldn't step on a man if he could possibly avoid it and, number two, even if a man was killed that way, it sounded funny. The scene as I rewrote it had

189

the horseback riders asking her for directions to a phone to call the Coast Guard: they had come upon bodies and wreckage on the beach. Going back with them, she had discovered her husband. Her traumatic condition was explained in the line (somewhat poetic), "It was almost as if in death he had tried to come back to me." Frankly, I was kind of proud of it. After all, it was a basis for believing in ghosts when you stop to think he could have drifted in on any part of four thousand miles of coastline.

It's typical Hollywood that the producer kept the scene but said to the director, "My God, don't ever let an actor get a pencil in his hand!"

CHAPTER

12

Continuing carefully to backtrack in my own footsteps to deceive the restless natives of Hollywood, I'd like to go on with what was occurring in my own work, which at times seemed to be a sideline, what with everything else that was happening. I played a series of romantic leads, first in the movie version of the Broadway play, *The Voice of the Turtle,* in the spring of 1947. Later on in the summer of the same year, I worked in *That Hagen Girl.* Another Broadway hit was filmed in the winter of 1947-48, and I played John in *John Loves Mary.* The following summer, a modest little picture that turned out to be a box-office phenomenon, *The Girl from Jones Beach,* was added to the list. Then, for reasons which will become clear, I went to England—my first time abroad—to do the film version of another Broadway play, *The Hasty Heart.*

There were probably signs and portents of changes to come, but I wasn't one to read them. The industry itself would reel and stagger when postwar readjustment ended the near-monopoly it had enjoyed in the harvest of the entertainment dollar. Mac and Mabel Citizen discovered a lot of things they could do when rationing ended, and their plans didn't include two nights a week at the movies.

My personal life was due for some changes. For one thing, I closed down a picture in the last weeks of filming (a first for me) to have pneumonia. I was notified I was going to be a bachelor again—and this, I thought, only happened to other people, and you read about it in the papers. And like the story, "you think you've got troubles," I came home from England and broke my leg in half a dozen pieces.

Meantime, back at the Guild, we were involved in the longest and most involved negotiations in the history of our union. As president of the Guild, I also put in appearances in Washington before the House Committee on Un-American Activities, and in Los Angeles before a special subcommittee of the House Committee on Education and Labor, headed by the late Carroll D. Kearns. These hearings were, of course, part of the strike aftermath.

Looking back, I realize that all of this extracurricular activity prevented me from giving full thought to my career. For example, I should have settled down happily and gratefully in *The Voice of the Turtle*. Instead, I fussed around trying to get out of it. Jack Warner had bought the rights to this reigning play by John Van Druten a long time before and had earmarked it for me while I was still in service. I've since learned that he stubbornly hung on even when stars like Cary Grant were offered. Perhaps the fact that I didn't know this at the time points up one of the shortcomings of our business: we just don't talk things out with each other. Here was Jack feeling rebuffed, and all because John Huston had dangled a role in his now-classic picture, *Treasure of the Sierra Madre,* under my hammy nose. Both pictures would shoot at the same time, so it was one or the other—there was no way to have both.

I wanted to work with Huston, one of the real geniuses in our world. I'm sure John still believes that if I had stamped my foot firmly before the front office brass, I could have had my choice. What he doesn't know is that I *did* put my foot down. Then the studio put its foot down—on top of mine. I was under exclusive contract: if I said no to *Voice of the Turtle,* there would be no part in *Treasure* because it was a Warner picture too.

So there I was, back in uniform, unhappy but luckier than I deserved to be. If the "uniform" line is confusing, let me recall to your mind that *Voice of the Turtle* concerns a lonely soldier on furlough. The girl the soldier inevitably meets and romances was played by Eleanor Parker, and even here I was a sorehead. A number of new performers had come along while I was flying my Air Force desk and she was one of them. To me she was unknown, and I wanted the studio to borrow June Allyson from MGM.

It took only one scene with Eleanor for me to realize I'd be lucky if I could stay even. She is one of the truly fine actresses in motion pictures, as four Oscar nominations attest, and by my vote at least a couple of those nominations should have been crowned with victory.

I tried to turn down the next script offered, *That Hagen Girl.* Every so often now it pops up on the Late Late Show, and I'm reminded of how right my first actor's instinct was and how wrong I was to go against that instinct and do the picture. But I had lost a lot of weight on my side because of my ill-considered objections to *Voice of the Turtle.* When Jack Warner called me in and laid it on the line regarding the big investment they had tied up in the screenplay (actually *screenplays*—this was the fifth rewrite in an effort to get a picture out of the book) and then asked for my help as a personal favor, I was all out of arguments.

That Hagen Girl was Shirley Temple in her first grown-up role. She was grown up in truth, and a wonderfully warm, sweet young lady. Unfortunately the public was not ready to give up their *young* Shirley Temple, particularly to a man old enough to be her father. That was the theme of the story. I played a lawyer, a returned war hero who was suspected of being the father of this schoolgirl, frowned upon by the town because of her lack of legal parentage.

Even after I'd agreed to do the picture I tried to talk the director into a sixth rewrite that would have put Shirley in the arms of her schoolboy romance, Rory Calhoun, and matched me with a schoolteacher in the story. Trying to put this over, I spoke one sentence too many to Peter Godfrey, our director. I said, "You

193

know, people sort of frown on men marrying girls young enough to be their daughters." He gave me a long, level look and answered quietly, "I'm old enough to be my wife's father." That didn't leave me much in the way of an answer.

I won the argument at the sneak preview, but it didn't make me happy. Came the moment on screen when I said to Shirley, "I love you," and the entire audience en masse cried, "Oh, no!" I sat huddled in the darkness until I was sure the lobby would be empty. You couldn't have gotten me to face that audience for a million bucks. Before release the line was edited out of the picture, leaving us with a kind of oddball finish in which we climb on a train—Shirley carrying a bouquet—and leave town. You are left to guess as to whether we are married, just traveling together, or did I adopt her. Maybe a late night TV sponsor can run a contest: "Was I passionate or paternal to the present Mrs. Black?"

Before sneak and release or even finish of the picture, however, there was an interruption. Warner's had a premiere one night at the Carthay Circle Theater. It had been an unusually hot day and I blamed the heat for the fact that I had no appetite for dinner, but when we stepped out of the theater into the night air I coughed, and I was sure someone in the crowd had stabbed me in the chest. I couldn't remember ever hurting so much in quite that way.

I was sure I'd be back on the set the next day, but I left the house on a wheeled stretcher, headed for Cedars of Lebanon Hospital. It was not only virus pneumonia: it was that brand for which the miracle drugs will perform no miracles. I can't blame the studio for suspecting a hoax—after all, I'd been less than happy about doing the picture. But while the studio was sleuthing around the hospital to see if I was really there, my next of kin were being notified that the hospital might be my last address.

Of course I knew none of this or much of anything else; not even that in another hospital my then-wife, Jane Wyman, had lost our child by miscarriage. Days and nights went by in a hazy montage in which I alternately shivered with chills or burned with fever, and even insisted that I be wrapped in blankets and fed hot tea through a glass tube when the fever struck. The nurses could not be expected to know that I was harking back to a memory of Nelle doing this to us kids when we had a fever.

Came one night when I seemed to see a street lamp and a lonely patch of sidewalk. Humphrey Bogart appeared, and we played an interminable scene exchanging and wearing innumerable trenchcoats, and trying to say lines to each other, always with a furtive air of danger in the surrounding darkness. Someone else can take a crack at analyzing what this Freudian delirium meant. This was evidently the night—"Big Casino, bet or throw in." I was cocooned in blankets, waiting for the blessed sweat that would end the fever. Only it didn't end: it just reached a new high. Finally I decided I'd be more comfortable not breathing. I don't know what time of night it was when I told the nurse I was too tired to breathe any more. I wish I knew who she was—God bless her. There in the dark she leaned over me, coaxing me to take a breath. "Now let it out," she'd say. "Come on now, breathe in once more."

This went on, over and over, with her arguing me into another breath when all I wanted was to rest and stop making the effort. Wherever she is and whether she remembers our midnight contest or not, I don't suppose I'll ever know, but the memory is vivid to me. She was so nice and persistent that I let her have her way, and kept breathing out of courtesy. The sweat came and washed me back down the divide I'd been climbing.

The ambulance ride home made quite an impression on me. I couldn't get enough of looking at the world as it went by, and even the most ordinary, everyday things seemed strangely beautiful. I was seventeen pounds lighter and plagued for weeks and weeks by lack of strength. Even the lightest effort brought on a shortness of breath and a clammy perspiration. In an effort to stimulate my appetite, the doctor suggested a glass of wine with dinner. He probably didn't have hobby lobby in mind, but that's the way it turned out. I liked the wine—then decided I had to learn how to

195

find the good ones, and wound up with an interest that has given me great pleasure these many years.

I was still battling the shakes when the studio decided to finally wrap up *That Hagen Girl*. The doctor imposed a 3 P.M. curfew on them, but even this curfew couldn't control what went on before three. My first day back on the job I had to run through a driving rain and dive fully clothed into a murky, ice-cold tank to rescue Shirley. The only thing that made me accomplish this was the horrible thought that if I folded before the scene was completed I'd be known forevermore as the guy Shirley Temple saved from drowning.

I don't know how much my double life had to do with what had happened, but during all this picture-making I was spending five nights a week at the Guild. For months we had been getting ready for our big negotiations with the producers.

As a new union, SAG had signed a ten-year deal in 1937. Time and experience had revealed a number of burs under the saddle, so this negotiation was going to be a real reform movement. Fact-finding committees had been set up in each of the various classifications into which our members fell: day players, contract actors, free lance, stuntmen, multiple-picture players, and on and on. Each group had gall spots where the harness rubbed and yet we had to keep the whole picture in perspective so that we didn't solve one group's problem at the expense of creating a hiring advantage or disadvantage for some other class of player. By the time we were ready to open negotiations, we had a sizable printed book filled with complaints and proposals for cure, ranging from a request for a "200 per cent increase in salary of bit players," to the reasonable demand that performers be given twelve hours between calls. The point involved here, of course, was that any actor's face was his fortune and it was foolish to spend a king's ransom on make-up departments and camera geniuses and then grind the actor down to where nothing could hide the fatigue circles and bloodshot eyes.

The negotiations opened on April 15 and carried on for five

months. All of us had a darn near perfect attendance record, which was broken in my case by the pneumonia bout. In addition to this chore, we were the same officers and staff members who had to gather at odd hours on weekends for the run-of-the-mill activities that went on regardless of negotiations.

During the negotiations, in typical labor management tradition, we asked for the moon and they offered green cheese. Then we wiped out some of the decoy bargaining points and got down to business. Our contract ended May 15 but we agreed to extend it thirty days. Then, because both sides were honestly trying to treat with the ten-year accumulation, we continued granting extensions.

The negotiations were a whole new experience to me. I suppose I really walked in believing we'd get what we asked because we asked for it. First surprise was discovering that the fellows across the table had ideas of their own. I was unprepared for the respect and courtesy involved, or the bullheadedness that could be encountered. I knew I'd never realized the ultimate reasonableness of such bargaining, or the physical endurance required.

I was surprised to discover the important part a urinal played in this high-altitude bargaining. When some point has been kicked around, until it swells up bigger than the whole contract, someone from one side or the other goes to the men's room. There is a kind of sensory perception that gives you the urge to follow. It really is a kind of intuition and certainly not the result of any agreement or hanky-panky. Then, standing side by side in that room that levels king and commoner, comes an honest question, "What do you guys really want?" No bargaining here —each tells what is the settling point, what they must have if they are to win ratification by those they represent. Back in the meeting, one or the other makes an offer based on this newly acquired knowledge. There is a little more table thumping, a few unprintable words. Then the other returnee from the men's room says, "Can our group have a caucus?" That is the magic word, like

197

the "huddle" in football—it's where the signal is passed. Slowly, point by point, men's room to caucus, you get on with it.

We shook hands over the debris of conference indispensables such as cigar butts, notepaper, chewed-up pencils, and paper coffee cups. Actors had gotten raises ranging from 52 to 166 per cent. Working conditions had been vastly improved and we had wearily agreed to a stopgap clause that settled nothing with regard to movies someday being reissued on television—but then everyone said they'd be crazy to sell their movies to a competing medium.

I must tell of one negotiating experience, however, to illustrate the really fine relationship we had in these bouts. Studios can call an actor back after a production is finished for needed closeups and added shots that weren't anticipated during regular shooting. Under such circumstances, they don't have to pay for the intervening period. Some of the "quick buck" producers had developed a nasty habit of deliberately shortcutting and then getting a free ride by pretending they were calling the cast back for "added closeups" not contemplated during scheduled production. After a bitter battle, we won the producers' consent to no more such free rides. As the negotiations went on to other points, we were uncomfortable among ourselves about our victory. We realized that in blocking the "sharpies" we had made legitimate added "closeups" so expensive they just wouldn't be made. This violated point three of our code: "Was it fair to the public?" Hadn't we done something to prevent the public from getting as good a picture as it was possible for all of us to make? The last day of negotiations we brought up the point again, much to the producers' surprise, and we handed it back to them.

Frank Freeman, their chairman, asked what we were going to do to protect ourselves from chiselers. We answered that we'd just have to take our chances, but it wasn't fair to penalize responsible companies for the misdeeds of a few. The producers said we were being unfairly treated in this and ended up creating a committee of their own to police the industry and protect actors

198

from that kind of chiseling. The membership approved the results of our negotiation—3,676 to 78. But unlike the pictures we make, the house lights didn't go on and everyone live happily ever after.

Other items on the agenda were catching up to SAG. George Heller, the small, dark, intense secretary of the American Federation of Radio Artists, came to Hollywood to explain something about a new plan for unionizing television. We didn't pay him as much attention as we should have at the moment—and we paid for it later. Old movies began to turn up on TV; the movie box office itself slumped. Zenith came along with the idea of squirting television programs over telephone wires. Another Hollywood committee suddenly popped out of nowhere—the Hollywood Arts, Sciences, and Professional Council of the Progressive Citizens of America, or HSPCPCA. It was to deal with examining "thought control" and the "relation of the actor to film content." Nobody called and asked me to be on the board of this version, although I noticed names once listed as belonging to HICCASP turned up as members of HSPCPCA. Does Freud say anything about why these outfits choose such unwieldy names?

We weren't through with the little Red brethren by any means —they may have been in the process of taking Mr. Lenin's one step back after about ten or fifteen years of taking two big steps forward, but they were going to shuffle their feet for a while. It was almost anticlimactic to find ourselves back in the atmosphere of the late unlamented strike, but we shook ourselves and tried to recapture the flavor for the long-awaited fireworks with the Kearns Committee in August of 1947.

When the smoke had cleared, the hearing had been indefinitely postponed and Congressman Kearns had been recalled to Washington on urgent business.

There wasn't much time to brood about this latest revelation of cracks in the marble halls of justice. Kearns had told us at the start of the hearing that no one could mention Communism. Roy Brewer had protested that you couldn't talk about the strike without talking about the Communists. But it seemed

199

that even Congress had jurisdictional lines and that subject belonged to the House Committee on Un-American Activities.

Suddenly subpoenas descended on Hollywood like a first snow of winter. It seems we were all going to Washington as guests of HUAC. Some of us were going advertised as friendly witnesses, and a lot of people were just going. The Committee was—and still is—the target of Communists. Communism's greatest weapon is our ignorance regarding Communist tactics, strategy, and goals. Naturally, any agency attempting to dispel that ignorance is on the Red hate list. Anyone who took the Committee's side was a "crackpot" or "Fascist." The congressmen themselves were "witch hunters and Gestapo."

The situation was made to order for the "Commies"—they organized one of the most successful operations in their domestic history: "The Committee for the First Amendment." Literally the whole industry appeared on a giant radio show and, of course, there was the famous planeload of stars to Washington. Today some self-appointed "Red hunters" still use participation on that junket as proof of pro-Communist leanings. The truth is they got Hollywood so steamed up about defending the town's good (?) name that the Communists in their own circles insisted that *no* party member be on the plane: it was for suckers only.

Nevertheless, be it noted for the record, the Senate Report on Un-American Activities in California for 1955 declared that the Committee was a "Communist-dominated front," infiltrated by Communists, flavored by Communists, and—I suppose—tasted by the public.

The hearings aroused the American people as they've never been aroused before or, sadly enough, since about Communism. Perhaps part of it was the thought of shelling out money at the box office to support some bum and his swimming pool while he plotted the country's destruction. A lot of customers laid it right on the line and asked Hollywood, "What now?"

The producers, meeting en masse in New York, put out what was called the "Waldorf Declaration." They agreed none of them would knowingly employ Communists or those who refused to answer questions under oath about their affiliations. The Communists were among those who reacted in Hollywood by distorting any facts they got, claiming they were victims of a "blacklist" —when they were actually working members of a conspiracy directed by Soviet Russia against the United States. In war, that is treason and the name for such is traitor; in peace, it is apparently martyr. It is easy to call oneself a "political party" and hide other motives behind it: the Mafia can do it, so can a Chicago mob of gangsters. My own test for the time when the Communists may call themselves a legitimate political party is that time when, in the USSR, an effective anti-Communist political party wins an election. At that time, I shall withdraw my objections to labeling Communists "political."

I arrived home from the Washington hearing to be told I was leaving. I suppose there had been warning signs, if only I hadn't been so busy, but small-town boys grow up thinking only other people get divorced. The plain truth was that such a thing was so far from even being imagined by me that I had no resources to call upon.

Jane Wyman and I met in 1939, making *Brother Rat*. We became engaged during a cross-country tour with Louella Parsons who, incidentally, came from my home town. Louella took a group of us on a nine weeks' vaudeville tour as her picks for future stardom. She picked pretty good too: June Preisser, Susan Hayward, Joy Hodges, Arlene Whelan, Jane, and me. I think I should interject that through all that followed Louella remained scrupulously fair and grieved, as she always does when fate knocks some of us Hollywoodians kicking. We may be grist for the newspaper mill, but we are also friends in her book and the only way we can lose that is if we "betray the industry."

Divorce happens in every town, but somehow people reserve a special feeling for it when it happens in our town. I think that some of our less stable (and they are a very small percentage) glamour peddlers with a frequent repeat pattern have given the public an impression that it isn't tragic here—that no one takes it seriously. That, of course, isn't true: if you hit us we bruise, if you cut us (forgive me, Shakespeare) we bleed. When we have a domestic problem, we can't tackle it in any atmosphere of privacy. I have never discussed what happened, and I have no intention of doing so now.

The problem hurt our children most. Maureen was born in 1941 and Michael came to us in March of 1945—closer than a son; he wasn't born unasked, we chose him. There is no easy way to break up a home, and I don't think there is any way to ease the bewildered pain of children at such times.

CHAPTER

13

Picture a reasonably young man working with and among the most beautiful girls in the world—plenty of money in his jeans, a Cadillac convertible, and an apartment. Sounds like an adolescent's daydream come true, doesn't it? The only trouble was, I wasn't an adolescent and I didn't exactly know how to be a bachelor all over again. Actually I had very little previous experience at being a gay blade around Hollywood. In my early Hollywood days I was too busy and too scared to collect phone numbers.

Like most people, I assumed that the well-known glamour girls in our business lived in a whirl of glittering parties and wouldn't even take a call from a newly arrived ex-sports announcer. In my second bachelorhood I knew better. A lot of famous, beautiful, and very nice girls are also the world's loneliest. Figure it out: how many guys are around to ask a girl for a date when it's public knowledge her annual income is anywhere from $200,000 to $500,000? Oh, there is a certain type of fellow who finds that no drawback, and some of that kind circle the fire in Hollywood, waiting to pick up a stray lamb—but most of the lambs prefer loneliness to subsidizing these male camp followers.

So now I knew better, and my pay check matched theirs, and I still wasn't collecting phone numbers. You don't go through a bath of printer's ink with news items based on whether you smiled or cried, without getting a little headline-shy. A newly created bachelor is watched like a hawk, and a simple dinner date becomes a new romance. A second dinner date with someone else is good for two stories: the first tells of the end of your romance with your previous dinner date, and the second starts a coy whisper about the new romance. Where in the world do the people of pictures go to be anonymous?

Fortunately (in one way) Warner's put me to work in a picture called *John Loves Mary* with a newly arrived actress, Patricia Neal, Jack Carson, and Wayne Morris—and yes, my comrade-in-arms, Eddie Arnold. There were some facets we could describe as unfortunate—one of them the play itself. It had been a great hit on Broadway, although playwright Norman Krasna was the first to admit it had one joke, and if you slowed down long enough for the audience to think, they'd ask why John didn't tell Mary the truth and your play would be over. As a matter of fact, that's exactly how the play ends, but you first have to keep the audience laughing for two hours or you have a one-reel short. We did this pretty well but a fear of mine proved justified: it was great for two years on Broadway, but wasn't the "returning serviceman" theme a little old hat by the time we brought it to the screen? It was. If you are wondering why I didn't turn it down, you'll perhaps recall an experience of mine in trying to turn down another smash Broadway play, *The Voice of the Turtle*.

The picture springboarded me into another starring role that didn't take a lick of work. In one scene, where I'm changing into civilian clothes in Mary's home, when her father, the Senator (Eddie Arnold) enters, my zipper stuck. The camera kept grinding and I kept tugging until finally I looked up at the camera and yelled, "The damned thing is stuck!" This became the featured running gag in the annual "blowup" film.

My next role went a long way toward solving my social problems. I was cast as a modern painter of the Vargas or Petty type in a picture called *The Girl from Jones Beach*. Virginia Mayo was "The Girl," and Eddie Bracken played my sidekick. The solution to my off-screen problem lay in the fact that the plot called for me to have and romance an even dozen gorgeous models. In one scene, Eddie got so goggle-eyed he stepped on my heels, tripped me, and cracked my coccyx. It was my first experience with the pain of a broken bone, but, as it turned out, not my last.

The late Peter Godfrey, the same polite Englishman who'd directed *That Hagen Girl,* called the shots on this one. For some reason he never saw the humor of the story and used to wind up a rehearsal sighing and muttering, "I don't see what's funny about this, but let's shoot it." I'm sure he didn't mind that he was wrong. The picture was a slick and very funny comedy but, more important, it rang box-office bells—even breaking the opening week record for the Warner Hollywood Theater.

Still, there were strange quakes in the Hollywood Hills, brought on by front office trembles. Cocktail parties were given over to guessing what kind of pictures people wanted. My own idea was that a public that had been geared up to a war for four years would not suddenly go back to parlor, bedroom, and bath. Granted they didn't want World War II pictures—they still wanted adventure and excitement. I was a "cavalry-Indian" buff. I thought then, and think now, that the brief post-Civil War era when our blue-clad cavalry stayed on a wartime footing against the plains and desert Indians was a phase of Americana rivaling the Kipling era for color and romance. Evidently someone else thought so too: Hollywood started making cavalry-Indian pictures, and John Wayne, saber in hand, rode right into the number one box-office spot. Ray Milland took sword in hand; so did Gregory Peck. Everyone rode into the sunset behind fluttering cavalry guidons. Warner's told me I was going to ride to England to play the comic "Yank" in *The Hasty Heart,* another smash Broadway hit by John Patrick.

The story takes place in a hospital compound in Burma, so we shot it in a London studio. The reason can be summed up in a phrase that was becoming a household word in Hollywood: "Frozen Funds." War-torn Europe, and particularly England, was trying to turn the money tide from out to in, and sometimes it seemed the picture business would do it singlehanded. Country after country placed limits on the number of American pictures they would play; then special taxes—some as high as 75 per cent —were slapped on only our pictures, and finally they froze what revenue remained and told us we couldn't take it out of their countries.

Warner's were going to thaw some of their frozen revenue in a co-production deal with Associated British Pictures. I was less than happy: first of all, this kick in Hollywood's collective teeth seemed like a poor reward for bond drives, charity benefits, and a long history of tax discrimination, censorship, and general second-class citizenship. I was also mad because of my own career situation. I still wanted that outdoor epic, and my complaint was that if I couldn't ride a horse on screen, I could ride my own off screen, but not if I went to England. Departure time was drawing near and I was sulking. The studio knew it couldn't shanghai me and drop me in England if my sulk persisted, so I was told in the friendliest way that the studio was looking for an outdoor property for me. Maybe they hadn't anticipated how helpful I was prepared to be. I had a story in mind, *Ghost Mountain* by Alan Le May. Twenty-four hours later, Steve Trilling called and said, "We've bought it," and I replied, "Send me the boat tickets."

A long time back a small voice had whispered in my ear that all my flying time had been used up, so England would get me by rail and ship. Even without this hunch it was right that I should make my first trip abroad by ship—what kind of experience would it be to see the Atlantic from thirty thousand feet, when I'd never been farther offshore than Catalina Island?

To me the entire trip was a grand adventure to be savored, swallowed, and digested. There was a dock strike in New York so at the last minute I was switched from the Super Chief (that's a train) in Chicago, to the Canadian National for the long journey to Halifax, Nova Scotia, where I was to board the S. S. *Britannica*. This was my first visit to our northern neighbor and it included a stopover in Montreal for a reception arranged by the local

206

theater owners. Then for a couple of days I pressed my nose against the window, drinking in the endless miles of birch forest. My arrival in Halifax was a little startling, with quite a crowd plus press and radio on hand. I'd like to think I was that important, but in truth I was the beneficiary of some built-up excitement. In addition to doing *Hasty Heart,* the studio had shipped me early to participate in London's Royal Command performance. A number of Hollywood stars had preceded me to Halifax and departed for England in the week before my arrival. The city was enjoying playing host to these familiar faces they were seeing for the first time in the flesh.

My schedule called for an overnight stay and sailing time midnight the following day. After the police-escorted struggle through the depot crowd, with all the heart-warming scramble for autographs, I was told the "following day" happened to be Harbor Day, a pretty important civic affair. My informant was the manager of the "Famous Players" theater in that area, and one of the most unforgettable persons I've ever met, Bob Roddick. A Scotsman with that undefinable brogue that is pure Nova Scotian, he gently sounded me out on joining Harbor Day as a sort of honored guest. Nothing could have suited me better: I saw the city, toured the harbor in the police boat, bought a whale's tooth at the world-famous waterfront store where you can rummage through tons of fascinating merchandise and come up with anything from a pirate's treasure map to a thousand pounds of anchor chain.

A cold drizzle fell all day, but the natives took it in stride so I could do no less. As darkness fell we said good-by to the Mayor and all the other dignitaries and drove to Bob's home, where his wife Miriam was already at work on dinner for the three of us. He and I shucked out of our wet coats and shoes, and sat, glass in hand, before the fire.

Bob was a storyteller of great ability and with a wide range. I was shown wood and cement from the mysterious shaft where three generations have sought treasure on Oak Island. He later shaped the wood into a chest with a chunk of the cement as an

207

insert, and sent it to me with a history of the mystery of Oak Island. In addition to everything else, he was an accomplished woodworker and builder of fine furniture. By far, however, his greatest hobby was people. His wife said he "savored people like a suspicious husband tasting a new pot of soup."

Much later, on a drab, dreary day in London, I received a letter from him that began, "Well, here we go again, and if you think I'm writing to you as a film fan, then to hell with you once more. Something I've never done twice over is to write to a person without being asked, and why I do it now I can't say, except that somehow I feel you're a lonely soul who has his dark hours, and if such is the case then take the lift that is found in friendship."

His aim was better than he knew. All of us, I suppose, have a lonely inner world of our own, but I didn't want to admit to mine. Don't read something into this that isn't there: I had no desire to backtrack and that was not whistling in the dark. My loneliness was not from being unloved, but rather from not loving. Looking back, because at the time I wouldn't admit it to myself, I wanted to care for someone—yet I was building a sizable resistance to doing that very thing. Today I get homesick if I'm away from the family two hours, but there is a warmth even to missing them. Real loneliness is not missing anyone at all.

In this day of hors d'oeuvres on one continent and dinner on another, it perhaps sounds silly to talk of a trip to Europe as adventure, but in every way it was a first for me, including the moment I crossed the Canadian border, and I intended tasting it like a gourmet feast. Midnight found me hanging over the rail, fascinated by the fact that a strong gale had the *Britannica* pinned broadside to the dock, making her departure impossible until about 2 A.M. when the wind shifted.

The North Atlantic even staged one of its worst storms in years as a highlight of the trip. We docked in Liverpool and took the boat train to London, where again something of a first awaited us—the worst fog in a hundred years. It's actually true that buses trying to run in the heart of the city creep along in such a fog

208

behind a man on foot carrying a flaming torch. Somehow, though, our Sherlock Holmes movies had never prepared me for the smell. I expected the fog to be damp, breathable mist—to discover it was almost combustible, so thick was it with soft-coal smoke, was a shock to my smog-sensitive sinuses. It lingered for almost a week until a kind of claustrophobia threatened to drive everyone stir-crazy.

This was England's time of austerity under the Labor-Socialist government. No billboards, window displays, or marquees were permitted lighting. The only outdoor illumination came from dim and inadequate street lamps. A city can be a pretty dreary place under those circumstances, and the additional severe limitation on food didn't help. My first dinner at the Savoy Hotel found me braced to give the menu a rundown to see what I'd be up against for the next several months. With pleasant surprise my eye stopped on pheasant. Now life couldn't be too fraught with hardship if a fellow could get pheasant under glass. At least that was my thought until the pheasant arrived. It seems that merry old England cherishes some of the traditions of the gourmets of antiquity in serving game. The bird was served, complete with feathered ruff and head and yellow legs. I looked at it and it looked back at me. Somehow it seemed that if I so much as touched it with a fork, it would cry out in pain.

A few days later, Mike O'Shea and his wife, Virginia Mayo, arrived for the Command Performance. We had dinner together that first night, and I saw Mike's face light up when he spotted pheasant on the menu. I waited eagerly, anticipating his reaction when dinner arrived. But Mike was equal to the occasion: he and the pheasant looked at each other; then Mike called the waiter back and said, "Bring me some liniment and I'll have this bird flying again in fifteen minutes."

After the Command Performance, many of us did repeats in Cardiff, Wales, for their actors' charity, and in Dublin. Nothing could down the "Joe Tourist" in me, even running out of shillings one cold night in Cardiff. The heat in the hotel rooms was provided by gas heaters, like slot machines, that required a shilling every couple of hours. I ran out about 2 A.M. and finished the night wrapped in my overcoat.

Seeing a country as a guest of the government does have its advantages, such as an audience with Eamon de Valera, dinner with Ireland's President, and a visit to the world-famed Abbey Theatre. But even the quiet moments between scheduled events offered something: the Irishman who took me down the street from the Gresham Hotel to show me the bullet marks on the store fronts, souvenirs of the bloody Black and Tan strife in 1920. That night I followed the sound of music to the entrance of a ballroom and peered in at a University of Dublin dance. Every man was dressed in white tie and tails—every girl in a full-skirted white gown. I watched them do a graceful whirling waltz that looked like something we'd stage for a big musical, and I wished that my own country could slow down just a little to have time for such graciousness.

The Hasty Heart took almost four months to make, and, as one Englishman warned me, "You won't mind our winter outdoors—it's indoors that's really miserable." I discovered what he meant on that Elstree sound stage. Our wardrobe for the entire picture was either pajamas or shorts, and we froze most of the time on those long working days. English picture-making is a strange combination of tremendously talented, creative people and incredible inefficiency that makes everything take longer than it should. Our set was a marvel of design and perspective, our cameraman without a peer, the cast truly professional to the smallest bit part, but we could spend half a day getting a simple dolly shot because no one could eliminate a floor squeak on the most important line in the scene.

Pat Neal was again the girl and we became fast friends. The difficult role of the Scotsman was played superbly by Richard Todd, an ex-paratrooper who started the picture as a young unknown, earning about eighty-five dollars a week, and emerged from the preview an established star and deservedly so.

We were on a five-day week so there were Saturdays and Sundays to prowl and explore. Sometimes I stayed in London and sniffed my way in and out of little shops on Drury Lane, where for a few shillings you could buy old playbills advertising stars and plays of a hundred years ago. I got so steeped in atmosphere I almost expected to run into Nell Gwynne slipping in or out of the royal carriage.

By far my favorite weekends were the ones I spent touring the countryside in the luxury of a chauffeur-driven Rolls-Royce. As my homesickness grew, so did my resentment against the studio for cooking up the idea of an English picture. I hired the car and driver, putting the tab on the hotel bill, which I justified on the grounds that if I were home I'd have my own car to drive and besides, if Warner's wanted to unfreeze their refrigerated money, I'd help unfreeze a little extra. You are right: it was wrong and I'm ashamed of myself—but then, I'm not hungry and cold and six thousand miles from home now.

We finished shooting with about eight days before we were due to sail on the *Queen Mary*. I was obsessed with the idea of sunshine and warmth. One of Warner's representatives in London, an American married to an English girl, caught my fever and agreed that the three of us should take their car across to France, and we'd drive to the Riviera. With the car and luggage all loaded on the Channel ferry, his wife discovered we should have brought the hall table—that's where she'd left her passport. With the gangplank already being lifted she made a dash for the dock, calling that she'd have it (her passport) sent down to Southampton by the next train and meet us in France later that day. On the boat ride I discovered to my horror that my companions were as green about European travel (outside of England) as I was, in addition to which any chance we had of licking the language problem depended on what I could remember from two years' high school French.

Our first challenge found us red-faced and wordless. We had drawn a woman customs inspector, and the first suitcase she opened belonged to our missing partner, Margaret, still back on the English beach. There couldn't have been a more feminine bit of luggage, and only a Frenchwoman could have played the scene as our customs inspector played it. Gently, with just a touch of exaggeration, she lifted the delicate unmentionables and dropped them one by one back into the bag. Then, almost with a flourish, she dropped the lid, looked up at us, and murmured, "*Très jolie.*"

Our short trip was a huge success, even to winning wads and wads of paper francs at Monte Carlo, which turned out to be about sixty-five dollars when translated into real money. On the ride south our heads were on swivels, turning from burned-out tanks that still could be seen in peaceful grain fields, to temporary graves along the road, clusters of white crosses, each hung with a helmet. Then, on a more cheerful note, we drove through the wine country and got a tourist's kick out of gateposts bearing famous names we'd seen only on bottles.

In spite of the homesickness, the hunger, and the annoyance at Socialist bumbling, my farewell to London held its measure of regret. After all, there was Lord Napier looking proudly out from his pedestal in Trafalgar Square. Our old family Bible carried a handwritten account of his daughter disowned for marrying beneath her station, and the migration of the subsequent family to the new world where eventually Nelle would be produced. There were friendships made and cherished to this day with these wonderfully cheerful, warmly humorous people. Someday I want to see the old lady, London, now that she is bedecked with lights.

The trip home on the *Queen Mary* was a pleasant reversal of my more adventurous voyage on the *Britannica*. Back in New York, I discovered things in the picture business were normal, which means all messed up. *Variety* carried a story the day we docked that Warner's had slated *Ghost Mountain* for early production—with Errol Flynn in the starring role. Without waiting for my adrenalin flow to return to normal, I fired off a wire to the studio, quoting the story and declaring I, of course, didn't believe it. The truth was I did believe it—in fact, would have made book on it using borrowed money. The second booster that really put me into orbit was learning that the studio justified its action on the poor box office of—you've guessed it—*That Hagen Girl.*

I was too far out to listen to my agent, Lew—we weren't even on the same wave length. I dared the studio to put me in a picture, any picture—the implication being that I'd pull all the tricks that had ever been invented in past studio feuds to induce ulcers at the executive level. It has often occurred to me since that all of us have a behavior pattern shaped and molded by a lifetime of actions and reactions. If the studio had taken my dare, I'd have probably dreamed up all sorts of fiendish delaying tactics, but would have reported for work every day on time and with lines learned. The picture would have finished on time and I'd have the ulcer, because it would have been impossible for me to pull my fiendish tricks in the face of director, crew, and supporting cast who had nothing to do with my quarrel.

But that is hindsight: Lew had foresight and a more practical approach. My contract had three years to go. Lew rewrote it to read one picture a year for three years, at a salary for that one picture equal to half my yearly income, and full rights to do outside pictures. In other words, I was at last a free lance. My face was saved and the studio wasn't hurt because every studio in town was really trying to unload contracts as the result of the anti-trust decision. One week later Lew added a five-year, five-picture deal at Universal, and I bellied up to the bar like a conquering hero ordering drinks for the house. You could hardly see my wounded ego under all those $75,000 plasters.

Universal wasted no time: they came up with an exciting crime thriller teaming Ida Lupino and myself. Shooting was to start on a Wednesday early in June. On the Sunday night preceding the starting date, I participated in an old Hollywood tribal custom, a baseball game between comedians and leading men, to benefit the City of Hope Hospital. Before the end of the first

213

inning I was lying just off first base with a comminuted multiple fracture of my right thigh—translated, that means my thigh bone was shattered and we could see six separate pieces in the X-ray.

Little did I know I was headed for two months of traction, more months of cast, then a steel and leather brace, crutches, canes, and almost a year of therapy, before my leg would function and my knee recover about 85 per cent of its normal bend. My problems were too immediate for long-range planning. My leg was sheathed in layers of tape and moleskin with straps from these mummy wrappings hitched to a thirty-five-pound weight by way of a pulley. Twenty-four hours later my eyes were swollen shut, my teeth hurt at even the touch of my tongue, and I itched and peeled all over: I was allergic to the wrappings. For a week or so the massive histamine doses kept me only semi-conscious; then I settled down to weeks of discomfort because there was no removing the bandages.

The doctor hadn't warned me about a muscle spasm that can occur when movement takes place during the early days of a broken bone. The first time I attempted contact with the hardware the hospital offered as alternative to the bathroom, such a spasm occurred and I thought my leg was breaking all over again. To me the solution was simple: I just wouldn't move any more. Talk about mind over matter—I remained motionless for five days.

It's a funny thing about a long hospital stay: I'll never be quite so sorry again for the long-time patient as I once was. You get hospitalitis, settling into the routine, absolutely free of any responsibility with your whole world narrowed down to you and one room. Finally, blasted out of my warm cocoon and balanced between a fancy pair of aluminum crutches, I was back in the outside world. There was a period of having to guard against going over backward. Because of the traction, my bed had been propped up twelve inches higher at the foot, and so adaptable is the human animal that I adjusted until the bed seemed to me perfectly level. The result was that, on my feet, I kept on straightening up until I'd go over backward. Discarding the crutches was

214

a joy, as was dropping the first cane, but I must confess giving up the second cane was with regret. Maybe our fathers' generation had something in their fashion of carrying a walking stick, and we'd do well to revive the custom.

The late Jerry Wald saw that my first picture was number one of the three I owed Warner's. He called and said he didn't mind if I limped, or even used the cane, since I was playing a small-town lawyer in a picture called *Storm Warning* that teed off on the Ku Klux Klan. The girls were Doris Day and Ginger Rogers.

Some of our first scenes were shot at night in a small California town that is rumored to be the center of Klan activity here on the coast. The studio was understandably nervous and halfway expected some kind of incident. About three o'clock one morning, shooting a street scene, I thought maybe the studio was justified in its concern. A little character sidled up to me and whispered out of the corner of his mouth, "I hear this movie is about the Klan." I allowed as how it was—getting ready to yell, "Hey, Rube" —when his next line stopped me cold. He said, "Well, I'm in the local outfit and if you need to rent some robes, let me know."

My deal at Universal finally got under way, thanks to a wonderful guy and a great producer, Bob Arthur. Bob had a picture called *Louisa* that offered about as fast company as a performer could find: Spring Byington was Louisa, courted by Charles Coburn, and Teddy Gwenn. Ruth Hussey played my wife and we had a daughter from the studio contract ranks, Piper Laurie. This couldn't help but be a funny and successful picture.

My picture career was under way again, but at the risk of your saying, "This is where I came in," it had to share time with another Guild crisis and something new in my private life. First let me chronicle the pictures, because both the other subjects take some telling.

Louisa was good and a healthy plus to any list of screen credits, but I still wanted a crack at that outdoor stuff. Added to my frustration was the certain knowledge that the cavalry-Indian cycle was wearing thin, due to overexposure. Out of the blue came two fellows from over Paramount way, Bill Pine and Bill Thomas, with a story called *The Last Outpost*. It wasn't an epic, even though it was based to a certain extent on history: the little-known efforts of the Confederacy in the Southwestern desert seeking to intercept gold shipments to the Union. But it was in color, it was loaded with action, and I played a Confederate cavalry captain. The two "Bills" thought of everything, including shipping Tarbaby to Tucson, Arizona, to be my mount in the picture. That was no small part of my pleasure. That first morning some of the local cowboys, outfitted as soldiers, had a few derogatory remarks to make about Tarbaby and what she'd be like after a workout in that hundred-degree desert heat. Those boys just didn't know that a thoroughbred can do anything better than any other horse except quit. By sundown there were picture horses scattered all over the cactus patch, so beat we had trouble mustering enough for background in the close shots. But old Baby was not only picture-acting—she was kicking those beat critters out of the way. 'Twas a proud moment for her owner.

Warner's followed up with a musical remake of *The Male Animal* which they retitled *Working Her Way Through College*. Virginia Mayo, Gene Nelson, Pat Wymore, Don De Fore, Phyllis Thaxter, and I did this retread in Technicolor and discovered that when you have a solid story line, as we had from the original play, you just have to be successful. You know a picture is a success when the studio rushes into production with a sequel. I skipped the sequel which, of course, lacked the magic ingredient—that good story.

I'm afraid J. L. and I had kept a feud going since our '49 parting, so that when the studio and I disagreed on wardrobe for my role as the professor, I was something less than cooperative —I was downright rebellious. Things reached a peak about midnight one night when I received a telegram citing my contract and the studio's legal rights with reference to wardrobe. My first reaction was another explosion but, as the sleepless night wore on, something else began pecking away at the back of my head.

It didn't let up during the day's shooting, so when I was walking across the dark studio to my car that evening, I suddenly stepped into a phone booth and called Jack Warner in his office. When he heard my voice he was understandably wary and ready to duck a verbal swing, but I was all through swinging. "Jack," I said, "when I got your wire last night I felt pretty foolish. We've been together thirteen years and something is awfully wrong if we have to start sending telegrams to each other. I've done a lot of things for which I'm sorry, and I want you to know there won't be any more." I'm happy to say Jack matched me regret for regret, apology for apology, and somewhere under a studio phone booth there is a deeply buried hatchet. I left the phone easily a hundred pounds lighter: hate and resentment get to be a heavy load.

Universal, where I was supposed to realize my action ambitions, came up with another comedy. Diana Lynn, Walter Slezak, and I fought a losing battle against a scene-stealer with a built-in edge—he was a chimpanzee and he even had us rooting for him. The picture was called *Bedtime for Bonzo,* and he was Bonzo. Like all really good comedy, this one was based on a solid, believable foundation. Briefly, Bonzo was an experimental animal at the university where Walter and I were professors, and I embarked on an experiment of the kind actually conducted at Duke University.

The idea was to raise Bonzo in a home exactly like a child, and see to what level environment could lift his ability to learn. On the set he learned our business so well that going to work was a fascinating experience. Naturally his trainer was on the set, and the normal procedure called for the director, Fred de Cordova, to tell the trainer what we wanted from Bonzo. But time after time Freddie, like the rest of us, was so captivated that he'd forget and start to direct Bonzo as he did the human cast members. He'd say, "No, Bonzo, in this scene you should . . ." Then he'd hit his head and cry, "What the hell am I doing?"

My next scene-stealer was human and a master of the art with-

217

out even trying. *The Last Outpost* was the biggest money-maker Pine and Thomas ever produced, so they wanted to go again with a picture called *Hong Kong*, again teaming Rhonda Fleming and myself. It was action and a kind of unshaven part for me, besides which I was grateful to them for letting me do a sword and saddle role. The scene-stealer was a four-year-old Chinese tot, Danny Chang, who played the role of a four-year-old Chinese tot, lost and alone among refugees fleeing the Chinese Reds.

Working for the two Bills meant keeping to a schedule that didn't allow much time for socializing between setups. Under the pressure, Lew Foster, the director, sometimes grew a little harried since he was ordained by his position to be the man with the whip. Danny, of course, had to approach his role as some sort of game, being too young to understand what acting meant. I stood in admiring awe of his method for resisting pressure. When Lew's patience wore a little thin and a sharpness crept into his normally pleasant voice, Danny would quietly whisper, "I want a drink of water." Then, with inscrutable Oriental calm, he would sip that water, taking twenty minutes to a glass. It was like Russian roulette, watching that expressionless little face for a hint as to whether he'd ask for a second glass.

One day, when things were particularly rough and he was full of water, he came up with a new one: he sat down in the scene, quietly closed his eyes, and no one could persuade him to open them. He had just disappeared into some quiet mental Chinese garden. A. C. Lyles, who was handling publicity on the picture, saved the day with a pretty good ad-lib crack at child psychology. "If Danny doesn't want to do it," he said loudly, "let's go ahead and play the scene with his stand-in." Two eyes opened in a long, direct look at A. C.—then Danny quietly took his place in the scene, ready to work.

There were more pictures to come, but—meanwhile, back at the Guild . . .

CHAPTER

14

Actors wear a lot of different hats in the offstage world of organized labor. Actually the various performers' unions do make pretty good sense, even if the actors themselves don't always see it. "Equity" is the union of actors who perform in the legitimate theater and, incidentally, is the one from whence sprang all the others.

Vaudeville—with its host of variety performers appearing in a variety of places—is an entirely different world. So is radio; so is picture-making, or the concert stage. Only the performers in each field know the questions that must be answered if they are to receive a fair day's pay for a fair day's work.

Still, because so many of us cut across lines—picture people doing a play, stage actors a vaudeville tour, all of us guesting on the airwaves—the dream of one union card lingers on. An actor's first reaction upon moving into another field for a temporary engagement is to protest having to take out a "card" in the union administering that field.

Actually it isn't as ridiculous as it appears at first glance. First of all, we do have a parent organization supported by per capita dues of all the performers' unions. Usually referred to as the Four A's, it is "The Associated Actors and Artistes of America." Like the AFL-CIO of which it is a part, it is a somewhat powerless federation offering us a forum and method of cooperation but with no binding authority. Still, through this federation, we have worked out a system of interchangeability whereby performers have membership in one union covering their principal work and the right to join all the others without initiation fee and at a certain discount in dues.

All of this we learned the hard way. Contrary to what some diehards of the one-card school say or think, the SAG took more action than any of the Four A's members in exploring the feasibility of one big union. Back over the years the Guild at various times hired economists, labor experts, UCLA professors, and others to research and come up with a workable plan for single membership in one big entertainment union. In every case the findings were negative.

These experts noted something we should have been able to see for ourselves. The membership of Equity is predominantly in New York, and therefore can meet and settle things in a kind of town hall atmosphere. SAG is predominantly Hollywood, except for a solid block of members in New York, so again the advantage of local control is evident. By contrast, AGVA—the vaudeville union—has a membership constantly traveling and scattered, making for a union run by hired hands. Many times in years past the presidency of AGVA has been a sort of honorary title, a hollow crown. AGVA has a sorry history of upheaval and strife on occasion, brought on by exposure of corruption here and there among its hired hands.

Our last try (but one) at the one-union dream took place in 1948. We spent eighteen thousand dollars on experts who conscientiously gave us our money's worth by presenting half a dozen alternative plans for merging the seventeen entertainment unions. In each case, however, being honorable men, they pointed out that nothing would be gained that was in any way an improvement on the arrangement we already had. Our 1948 effort to exorcise the ghost of "one union" didn't exactly meet with universal acceptance, but then the United States Constitution wasn't an immediate hit either. In 1949 the stuff hit the fan. Television had been coming on but we were looking the other way. Only Walter Abel of our board, who was commuting pretty regularly between the coast and New York, tried to turn our gaze tubeward.

There were some independent film producers talking about filmed shows, although the major studios refused to consider this medium. Generally, TV was live and we didn't really think it was our baby.

All our sister unions had protected their interests: not so much by claiming jurisdiction as by stating they would not relinquish such a claim. We, on the other hand, had made no secret of the fact that we laid no claim to the new medium, but would help in any way we could to get the field organized and policed for the protection of all performers. We were a little puzzled by the insistence of our Eastern colleagues that we join them in their joint planning, but we laid it to excess enthusiasm born of being closer to the fire. We went along when they formed a group called the President's Committee of Television Authority, which shortly became known as TVA (no relation to the government power octopus of the same initials).

George Heller, the executive secretary of AFRA (the radio guild), was the moving force in TVA and he was urgent in his invitations to SAG to come back to New York and log some meeting time. Television sets were selling at the rate of 200,000 a month. More than forty cities had stations and the nightly audience was estimated at 9,000,000 by that fall of '49.

We finally decided to send Jack Dales and Ken Thompson back, partly out of curiosity and partly to prove we were sincere in our offer to be helpful. When they returned and reported at the first board meeting, the Cal Tech seismograph must have recorded the quake. Jack told us that in the New York meeting they had suddenly become conscious TV was being talked of as a single medium involving both film and live. He and Ken had politely interjected the Guild viewpoint that we did not feel we were justified in making any claims to jurisdiction in the new medium, but that we certainly would continue to represent actors making film, even if that film was eventually exhibited on television. This statement apparently was accepted by the assemblage,

221

which included a goodly number of performers. It was after adjournment that the gauntlet was flung. George Heller caught up with Jack and Ken. "I don't want you to get the wrong idea," he said bluntly. "No matter what they said in there—TV means both live and film, and SAG will have no jurisdiction over film made for TV." We exploded—but there was a kind of here-we-go-again flavor to the eruption.

Our contracts with five hundred film producers included and reserved the rights to TV use with our consent, no matter where it was exhibited or what technical devices—celluloid, acetate, tape, or anything else—might come into vogue. Our rights covered all commercial and industrial and advertising film—just as long as there were actors engaged in producing it. And, since about 80 per cent of all American film production was in Hollywood and nearly 90 per cent of the actors based themselves there, we of course used that as SAG headquarters.

We girded ourselves for battle, but so we could be completely secure in the knowledge our cause was just, we did a lot of soul-searching and were reassured in our belief that we had no basis for even pretending a claim to live TV. Among ourselves we came to the conclusion that logically AFRA (the radio union) should expand and take in TV, and the other guilds and unions would do well to follow our lead in forsaking any claims. After several years of expensive bickering, this is of course what happened, and AFRA became AFTRA—the American Federation of Television and Radio Artists.

We went into the battle confident as always because, as always, we had kicked the subject around until we knew our position was sound and honest. The series opener in what would become another round of endless battles was scheduled for New York. Everyone flew but me (the Kiwi), and what a train ride that was. I was still on crutches and wearing a steel brace, so once that train started moving there was no going to the diner or club car. It was a long sit—but maybe I needed conditioning for the meetings that followed. My crutches were aluminum and became a kind

222

of identification for one of the characters who was representing AGVA. He waged a hate campaign against everything the Guild suggested and, while he had no difficulty referring to the other members of our delegation by name, he always referred to me (in front of me) as the "guy on the silver sticks." I had a lot of names for him, but only aired them in our own caucuses.

Gradually we became aware of a familiar sound to the dialogue. After our experience with the CSU strike, we had a sensitivity to a kind of jargon delivered in an emotional holier-than-thou tone. A prominent radio announcer couldn't argue TV without some way-out reference like (and this was actually one), "If the House of Morgan should decide again that we must go through a blood bath of the kind they forced us into in 1917, and again in 1941 . . ." Seems a far cry from "I Love Lucy" and "Kukla, Fran and Ollie," but some of those jokers could drag it in.

Let me make one thing plain: I am not suggesting the TVA movement was a Communist plot, but just that a controversy of this kind was catnip to a kitten where the little Red brothers were concerned. They had to latch on and do what they could to cause trouble—particularly for SAG and also because "one big union" is right down their alley. The party line will always back anything that simplifies and centralizes. It's easier to subvert one organization where policy decisions are far removed from the rank and file than it is to take over a dozen groups. Further evidence that we weren't dreaming this up was the way our own little cell in the Guild had reacted to the jungle tom-toms. The same group that had pestered us in the CSU mess was back in uniform, ready to lead an assault from the rear on the Guild board.

And, finally, Victor Riesel, the labor columnist who was blinded by acid for his forthrightness by some unknown criminals, came out with it in November, 1949.

"It was the SAG which drove the Capone mob out of town and chased the comrades [Communists] back to their swimming pools," he wrote. He went on to say how "significant was the support that the TVA got from the studios' leftists—who, apparently, concluded it will be easier to move in and capture one big juicy outfit than a string of smaller outfits."

He was more candid than we dared to be. None of the SAG negotiators ever identified the political affiliations of a few of the TVA people.

We began to run into the same unauthorized press releases and evidences of bad faith. Because George Heller and I found ourselves nose to nose most often in the debates, I got a fair share of space in the whisper and mimeograph news service. One whisper that really upset me was a charge of anti-Semitism because George was of the Hebrew faith. First of all—this was my first knowledge of his religion—it just would never occur to me to ask or even be concerned with anyone's religion. Second, this is a charge against which you are absolutely helpless. You can state your views, but how do you prove them to a hostile doubter?" If you list friends who are near and dear to you, it is twisted sneeringly into the old cliché, "Some of my best friends are . . . "

We even had trouble with our New York membership. Most of them were also members of Equity, AFRA, and the others, so they were getting a pretty good indoctrination when they wore those other hats. We met with our New York board and, after a few brief, uncomfortable moments, one of them—with a sort of "let's clear the air" attitude—said, "I think we'd all feel better about this meeting if our president, Mr. Reagan, would clear something up." I said I'd be happy to. Then to my astonishment he said, "We've been informed that you have an office and an executive position at Warner's as a reward for your services to the Producers Association during the recent labor difficulties." When I could finally speak, this one was easy to answer. Jack Warner and I had not yet healed our quarrel, and I could truthfully say I wasn't even very welcome out Burbank way.

After we had battled through a number of sessions with the president's committee, it was felt we should report to our New York membership. Here again the old familiar pattern emerged.

For more than two hours, I presided at a meeting of 289 members. For most of the two hours the Guild policy was assailed in language that was pure vitriol. Jack Dales was on the platform, and at one point I whispered to him that if the motion to support our policy was put to a vote, we'd be clobbered. Once in a while I recognized and gave the floor to a member who made a pitch for us—at least he or she tried to make a pitch, between interruptions in the guise of parliamentary procedure. Somehow our opponents always seemed to be well versed in *Robert's Rules of Order.* The chairman must always recognize a call for "point of order, point of information, or point of personal privilege." Any time a speaker from the floor started making headway on our side, there would be a cry of "point of order." I would silence (reluctantly) the speaker and ask the interrupter to state his point of order. Nine times out of ten it wasn't legitimate, but he was successful in halting the speaker's progress. One or two sentences later the whole business would be repeated with "point of information" or "personal privilege." It's an old trick and very effective. When the discouraged and discomfited speaker sits down, up go the frantic hands again.

In presiding, a chairman—in an effort to be fair—will usually recognize the hand raisers in a kind of pattern: first from one side, then the middle, the other side, the back, down front, etc. The Communists know this, and so they scatter their people out with orders to raise their hands every time the floor is relinquished. Thus, no matter where you point, the odds favor one of them getting the call.

I was familiar with this. Still, it took me a long time in that meeting to realize that what seemed a great majority was making no move to put the motion to a vote. When it finally did penetrate, I had little trouble indicating we should "call the question." Jack and I thought we had seen all the tricks of rigging a meeting, but never before or since has there been a better example of how a determined and well-organized minority can fool the people. The vote was 278 to 11—in our favor. Eleven disciplined opponents had used the same tactics that the Communists used and had dominated the discussion for two hours and had given the impression that they were expressing the majority viewpoint.

But that came later. In the meantime, we were meeting in hotel conference rooms, hour after hour, until I was convinced my life was a drab picture of cigarette butts and crumpled coffee containers. After a while the coffee becomes identifiable as liquid cardboard.

We kept asking why we couldn't meet with more of our fellow performers. We never got an answer. Once we hit them with actual reports they had printed in their union papers, and in information letters which purportedly were the stories of our meetings. We had all been in the meetings together: there was no way they could sit face to face with us and justify their position but they tried.

Once Bill Holden and I succeeded in getting some of our friends on the board of Equity to invite us to a board meeting so that we could give a true account of the Guild's position. We had just started when the door opened and the Equity executive secretary, Phil Loeb (a stanch number two man in TVA), walked in—leading George Heller and two or three others he had invited on his own. What was to have been a simple statement of the SAG position became a repetition of the debate that had been going on so endlessly—this time with the Equity board as an audience. Moreover, Bill and I were finally excused while the others remained to top things off with a final word.

The argument went on a long, long time. There were dozens of meetings in New York and in Hollywood, and back to New York. Merger, cooperation, partnership—all were discussed. The reef on which we always broke up was the fact that TVA insisted we surrender our jurisdiction over film. They said over and over again, "The new medium of television is indivisible." To us it seemed so obvious that something would be really cockeyed if an actor in Hollywood got a call from Universal or Paramount to work in a film, and had to ask "Where are you going to show this film?" The answer would determine whether he worked as a Guild member, or as a TVA member under different rules and pay scales, yet he would be doing the same work he'd always done, for the same employers, in the same studio. The plain truth was and is that television is not a new art medium at all: it is simply a new type of theater. If that theater shows movies, the movies are made in the same way as for a drive-in, a downtown palace, or a box in which you insert a nickel and squint through a peephole. Unfortunately only SAG and our loyal allies in the Screen Extras Guild could see this rather obvious fact. The others wanted an expensive, top-heavy, new union.

In a New York meeting on October 5, 1949, at the Hotel Astor, I presented our resolution. It said simply that there were two areas in TV, one on film and one live. Between them, I said, there was a "so-called gray area" of film spot commercial announcements and film inserts. I proposed that: (1) TVA be established by the International Board of the Four A's to have jurisdiction over live TV including simultaneous kinescopes of such shows; (2) that SAG and SEG have jurisdiction reaffirmed by the Four A's over filmed TV; and (3) the "gray area" be submitted to mediation.

It was the same proposal we had been making, the one we thought both fair and just to all parties. It had received nothing but the coldest reaction from the other groups. Imagine our astonishment, then, when Nelson Case, president of AFRA, called for the floor and stood up. Here is what he said, from the record:

"Mr. Reagan has only this advantage in that his is all written out and mine isn't but, thank God, there is some sign we are now within talking distance of each other. From my corner of the table, I am very grateful and I would like to see us now pursue this thought to some kind of logical conclusion." He went on—to a somewhat numbed audience: "I, for one, if we can reach an agreement which will protect all our interests in the live field and in the shadowland, am certainly willing to go to the New York local of AFRA, which is a large local, and say to them that I am

227

willing to trust SAG in the negotiation of film television." There began to be some pained noises from his confreres. Case raised his voice and continued: "I do not feel that the television actors will be exploited if their film antics are looked after by SAG." He wound up by saying, "I certainly applaud heartily the resolution of the SAG and I would like to see us move forward and get this into some kind of shape."

As Case sat down, there was the damnedest hubbub you ever heard. Up jumped Louis Simon, the Equity lawyer, and demanded a recess of indefinite length. It was granted. Simon and his friends almost literally dragged Case outside—and the recess lasted for three hours, from 9:35 P.M. to 12:35 A.M. My fellow SAG members and I spent a joyful time imagining what must be going on in their huddle—we shouldn't have been so happy. What was our super-amazement, when we gathered once more to discover that Paul Dullzell, the Four A's president, had given up the chair and Simon had assumed it. Case got slowly on his feet and asked for the floor. He did not look at us. His face was a solid beet-red.

"I think it is incumbent upon me," Case began, in a stammering tone, "to say some words of explanation to SAG. So far I am the only speaker on the resolution. I must explain first that certain remarks of mine, when I got to reading over the resolution on which I remarked, struck me as quite strange, even to me.

"This is difficult to explain except on the basis of a mental lapse, I cannot blame it on fatigue or on a Martini or anything. But I had been thinking of a resolution embodying much of the identical language in that resolution and somehow I mentally inserted that language.

"My enthusiastic endorsement, unfortunately—and *not* because of pressure by any fellow member—did diminish strongly. During the interim, we have been considering . . . " He hesitated, then muttered, "This is difficult to explain because, being a human being, one is embarrassed to say that one has had a brainstorm."

We were too stunned at this about-face to say anything. Nor did he say much for the rest of the night on the record. He had

228

been voluble before; now, perhaps he was embarrassed. But his TVA fellows kept pitching.

We went back to Hollywood and called a mass membership meeting to report as fully and frankly as we could the outcome of our struggles. Once again we looked down from our position in the ring at the Legion Fight Stadium to the more than fifteen hundred members gathered at ringside. Because of our multiple memberships we knew there would be opposition from some whose parent union was on the other side of the hassle, but we could still be surprised at some of the rôles they could play. There in the crowd were two or three members of the TVA committee we'd been battling. They had flown out from New York, put on their SAG hats, and now would participate in the discussion without one word to their unsuspecting fellow members about what they'd been doing in New York. I am still bothered by the fact that we didn't expose them and sometimes even now I wonder if this wasn't carrying fair play to a rather ridiculous limit.

TVA took the bit in its teeth. It signified that it had got the consent of the Four A's to go ahead. It announced in April, 1950, that it would put into immediate action its so-called authority over *all* television. The Four A's seemed really serious about vesting authority over all television in TVA—creating a new union to infringe upon the already established SAG and SEG jurisdiction over film in that medium.

When the smoke had cleared two years later, not one of the companies with whom TVA bargained had signed an agreement to use their members. They then had recourse to the National Labor Relations Board. The NLRB elections became more or less of a standing joke among SAG members as they turned out time and time again to cast their ballots. In desperation, at one point, three of our executives were sounded out for top jobs in any new organization "if they would help swing SAG."

The major negotiations—which SAG figured had cost them more than $250,000 out of pocket, to say nothing of the lost

229

salaries by non-working actors—were over but the informal sessions dragged on. It had got to the pared-down essentials that, as Riesel had pointed out, was on our part "a private war against concentrated power—to keep the union free of any outside rule."

On September 10, 1952, before the International Board of the Four A's, the whole miserable affair came to an end. The facts in a resolution presented before that board at that time by SAG speak for themselves.

We said that an "unfortunate and bitter dispute" had roiled the organization on the question of TV jurisdiction. We pointed out that on the unlucky day of April 19, 1950, more than two years before, the same board had given total television jurisdiction over all TV to TVA—and since that time that organization had not been able to get a single film television contract for its members. It had been successful in the live television field alone —and there only through the abstention of SAG from competing and from the actual help of SAG in organizing. We also declared that the separation of live and film TV had been certified by several NLRB elections—all of which were brought against SAG by TVA and all of which SAG won.

SAG asked the Four A's to rescind its April gift of authority to TVA. It demanded that another resolution be passed declaring that "jurisdiction is hereby confirmed in SAG over all actors (including singers, announcers, stuntmen, and airplane pilots) employed in the motion picture field, including, without limitation, all motion pictures produced for use over television."

It was passed without dissent. It was a victory even more complete than we had hoped, along the identical lines we had predicted. It stabilized the SAG position in the movie industry for once and all. We could not know it then, but TVA was doomed to wither on the vine itself and gradually be absorbed by AFRA which was to become AFTRA—and dominate the live television field which TVA had once so arrogantly claimed. TVA itself dissolved like smoke.

Through all the battle my personal interest in television was

230

nil. Certainly I never dreamed the next big chunk of me was to appear precisely in this medium—as one of the first established motion picture stars deliberately to choose it for my own field at a time when everyone of stature in Hollywood was delicately holding their noses about it.

CHAPTER

15)

I have been asked now and then if all the years of Guild activity hurt my career, and if I'd do it all over again, given a second chance. The answer doesn't come easy, but it is yes to both questions.

Did it hurt my career? In a lot of ways, a number of which were my own fault. Ours is a highly competitive business: there is no doubt I missed a lot of career opportunities because of my mental absorption with the Guild. Then there is the problem of type casting. Most people think of this as continuing to put an actor in a role he has successfully portrayed. There is more to it: ours is a small community and an actor can acquire an image as much from his off-scene role as from his work on screen. I think I became too identified with the serious side of Hollywood's off-screen life—there were too many people who saw me only as a committee member. I once remarked that if someone was casting a Western, I'd be the lawyer from the East. Last—there can be no doubt that a lot of Hollywood's front office people like to call on you when they need a hand with their pet cause or charity, but they'd just as soon have you working for someone else.

Would I do it again? Yes—this has been the best of all possible lives for me and I think you have to do something to pay your way in life. The pattern for me had already been established by some pretty unselfish guys who set up the Guild in the first place.

Most important of all, however, is a dividend that makes all the long hours of meetings, the fighting and strife, the lost career opportunities, the biggest bargain of my life. It was because of the Guild and, more precisely, because I was president, that I found myself standing before an apartment door in Westwood one pleasant fall evening. When that door opened, I found all the rest of me I needed to find to give me more happiness than any one person could possibly deserve.

There was a lighter side to life and I was giving it some attention, according to the call I received from my business manager. In a somewhat worried voice he informed me my nightclub bills were running $750 a month. Unfortunately, they were purely personal and thus not deductible for computing income tax. As he figured it, that meant I had to earn about eight dollars for every dollar I was spending. My only weak defense was to tell him that at least part of that money paid for my own dinners and, after all, while a fellow may not live by bread alone, you couldn't do what I was doing on Wheaties.

Looking back, I know I thought my routine was normal, and probably a permanent way of life. I had a comfortable apartment from which, on a clear day, I could see the Mocambo; I was within walking distance of the Friars Club where, now and then, I could enjoy a change of pace by dining with the habitués of that theatrical club, when they happened to be between gin games; my phone was unlisted, but a collection of numbers weren't. Obviously this pattern of living was acceptable if you didn't look more than forty-eight hours ahead.

One day I received a phone call from Mervyn Le Roy, the director. As soon as I got over my disappointment that he wasn't paging me for one of the many fine pictures he did so well, I gathered that he was calling in behalf of a young lady under contract to MGM, who was working in his picture. (It should happen to me.) It seems that this young hopeful, Nancy Davis by name, was very much distressed because her name kept showing up on rosters of Communist front organizations, affixed to petitions of the same coloration, and her mail frequently included notices of meetings she had no desire to attend, and accounts of these meetings as covered by the *Daily Worker*.

Mervyn wanted me to call the young lady and have a talk with her about this problem. He guaranteed that she was more than disinterested in Leftist causes: she was violently opposed to such shenanigans. I told Mervyn that I'd take care of it—having made the switch from Ronald Reagan, actor, regretfully to Ronald Reagan, SAG president.

Stopping in at the Guild office, I reported the call to Jack Dales. We did a little quick checking and could discover nothing detrimental to her. We were satisfied that Nancy Davis was in the clear, and we were in a position to defend her in the event of any unpleasantness. I called Mervyn and told him what we had learned and to assure the young lady she had nothing to worry about. I have since learned the extent to which the young lady can worry.

Being helpful with Mervyn is something of a hobby. He is happiest when he can help someone else. Whether it is steering you to a shirt tailor he's discovered, or getting you a table at a new café, Mervyn just loves taking telephone in hand and being helpful—so I shouldn't have been surprised when my call was followed by a return call. It seems the young lady was not satisfied with the secondhand report: please, wouldn't I call her and take her to lunch or dinner, and quiet her fears? I don't know why it took all of this to get me to call an unknown girl. She surely couldn't be repulsive and on the contract list at MGM. Mervyn finally made his point and I called.

I introduced myself on the phone, hastily explained that I had a very early call in the morning so, if she didn't mind a short dinner date, I'd be very happy to talk to her about her problem. She very pleasantly informed me that she too had an early call, and couldn't consider anything other than an early dinner date— so on that pleasant California evening there I was, propped up between two canes before that door in Westwood (this was back in my just-out-of-the-hospital days).

234

The door opened—not on the expected fan magazine version of a starlet, but on a small, slender young lady with dark hair and a wide-spaced pair of hazel eyes that looked right at you and made you look back.

Don't get ahead of me: bells didn't ring or skyrockets explode, although I think perhaps they did. It was just that I had buried the part of me where such things happened so deep, I couldn't hear them.

On the drive to La Rue's, where we were going to have that short dinner, we took up the business of her name and what to do about it showing up on those "bleeding hearts" lists. Since she was relatively new in the business, I made the obvious suggestion: "Why not ask the publicity department for a new one?" I, of course, figured they'd given her the one that caused the trouble in the first place.

Very simply she said, "But Nancy Davis is my name."

I've since come to know she has simple anwers like that for a lot of problems—the shortest distance from here to there is whatever is true. Without her amplifying the statement by a single word, I knew that whether there were three or thirty Nancy Davises, they could do any name-changing that was going to be !one. (Of course, changing her name was the eventual answer, but not in the way I suggested.)

Someplace between soup and salad I learned she had gone to Smith. If she learned arithmetic there, the board of trustees had better call an emergency meeting. When numbers start getting that comma punctuation, she has no names for the digits in between. She can make the national debt come out at three hundred thousand instead of three hundred billion—and what a lot of problems that would solve.

About the time I adjusted to the fact that her father (for whom she has a limitless admiration—which I have come to share) was one of the world's truly great surgeons, I discovered she had grown up calling people like Walter Huston "Uncle," and her godmother was Nazimova—all this by way of her mother, who appeared on Broadway as Edith Luckett.

It's amazing that I learned or remembered any of this, because I had discovered her laugh and spent most of my time trying to say something funny. A lot of George Burns and Georgie Jessel material got an airing that night, and not always with credit given to them. We hastily finished our early dinner—after all, we had those sunrise calls in the morning and, besides, she had never seen Sophie Tucker who was opening that night at Ciro's. I figured Sophie could help me make her laugh some more. She did: so much so that we decided to stay for the second show and then—since she had never before heard Sophie and because her mother had been a star on Broadway—Sophie came to the table and joined us for a late snack. We got home about 3:30 A.M., but it was all right because neither one of us really had an early call at all.

This story, I know, will be a disappointment to those who want romance neatly packaged. The truth is, I did everything wrong, dating her off and on, continuing to volunteer for every Guild trip to New York—in short, doing everything which could have lost her if Someone up there hadn't been looking after me. In spite of my determination to remain foot-loose, in spite of my belief that the pattern of my life was all set and would continue without change, nature was trying to tell me something very important.

In the months that followed it didn't even frighten me to discover our friends were taking us for granted, and automatically inviting us to dinner parties as a twosome. We went to the premiere of her picture, *The Next Voice You Hear,* and for the first time I found myself remembering that she was an actress, and at the same time discovered that she was a damn good one. Before we left the theater, remembering the first time I had ever seen myself, I told her she could go home and unpack—she'd be around for quite a while.

We had deserted the nightclubs to a great extent and many

236

of our dates were spent at the home of Bill and Ardis Holden. Someplace along here I know there should be a scene of sudden realization, the kind we'd write if we were putting this on film. It just didn't happen that way. To tell the truth, I'm glad— although I get scared thinking I could have lost her. Gradually I came out of a deep-freeze and discovered a wonderful world of warmth and deep contentment. My friends had been extremely patient, as I discovered one night at a meeting of the Motion Picture Industry Council. Bill and I, as Guild representatives, were seated at the huge round table in the Producers Association meeting room. For the first time I was strangely indifferent to all that was going on. Suddenly I picked up one of the scratch pads always available, and wrote a note to Bill: "To hell with this, how would you like to be best man when I marry Nancy?"

Right out loud he blurted, "It's about time," and that ended the meeting for us. To everyone's surprise we got up without a word and walked out, not caring that the producers would probably have a sleepless night, thinking that some new Guild crisis was about to hit the picture business.

Nancy's career wasn't flourishing—probably because her studio, MGM, wasn't exactly "busting out all over" with pictures that set the world on fire. Dore Schary was in charge at the big Culver City colossus and he seemed determined to type-cast Nancy in a series of "kitchen cabinet" epics in which she always ended up padded to indicate an expectant condition. He seemed resolved to midwife a cinematic population explosion, even if the offspring always ended up back on a shelf in women's wardrobe under P for pregnancy pad.

Of course, she managed to break out of the maternity ward a few times. She more than held her own with Fredric March in an episode of *It's a Big Country,* and you aren't exactly playing in a little theater movement when you swap lines with Mr. March. Probably the biggest disappointment was one of failure to properly exploit and sell a tremendous and sensitive job of film-making in which she appeared with Ray Milland and the late John

Hodiak. *Night into Morning* was one of those pictures that is Hollywood when it is grown up and good. Somewhere the selling job just didn't get done so not enough people saw the movie, but all who did loved it.

In a situation remarkably similar to my own studio hassle, Nancy found herself in a cooling atmosphere and walked away from Metro with more dignity than I had managed under like circumstances. As Judy O'Grady and the Colonel's lady are sisters under the skin, so is there a brotherly pattern to most studios in their dealings with performers. Nancy did a personal favor for Dore and appeared in a turkey she could hear gobbling when the script was delivered to her door. She let me read it to see if her reaction was sound, fearing she might be prejudiced because once again her wardrobe would have to allow for the pregnancy pad. I told her the only way this picture could be saved was by an ingenious cutting job—like up the middle. The finished movie was as bad as we thought it would be and, of course, the studio self-righteously cooled off on everyone they'd coerced into making it.

About the time I passed the word to Bill Holden that I was about to do the most sensible thing I've ever done, a picture came my way that I not only loved but that did nothing to set me back where Nancy was concerned. Warner's paged me for the last one of my deal—the life story of baseball's immortal Grover Cleveland Alexander. Nancy is a baseball buff: she comes by it honestly. Her birthday is July 6 only because her mother put off having her until after the Fourth of July double-header—at least that's her mother's story.

We had about a dozen big leaguers employed for the baseball scenes and I had a betrothed who was fidgeting from one foot to the other, waiting to be invited to the set. The first day she visited I told her I'd decided against a diamond necklace or a full-length sable but was going to get her a baseball autographed by our ballplayer actors. The funny thing was she really would have chosen the baseball over those other things. Then, however, I goofed;

getting a new ball from props, I told her to sit and relax and I'd be back with it autographed. Fortunately I glanced back in time to see her looking as forlorn as a kid who has just discovered Uncle Henry in the Santa Claus suit. There was a moment of panic on my part when I thought maybe she'd decided on the diamonds (which were only conversation). All I had to do, however, to make her happy was toss her the ball—she wanted to get the autographs herself. I tagged along just to make sure the fellows would understand she was under contract and not up for waivers.

Making this picture was as happy a chore as I'd had since playing the "Gipper." For three weeks before shooting I spent about two hours a day with Cleveland's Bob Lemon and Detroit's Jerry Priddy, pitching and learning the difference between throwing from the mound and just throwing.

Doris Day played Aimee (Mrs. Alexander) and the real Aimee was on our set as advisor. From her we learned a great deal about the tragic secret so carefully kept from the public during all those years of her husband's greatness. There was no secret to Grover's problem with alcohol, but his real cross was epilepsy and in that earlier, unenlightened day he felt keenly the stigma which today we are learning was compounded of ignorance and superstition. I've always regretted that the studio insisted we not use the word, although we did try to get the idea across. The trouble was that a frank naming of his illness would have the ring of truth, whereas ducking it made some critics accuse us of inventing something to whitewash his alcoholism. One thing we didn't invent was the love story between Alex and Aimee. He once pitched (and won) both games of a double-header so he could get a day off to be with his bride.

Came our wedding day and not one protest from Nancy over the fact that I cheated her out of the ceremony every girl deserves. It is hard for me to look back and realize the extent to which I was ruled by my obsession about the press and the fuss that would accompany a regular wedding. I can only confess that at the time

239

to even contemplate facing reporters and flashbulbs made me break out in a cold sweat.

On a lovely spring evening we went out in the San Fernando Valley to the Little Brown Church. Bill and Ardis Holden were waiting, and with them as matron and best man we were married in a beautiful and simple ceremony. Thank heaven for Ardis, because my plans hadn't gotten beyond "I do." Ardis had arranged for a cake at their Toluca Lake home and a photographer, so we have wedding pictures.

Nancy had grown up with a family tradition of a spring vacation at Phoenix, Arizona. To this day she confesses to a nostalgia whenever she smells orange blossoms, and it held true even with her own wedding bouquet. At least this I did right. From the Holdens' we headed for Phoenix, stopping over at the old Mission Inn at Riverside.

Later in our honeymoon, Nancy's mother and father came out and, being the remarkable people they are, this was exactly as it should have been—in case you are inclined to question parents on a honeymoon. The quickest way I know to get a punch in the nose any place in Chicago is to make a derogatory remark about Edie Davis. What a politician was lost in her! The cop on the beat, the cab driver, all the people who know the heartbeat of a big city, know Edie. The reason, of course, is simple. Edie knows the cop on the beat, the cab driver, and especially does she know any and every soul in need of a helping hand.

Meeting her father, the doctor, wasn't the easiest moment I ever had. After all, here was a man internationally renowned in the world of surgery, a fearless stickler for principle, and a man who could no more choose the easy path of expediency than he could rob the poor box. My fear lasted about a minute and a half after we met—which was as long as it took to fiind out he was a true humanitarian. Not the sticky, bleeding-heart kind, but the kind who could impress on the medical students at Northwestern that theirs was a sacred responsibility to cherish the human lives that, as doctors, they would hold in their hands.

240

Back in the mundane world of picture-making, we moved into Nancy's apartment temporarily, although I kept mine because there wasn't room for all our clothes in an apartment that had been chosen for an aspiring young actress. Incidentally, her career and what would happen to it had entered my mind once or twice, and while I knew I'd be happier if the career ran second—way behind—I knew also I could never say "give it up." She was too good: her drama training at Smith had led to summer stock, road shows with the late Zasu Pitts, and Broadway in *Lute Song* with Mary Martin. I shouldn't have worried—she was her mother's daughter and it was ingrained in her to simply say, "If you try to make two careers work, one of them has to suffer." She was fair. She said, "Maybe some women can do it, but not me."

My own career was due for some rough sledding and, as usual, partly because I couldn't say no. The two Bills (Pine and Thomas) corralled me and talked me into doing one of those sand and banana epics called *Tropic Zone*. I knew the script was hopeless, but there was a little matter of a debt of gratitude because they had given me *The Last Outpost* when no one else would let me get outdoors.

With the picture out of the way we started house hunting, intending to find something more or less temporary until (hopefully) one day we could build. In the meantime, our two-apartment situation made for some peculiar scheduling. If we were having dinner with Goldie and Bob Arthur (which we often did) I'd read the evening paper while Nancy dressed—then we'd drive to my apartment and she'd read while I dressed, and we'd arrive a little late at Chasen's Restaurant.

Even though I'd done a picture for Bob, it was Nancy who really brought me into the warm circle of their friendship. Bless baseball, she'd met them at a World Series game in New York and it was a sort of instant liking.

The first time she took me over to their house, she didn't—and I learned another fascinating thing about my wife. We were going to drop over after dinner and she'd show me the way.

241

At 11 P.M. we still hadn't found them, but we had ended up three times by a reservoir high in the hills off Mulholland Drive. When I later told her father of the incident, he looked at me rather peculiarly and asked, "Didn't you get mad?" I was able to answer truthfully that I hadn't. Then he said, "I think there is something you should know about Nancy." He told me that, having lived all her life in Chicago, the only way you could give her directions in her home town was to explain where a place was in relation to Marshall Field's. That store is still the one place she can find with no help whatsoever. It gets pretty complicated sometimes trying to explain to her how she can get to Dodger Stadium in Los Angeles, when you have to start by explaining where it is in relation to Marshall Field's in Chicago.

Early in the fall I closed out the Universal deal with a picture that I can only excuse because it was a Western. The title was *Law and Order* with Dorothy Malone and Preston Foster, and having said that there is nothing more to be said. However, I really didn't have my mind on much of anything at the studio because we had found a house out in the Pacific Palisades and Nancy was decorating one room as a nursery. We didn't get the living room furnished for another year and a half.

According to medical science, we were in the careful period, but still so far from the launching date there was no reason we should miss the International Horse Show at the Pan Pacific Auditorium. We had box seats, front row center, and should have been completely comfortable, except that Nancy whispered the baby was evidently practicing some unusual maneuvers. About the third whisper a warning bell rang some place in my head and this was one bell I was hearing. I told her to squeeze my hand whenever she felt this unusual move and, without telling her what I was doing, I began clocking those hand squeezes. At the end of the show she was squeezing my hand every eighteen minutes and I said, "Don't look now, but you are having a baby." Well, of course, she didn't believe me and insisted we go home, which was in the opposite direction from the hospital. We even went

242

through the motions of going to bed—for about seven minutes—and then we were back in the car and on the way to the hospital.

These somewhat unusual circumstances didn't end with that double ride. We were ushered into a room bluntly but correctly named the labor room. When they found that the pains were coming every ninety seconds, all hell broke loose. The next thing I knew, someone hung me up on a broken spring couch in a dismal cell off the broom closet, followed one quick glimpse of Nancy being wheeled farther into the mystery of the maternity ward.

It was two in the afternoon when the door opened for me—Patti had joined us. I know she'll understand if I confess that at the moment her arrival didn't impress me much. The only word I wanted concerned her mother. A lot had been going on all night and morning, culminating finally in a Caesarean delivery. For one who couldn't await her scheduled arrival time, Patti had certainly made sure the occasion would be remembered.

At the risk of sounding like a proud papa—which, incidentally, is not a bad part to play—I grew about six inches when one of the nurses confessed that Patti was a kind of teacher's pet in the nursery. I used to sneak up to the corner of the window and peek, and sure enough—whoever was on duty would invariably be doing her chores onehanded, and carrying Patti around in the other arm. It didn't take me long to understand why—she moved in on me with a pair of big brown eyes that had her mother's disconcerting way of looking directly at me.

She was not quite three when she completely deboned me and wrapped me up as her own personal possession. Crawling into my lap and fixing me with those eyes, she asked me to marry her. Weakly I asked, "Why do you want to marry me?" and while her answer was no brilliant utterance to be immortalized in stone, it was a factual reply, highly satisfactory: "Because I love you!"

CHAPTER

16

Home from the hospital, we were to spend practically the rest of 1952 close to our own hearth. The doctor had ordered Nancy bedded for at least six weeks. On our second day home, a neighbor called, a six-year-old from next door. "Mr. Reagan," he said, "I hear you have a new baby here." I allowed as how that was so, and then he asked if he could "see Mrs. Reagan." I had to tell him, "She's in bed and won't be up for some time." "Well," he snorted indignantly, "with a brand-new baby in the house, she certainly picked a fine time to get sick."

My timing wasn't so good either. Certainly, with a brand-new baby in the house, it wasn't the time to find my career less than flourishing. *Tropic Zone* and *Law and Order* both gave me that I-don't-want-to-go-out-in-the-lobby feeling I remembered so well from those early B pictures, and more recently from *That Hagen Girl*.

The plain truth was that all my years under contract to a studio had given me built-in reactions that were of no help in the freelance field. Under contract you read a script, biased toward doing it—after all, you are on salary and supposed to do what the studio asks you to do. If it is really bad, you put up an argument, but if it's only so-so your mind automatically looks ahead to the next one, because there will be a next one. The simple fact of free lancing is that "next ones" only happen if you choose the

244

right one each time. If you show up in a turkey, no one wants to help you remove the pin feathers.

I had said yes to a couple of turkeys. Now I sat down and looked myself in the career. One of the first signs of Hollywood chill is not only who doesn't call—it's who does. Producers complete with shoestring have a great script you ought to read. A short time before they wouldn't have called you because you were out of their reach. Now, having them on the line gives you the same feeling a fellow lost in the desert must have when he looks up and sees the buzzards starting to gather.

Nancy and I talked it over and decided to gamble that my mistakes weren't irretrievable. In other words, I'd say no to everything until, hopefully, the right part in a right picture came along. Of course, this presented some economic problems. True, I'd been making handsome money ever since World War II, but that handsome money lost a lot of its beauty and substance going through the 91 per cent bracket of the income tax. The tragic fact of life in this evil day of progressive taxation is that, once behind, it is well-nigh impossible to earn your way out. Like most fellows in uniform, I had taken advantage of the right to defer income tax until after the war, so I returned to civilian life with a good income, a high tax rate, and a debt. Incidentally, the government forgave this tax debt after the First World War and many of us had a sneaking hope the same thing would happen the second time around—foolish us. The day for repayment came and so did a polite fellow in a gray suit. When I opened the front door, almost his very first words were, "Where is it?" My second bump was the broken leg and six months of idleness. Incidentally, broken bones are costlier in Hollywood, like ten thousand dollars' worth. Now we were buying the ranch and our home out of income with two first and one second mortgage.

All of this adds up to the fact that sitting it out was dependent upon finding an interim income. There were plenty of opportunities if I wanted to pull up stakes and try Broadway. Sometimes it seemed as if the only place an actor was unwanted was

245

in Hollywood. At least half the shows that went on to New York success were dangled in front of me, until I made a flat "no New York" statement. And, of course, television was busting out all over: everyone had a great idea for a series. Here, too, I was stubborn. We had seen the series idea used on the screen in years past and, even though moviegoers saw only a half-dozen episodes a year, no series lasted more than about three years. When it lost public favor, the actors playing in it suffered from their identification with the roles they played, and other producers were reluctant to use them.

Lew had become president of MCA and now had to be concerned with running the circus. A real nice V.P. and a good friend, Art Park, inherited me and my troubles. Poor Art had to find me a living in a truly sick industry that had virtually ground to a halt, except for a handful of current favorites still in demand for the spectaculars. Ruling out the stage and TV didn't leave him much room for prospecting. Let me make one thing plain—there was no disagreement about my decision to turn down the pictures that were available. These were pictures they didn't want good—they wanted them Thursday.

Like other studios, Universal was in a stew, so it wasn't too much of a surprise when their next idea was about three stages worse than *Law and Order*. Art and I went out to the studio and said a polite "No." Then in true Hollywood style I sat in an outer office while Art and the producer talked about me. In about half an hour Art came out and asked one question, "Do you feel so strongly opposed to this script that you are willing to cancel the studio's commitment?" Here was the moment of truth: a few weeks' work and I could pocket seventy-five thousand dollars and then start holding out. But I knew if I was going to cure my problem, the medicine had to be taken without delay. There went picture number four of my five at Universal. A few weeks later number five was gone the same way. It didn't pay any bills, but there was some satisfaction in seeing both of those turkeys

246

later on and being glad it wasn't me up on the screen in plain sight.

Now, however, a real blow fell. Somehow we had neglected to tell the business office I was going into retirement, so in their usual routine they estimated my income as unchanged and paid the tax collector a twenty-one-thousand-dollar advance on what they hoped I would earn. Uncle Sam is a real bird dog when it comes to tracking down any tax due and unpaid, but evidently it hasn't left much time for organizing a rebate department. It took us almost a year to get that twenty-one thousand dollars back, but I must say when it finally did arrive, Hitchcock couldn't have topped it for suspense: we were exactly eighteen thousand dollars in the hole.

Don't gather from all of this that Patti was hollow-cheeked from hunger. Actually I was amazed then and still am, looking back at what a salable commodity picture stardom is, even when pictures won't buy it. I had ruled out a TV series, but there were a number of TV shows using guest stars, just as there had always been radio guest programs before TV. Art and the MCA team were like the cavalry to the rescue with a well-ordered scattering of guest appearances here and in New York. Naturally I only did this to dabble a bit in the new field and "get my feet wet" (I said to the world at large), but "bring the money" (I said to the boys at MCA).

It is an unwritten rule of show business that you must never show "need"—you are always flush and only interested in working for the love of the game.

For fourteen months I turned down such scripts as came my way. We trimmed our sails and rode as far as each guest fee would take us until my nightmare loomed as the day when possibly I might, from sheer necessity, have to accept something even worse than what I'd been refusing. Strangely enough, when the trial ended, I discovered my earnings had totaled almost as much as in the more prosperous years: the problem had been in spacing and lack of assurance as to whether there would be any. A long

247

period of no income would suddenly and unexpectedly be relieved, but during that dry spell there was nothing to reassure me in my fear that the drought would continue.

At the lowest point of all, just prior to Christmas, a script came from MGM. I'll swear it came down the chimney to the sound of sleigh bells and tiny hoofs on the roof. While it wasn't going to be a multi-million-dollar epic, it was respectable and as timely in subject matter as it was in relationship to my problems. The word had just reached America of the death march and the brainwashing of our soldiers captured in the Korean War. My part was that of an officer deliberately dropped behind the lines to learn what was going on in the prison compounds. For technical advice I had an Army captain who had gone into one of those camps at 175 pounds and emerged two years later weighing a hefty 82.

The picture should have done better. Every torture scene and incident was based on an actual happening documented in official Army records. Unfortunately, production and release were both rushed, with the idea the picture should come out while the headlines were hot. Another thing against the picture (and here I run the risk of being howled down as a wild-eyed radical) was the reluctance of extreme liberals to enthuse about anything that upset their illusions about "agrarian reformers."

Anyway, it was a major studio release on a subject that still needs a lot of telling, and I certainly didn't have anything else to do.

With Broadway and a TV series on my "won't do" list, the MCA troubleshooters had come up with another source of loot, and the suggestion seemed so outlandish I didn't say "no"; I just ran for cover, yelling over my shoulder, "You must be kidding!" What they had in mind was Las Vegas and a whirl at doing a nightclub act. Moneywise the suggestion was a beauty. The offer for a two-week stand was almost equal to my total pay for *Prisoner of War.*

Reluctantly, because the idea scared the hell out of me, I made

248

a date for the next morning. One of our good friends is Carroll Righter, who has a syndicated column on astrology. Every morning Nancy and I turn to see what he has to say about people of our respective birth signs. On the morning of the meeting I looked, and almost suspected an MCA plot: my word for the day read, "This is a day to listen to the advice of experts."

Cutting out the item, I walked into the meeting and, without even saying hello, asked, "Are you guys experts?" It was a little out of character for me after so many years as a satisfied client—they were, as the writers say, "taken aback."

Finally one of them tentatively ventured, "Well, I guess we—kind of are."

"Let's get on with it then—and the first question is, what would I do in a nightclub?"

They were ready for that one. "How many benefits have you done?" they asked.

"Hundreds," I had to answer.

"What do you do at those benefits?" was the next question, but they already knew what my answer would be: I always introduced the other acts.

They told me that was all I'd have to do in Las Vegas, I'd be introduced first as presenting my show and then I'd proceed to introduce the acts as sort of the impresario who'd put the whole show together. This still left me with a worry that somewhere around the climax of the show something would be expected of me to justify getting star billing. This, they said, would be solved by involving me with the top act in some special material we'd have written—after we decided on the top act.

The easiest chore was getting a booking. In twenty minutes Beldon Kattleman at the El Rancho was on the dotted line. As it turned out, this wasn't where we opened.

Nancy and I were unpacking in a Berkeley hotel room prior to a banquet where I was scheduled to address a lawyers' meeting in an effort to prove that actors didn't eat their young, when Art Park phoned to say Beldon wanted to move our date up to

249

Christmas. I needed the booking and certainly the money, but something inside me rebelled at the idea of hearing "Silent Night" in Las Vegas—and we said no. His next call was a demand that I simply appear as master of ceremonies at one of his regularly scheduled shows, and the show he had picked headlined a stripper. I'm sure the stripper was a nice girl—the kind you might even take home to Mama—but try as I would, I couldn't come up with an idea of how we could work together, in front of people. Like my Universal pictures, the El Rancho ended up a mutual cancellation. No harm done: in another twenty minutes the boys had a deal at The Last Frontier.

The key act was the one I'd be involved with, and we came up with a natural: a male quartet called The Continentals, who not only sang but did some sharp comedy material. As it worked out, they did their regular act, then returned for an encore with an added starter—me. Their writer was an old friend of mine and came up with a hokey but very funny sketch wherein I wound up with a straw hat and cane like a real song-and-dance man— only I never quite got to deliver. We followed this with a take-off on an old-time German vaudeville routine.

Still I felt the need of something more—particularly as an opening monologue. I've never believed that picture people are so in demand that they can appear in the flesh and get by with just saying, "I'm glad to be here." George Burns once expounded on truth being the basis of all good comedy, and he was right. With my own beginner's status (as a floor show entertainer) in mind, I started to put together several minutes of (hopefully) funny monologue. Greeting the audience, I spoke a completely truthful line: "When it was announced I was going to do a floor show, someone said, 'What's he going to do?' That's a very good question—I wish I had a very good answer—so does the fellow who asked me—he runs this place." Plain truth, but it got a laugh, as did the rest of my dissertation about type casting, my yen to be a "ricky-tick" floor show fellow, and my background of benefits

250

in which I always introduced other acts because I couldn't sing or dance myself.

We had a wonderfully successful two weeks, with a sellout every night and offers from the Waldorf in New York and top clubs from Miami to Chicago. It was a great experience to have and remember, but two weeks were enough. Nancy was with me and sat through every show, and when it was over we couldn't wait to get back to the Palisades and that tiny queen who had taken us over.

When we were back home, we thought of it as just so many more weeks we'd bought that we could hold out in our waiting game.

Taft Schreiber, who heads up the television activities at MCA, dealt me my next hand. He knew my feeling about a TV series, but asked me to hear him out on an idea they had cooking. According to his story, General Electric was in the market for a new show, and Revue (the MCA subsidiary) had an idea to sell but it involved me. They wanted to approach GE with a package calling for a weekly dramatic program featuring guest stars, with me appearing in no more than half a dozen of these plays as the star, but introducing all of them as Bob Montgomery had in his earlier TV anthology. The real extra, however, and the one that had drawn me into the picture, was MCA's idea to hang the package on some personal appearance tours, in which for a number of weeks each year I'd visit GE plants, meeting employees and taking part in their extensive "Employee and Community Relations Program." I had been tagged because of my experience in the Guild and the speaking I'd done in the industry's behalf along the "mashed potato" circuit.

Thus the "General Electric Theatre" was born, and a door opened on another part of me—a part which now has a choice of doors, some leading in directions I never before considered.

But while all this was in the working-out and still-unsigned stage, things happened in bunches. Along came a picture over at RKO. It wasn't earth-shattering, but it was a solid kind of

Western with two pluses: one, it would have a glorious Technicolor background of scenic Glacier National Park and, two, the title role of *Cattle Queen of Montana* would be played by a great actress and real pro, Barbara Stanwyck.

Somehow working outdoors amid beautiful scenery and much of the time on horseback never has seemed like work to me. It's like getting paid for playing cowboy and Indian. Once again, I'd be happy I was a train traveler, for the whole Northwest was new to me—as was the park itself. Our cameraman made the three-day trip with me when he found it was possible to escape the plane.

We had a day or two before actual shooting, so I talked the hotel owner's son into guiding me on a hike to one of the nearby scenic spots in the park. It was my first and last such jaunt. We came upon a bear, which I thought was an extra added attraction until I got a look at my youthful guide's face. "Keep walking," he hissed—and it seemed he'd suddenly lost a lot of his suntan. It was inconceivable to me that a bear could be wandering around in a public park, unless he was guaranteed noninjurious to tourists. Of course, this was a ridiculous idea, as a lot of mauled rubbernecks discover each year. Nature is awfully natural in our national parks—as it should be—and it's up to us to look, not litter, and keep away from wild animals.

As we walked, our pace getting gradually faster, my young companion whispered, "We'll probably be all right if she hasn't got a cub around." (I don't even know how he knew it was a she.) My eyes hadn't left the bear—which made it even, because the bear was sure as hell looking at us. Finally, deciding I ought to have some knowledge of what was protocol in this particular situation, I asked, "What do we do if the bear comes at us?"

His answer didn't exactly reassure me. "I've heard [that's the part that chilled me—he was giving me hearsay] we should run downhill."

"Why?" I asked.

"They say [there was that secondhand stuff again] that a bear gets top-heavy when he tries to run downhill fast."

252

Well, it was a long, tense walk—with no chase scene, thank heaven. I've got a sneaking idea I might be a little top-heavy myself, running downhill fast.

Glacier Park was new to me, but Hollywood was an old story to the natives up there. We rented our horses from the nearby ranchers and gave the ranchers jobs riding in the posse. It was the first time I'd ever seen the extras on classier horses than the stars. As it turned out, they had run a bunch of horses down out of the brush for rental to the picture people and kept the real saddle stock for themselves.

In one scene I was supposed to be crossing a stream as Barbara laid a shot across my bow. The script said my horse, frightened by this shot, would rear and nearly unseat me. We waded in, Barbara shot, and my trusty steed never twitched. I volunteered to gig the horse with my spur on the side away from camera on the next take. She shot, I gigged, and the horse just stood there. I'm not one for harsh treatment, but on take three I arranged for the prop man to sting this quiet performer in the fanny with an air rifle. We were statuelike in our complete lack of motion. A vague suspicion had become a certainty in my mind. I urged my mount over to the shore, and this wasn't easy. Sure enough, the poor animal was so footsore after a week of picture work (they were all unshod) that once he got in that mountain stream and felt cold water on his new bunions he wasn't moving for shots, spurs, or BB's. We rewrote the scene.

That fall the GE Theatre got underway on what was to be an eight-year run, with more "firsts" to its credit than anything on television before or since. We were the first to emanate from both New York and Hollywood on a regular basis, and the first to alternate between live and filmed shows. We always got a kick out of the arguments over the relative merits of live versus film: we were the only ones truly unprejudiced because we did both, but no one asked us. Eventually we went to all film for the simple reason that film gave better quality in every way. For one thing, we discovered that our scripts could run nine pages longer for

253

the film half hour than they could for the slower-paced live show, and nine pages can be pretty important to a half-hour one-act play.

Most people have never seen the studio end of a live show like ours—it's quite different from the musical or comedy program that plays to a live audience as it is being televised. In our live efforts, the various sets are built around the perimeter of the studio with three mobile cameras, sound equipment, etc., maneuvering in the cleared central area. One scene might end with a character obliged to run from one end of the studio to a set at the other end, peeling off a coat and tugging on another, to indicate (by costume change) a lapse of time. Watch those live shows—the pants don't change. This is what made for the slower pace: very often one camera would focus on a steaming cup of coffee, or the curling smoke from a cigarette on an ashtray. Twenty seconds would be wasted on this scenic nothing, while actors scrambled into a new setup. In film, on the other hand, you simply snip the film and glue it onto the next scene.

I could never quite keep my sense of humor when actors who should have known better would argue that live TV was more like the stage, in that you could sustain an emotion—while in film you had the long waits between shots, which broke your mood. The answer to that, vulgar though it may be, is "nuts." Nancy and I did a live half-hour for GE and she played the first ten minutes wearing two dresses. At one point she left a romantic scene with me—running like crazy for another set, while a wardrobe woman unzipped and removed the outer dress (pull one zipper too many and we'd be off the air). Her next scene called for her to be worried to the point of distraction. Now, what emotion did she sustain? What these performers really meant was that they got to a high, nervous, keyed-up pitch making all these mechanical didoes work without a foul-up, while acting at the same time (sort of like patting your tummy and rubbing your head), and they got a real happy reaction when the little red lights clicked off and they knew they'd made it. But we aren't

254

supposed to be in this business for our own kicks, and the audience doesn't really care how we manage the backstage tricks: they want to see the play without the seams showing.

By some miracle we survived our live period with no monumental catastrophes such as launched the first big "Climax" show. Dick Powell headed up an all-star cast as the detective who would expose the murderer at the proper dramatic moment— and he would have, too, except that the body got up and walked off-stage in plain sight of twenty million viewers.

We went on opposite top shows with budgets double ours, as the other two networks struggled for the prestige of number one at nine o'clock Sunday night, but for seven of our eight years we stayed out in front. Our secret wasn't any secret at all: we tried for variety and quality in our stories, and we cast with the best we could get—particularly from the world of motion pictures. In our eight years we starred half a hundred Academy Award winners—many made their first, and some their only, television appearances on our show. We discovered that stars supposedly forgotten in Hollywood were still much beloved by the people. And to those who see only a vast wasteland in TV, we did some pretty imaginative pioneering. Jimmy Stewart did Dickens' *Christmas Carol* as a Western; "Rider on a Pale Horse" was dramatized; and I think we brought several Bible stories to the viewers entertainingly, yet with dignity and taste.

Of course, like all marriages, this wedding of industry and art had its friction points, and we were no exception. Sometimes I've thought the sponsor should assign a new man each season to be his contact with the show-business bride. Usually the liaison man is to guard against us show folk innocently embarrassing the sponsor, and this he does—for the first season—but everyone has two businesses, according to old theatrical legend: his own and show business. By the second season the company man develops a C. B. DeMille quality and begins blue-penciling scripts because they aren't his type of story.

His original task is legitimate and necessary. Take us, for

example—the time we came up with an exciting half-hour play based on the danger to a planeload of passengers lost in the fog with all instruments out of whack. We needed someone to remind us GE made those instruments, sold them to the airlines, and said airlines would consider it tactless if GE told umpteen million potential passengers they might land the hard way.

On the other hand, when our "middle man" began playing producer there was an overwhelming urge to take him on location and not bring him back. We ran our operation on the pattern of a studio—hiring producers for special projects and groups of pictures. One season we were fortunate in lining up a very talented and capable picture producer with a distinguished record, Harry Tugend. Our sponsor's representative was unimpressed, challenging many of Harry's story ideas on the basis of taste. Now it is true that any story can be done vulgarly or properly, depending on the producer's personal bent. Harry thought his past record justified granting him a free hand, and he was right. When the blowup came, it was not my kind of spluttering blast but a beautiful job of erudite putting-in-place.

Harry went into a story conference with his tormentor. He said, "Here is a suggested plot. The play opens outside the Pentagon; a general just coming to work sees a convertible pull up with a young captain and his wife. They kiss good-by, and she drives off; the captain goes to his office. The general inquires as to his identity—all day he can't get the captain's wife off his mind. Finally, taking advantage of his rank, he has the captain ordered to duty in Korea and after a suitable time makes a play for the lonely wife, a play in which he is successful. Then word arrives that the captain has been killed, and the general realizes his lust has caused the death of the younger man. Do you think GE would O.K. such a story for the Sunday night show?"

Well, of course, the answer was a horrified "No!"

Very quietly Harry said, "I've just told you the story of 'David and Bathsheba.'" He had made his point about taste, because obviously we would have been willing to do the biblical story

256

on GE Theatre. Nevertheless, it didn't do any good—nothing changed.

Still, GE was a truly good sponsor, a vast corporation, but as human as the corner grocer. The tours I made of GE plant cities were part of an effort to meet two problems that seemed at first glance in diametric opposition. No large corporation has ever attempted decentralization on the scale attempted by GE. It was not only decentralization of physical facilities into 135 cities and some forty states, but decentralization of policy decisions and management to the point that various branches and departments were as competitive with each other as the company was with Westinghouse. It didn't seem at all unusual in GE to make millions of dollars in refrigerators and freezers, and at the same time have the X-ray branch experimenting like crazy to develop a method of preserving food without refrigeration.

This spreading out had created a couple of morale problems. One, how to keep employees in some distant small town from feeling they were forgotten by the company. Two, how to encourage management personnel in those scattered plants from isolating themselves from the community and thinking of themselves as on a temporary assignment with no civic responsibilities at all.

The first lesson we learned was that no one could do an eight-week tour without ending up a paper-doll clipper. After the second tour that year, which brought the total time to sixteen weeks, we settled for a greater number of tours but shorter—no more than three weeks at one haul. I know statistics are boring, but reducing eight years of tours, in which I reached all the 135 plants and personally met the 250,000 employees, down to numbers, it turns out something like this: two of the eight years were spent traveling, and with speeches sometimes running at fourteen a day, I was on my feet in front of a "mike" for about 250,000 minutes.

Headquarters, or rather the fountainhead of GE, had been picked for the opener, the huge turbine plant at Schenectady, New York. My first look was from a balcony outside the offices

257

down on thirty-eight acres of factory under one roof. The VP in charge escorted me down the iron stairs to the factory floor, and the pattern was established at that point. Probably the VP and his fellow executives had never witnessed a movie premiere, so they were unprepared for what happened. Machines went untended or ground to a halt; the aisles filled with men and women bearing their children's autograph books. I walked, signing, answering questions, asking a few of my own, and generally having a hell of a good time getting acquainted. About four hours later, back in the upstairs office, the reception was equally heart-warming—the execs were ecstatic: they knew how to evaluate the lost production time against a shot in the arm morale-wise. I was very well aware that anyone from Hollywood would have been given the same reception, but I wasn't about to volunteer that information. It was too good after the downbeat year and a half to bask in a little glory, whether deserved or not.

Earl Dunckel was the tour impresario that first year, and a good man to have along. For the most part we were hitting big plants, so the pattern remained eight hours of walking the assembly line, meeting the employees individually—stopping to visit whenever a group could gather around. This visiting led to another development which Earl was quick to capitalize on. He began calling ahead and, where a plant would lend itself to it, we varied the hike by shutting down sections of the assembly line and gathering the people in an open space where for twenty minutes or so I'd talk to them (usually signing autographs at the same time).

I knew I had to avoid a set routine or a canned speech which, although it would have been easier, could have ruined the whole wonderful reaction we were getting. I was sure that one group exchanged notes with the others about what took place in these twenty-minute sessions, and it wouldn't do to have them discover I had one twenty-minute pitch which was turned on and off like a record. Besides, at fourteen times a day I'd get pretty sick of it myself. The answer was a brief greeting and explanation of

258

why I was there, which of necessity had to be fairly pat, but then I freewheeled my way into a question-and-answer session and that really made for variety. One group would get off on the subject of stunts in movies, and how the fights were done; another (particularly the gals) wanted to know about what we did on Saturday night—and so it went. Believe me, it was stimulating. Sometimes the stage was a truck, sometimes a table in the cafeteria. The audiences were as varied: it was nothing at all to face the office gals at 8 A.M., the men in the foundry at 8:30, and at 9 the research lab, where everyone but me had a Ph.D.

The eight years and 135 plants have a way of melting into a montage in my memory, but some overall impressions remain. For one thing, it is too bad that a lot of people can't see the miracle of American industry at work. I know I should be impressed about Edison inventing the lightbulb, but Edison himself would be impressed by the machine that spins those bulbs out like peas from a pod. At Nela Park in Cleveland, where GE has headquartered its research and manufacturing of lighting equipment, you have the feeling you are on a campus, not in a factory. Beautiful landscaping and ivy-covered walls add to the impression. I asked the head man how many people worked there and he answered wryly, "Roughly about half."

He was joking, but this touches on a point that did much to shape my ideas and, in many ways, redirect them. These employees I was meeting were a cross-section of America and, damn it, too many of our political leaders, our labor leaders, and certainly a lot of geniuses in my own business and on Madison Avenue have underestimated them. They want the truth, they are friendly and helpful, intelligent and alert. They are concerned, not with security as some would have us believe, but with their very firm personal liberties. And they are moral. If I had to choose the one comment I heard most often about our show in those eight years, and I heard it from one end of the country to the other, it was usually in the form of a "thank you." They thanked us because we had never embarrassed them in front of their children. As a matter of fact, that oft-repeated remark influenced our program content when sometimes we were undecided.

Their hospitality at the plants, the ingenuity of the things they'd do to make me welcome, were beyond belief. I could do our home in plaques: I'm an honorary S-O-B (Supervisor of Burlington), an Ozark Hillbilly, a locomotive engineer, a pilot on the Confederate air force, a Duke, a Patroon, and yes, a Kentucky Colonel. This is Americana, a tongue-in-cheek jibe at titled nobility, but at the same time they are given in friendship and affection, and I treasure them. A few years ago when our ranch burned— while I was on tour—even the neighbors knew the plaques and framed greetings had top priority: they saved all of them.

The plant visits were never short of humor. There was always the grandmother the gang wanted me to hug and call by name, the foreman I'd use as villain in a demonstration of a movie punch, and the machine I'd be asked to run which ended with me getting a handful of grease.

In Owensboro, Kentucky, I faced some five thousand girls—General Electric's "ladies in white." Attired in sterile nylon gowns and caps, they work in a dust-free atmosphere making electronic tubes. Come question time, I heard the familiar "How do you-all like Owensboro?"

Trying to gag up my answer, I said, "Fine! How could I complain about being here with five thousand girls? But just think, next week I'm in Pittsfield, Mass., where there are thirteen thousand men."

A little cornpone accent in the middle of the crowd drawled, "You stay here and we'll go to Pittsfield."

I drove a locomotive, revved up a jet engine, watched a plastic bottle receive a million volts of X-ray, and fired a 20-mm. cannon so top secret at the time I couldn't even tell Nancy about it. Operating on the old Gatling gun principle, the gun was fired by an electric button. They handed me the button and challenged me to fire less than the drum of 150 shells. It still staggers my imagination to think of an intricate mechanical process operating

260

at such speed. In other words, I failed: my thumb pressed the button and in the one second it took to lift it, the 150 shells were fired.

One plant distributed over ten thousand photos, and in two days I signed all of them. It's the only time I ever blistered a finger just writing. In another town they had a reception and I stood in a receiving line and shook two thousand hands. After the first one thousand it seemed that everyone not only had an iron grip but managed to land their thumbs on the exact same spot, no matter how I twisted or turned my hand. It became the sheer agony of a bone bruise. At Appliance Park in Louisville, Kentucky, there were forty-six miles of assembly line—I walked all of them, twice. I had to meet the night shift too. I'm quite an authority on floors and what they do to feet; after forty-six miles of concrete I had to cut my laces to get my shoes off.

The trips were murderously difficult. I could lose ten pounds in three weeks and eat anything I wanted. The schedules were dovetailed on a split-second basis, and the demand on energy so great when you had to meet the fourteenth group with the same zip you'd shown ten hours earlier that I didn't really sleep until a trip was over. *But I enjoyed every whizzing minute of it.* It was one of the most rewarding experiences of my life. There was an understandable glow at being welcomed so warmly, but in addition it was wonderful to encounter the honest affection most people had for the familiar faces of Hollywood.

No barnstorming politician ever met the people on quite such a common footing. Sometimes I had an awesome, shivering feeling that America was making a personal appearance for me, and it made me the biggest fan in the world.

CHAPTER

17

Right from that first day in the giant turbine plant at Schenectady the employee relations phase of the tours was pretty well grooved. The community relations program was slower in taking shape. Oh, it's true I usually met the Mayor, received a key to the city, and had a few pictures taken, but I had anticipated a few after-dinner speaking chores or, at least, a ribbon cutting or two.

Then one day as we approached Boston, Earl hesitantly broached the subject, and the mystery was cleared. "You know," he said, "I've fended off some invitations for you to speak because, frankly, this trip is so damned hard I didn't want to get stuck in a hotel room writing speeches for you. But now we have a special employee meeting and I don't think we can duck it."

It seems that Boston was just going in for the United Fund type of charity campaign, and an effort was being made to line up the people in the GE plant on a salary deduction basis for once a year giving. The morning of our arrival had been designated as the day when the employees would be approached on this plan. I told Earl there was no problem, that just by chance this happened to be a subject with which I was very familiar. The motion picture industry had pioneered in the consolidated charity idea. There had been a time when you couldn't go from a sound stage to the café without being flagged down by some charitable group who had been granted permission to come into the studio and solicit. The causes were worthy but they and we suffered from this day after day solicitation.

The Guild had been very much involved in the research and study that led to the creation of the industry's "Permanent Charities Committee." It was very easy for me to do some twenty minutes on this subject because of my own part in the study and research resulting in the Hollywood plan. That settled the problem of community relations. Earl discovered that he could accept the speaking invitations in my behalf without laying a hand to a borrowed typewriter. From then on, when the noon whistle interrupted my treks up and down the factory aisles, I would be rushed into a waiting car, driven to the luncheon meeting of a service club, and introduced as the speaker—following which I'd be rushed right back to continue my hike. From then on, one spot in the day became my only moment of splendid solitude. In the words of the poet, it came "between the dark and the daylight when the night was beginning to lower." For all of five minutes, I could stand in silent meditation in the shower, before Earl rapped on the door and told me I'd have to get dressed for an after-dinner speech.

With all that I had heard of the timidity of sponsors, I was somewhat surprised that General Electric delivered me as often as possible on the mashed potato circuit, and never suggested in any way what I should talk about. Nor did they ever indicate I was singing the wrong song and should switch tunes. It was Earl's words about writing speeches that made me realize I couldn't be a mouthpiece for someone else's thoughts. Like in those days right after the war, and later on when I took to the road in behalf of the motion picture industry, speaking wasn't a gimmick to justify a personal appearance. I had to have something I wanted to say, and something in which I believed. Trying to correct some of the misconceptions about show people qualified as something I thought needed airing.

There are more than five hundred full-time correspondents assigned to Hollywood. This is more news coverage than is given any spot on earth, except Washington, D.C. In spite of this (I would never dare suggest because of it), there is a vast difference between Hollywood as it really is and the image in the public mind.

Of course, I couldn't impose on an audience to the extent of just singing Hollywood's praises, without tying the whole subject into the listeners and how they might be involved, so I followed my factual data with illustrations of what had happened to Hollywood. In years past, concentrating more on publicity than public relations, we had never refuted our detractors nor bothered to correct the record. The result has been that none of our fellow citizens feel the urge to go to bat for Hollywood when we are the victims of discrimination, particularly at the hands of publicity-seeking political figures. In a land of free speech, our portion of the communications industry is subject to censorship by many state and local governments and, because everyone thinks Hollywood is synonymous with great wealth, we have been and are discriminated against taxwise. In all the half million words that make up the senseless hodgepodge of the income tax law, there are only two references to actors. One says we are not entitled to the deductions granted businessmen because we are professionals and the other says we aren't professionals because we receive a salary instead of a fee.

The most dramatic part of my pitch, however, was the account of the attempted takeover of the industry by the Communists. In passing let me say it was dumfounding to discover, in spite of all the publicity, how completely uninformed the average audience was concerning internal Communism and how it operated. Here, I think, a useful purpose was served in awakening many people to the threat in their own backyards. This was especially true in those industrial communities where the emphasis was on defense. At least one of the unions in those areas suffers from Communist infiltration amounting to outright domination. It was easy to point out that, had Hollywood accepted its civic responsibility more positively and been more concerned with its

264

own public image, the Communists couldn't have come as close to success as they did, and Hollywood would not have appeared in such a bad light in the public view.

In summation, it made sense to suggest to an audience that if one group of people in America could be denied fair treatment, then the freedoms and rights of all were in danger. If they (the audiences) were so complacent as to think they could sit back and not lift a hand until the battle involved them personally, they were about as shortsighted as a fellow going into the poultry business without a rooster—they were putting a hell of a lot of confidence in the stork.

As that first year drew to a close, I discovered with great fear that Earl was moving on and up to another job. Sixteen weeks of this back-breaking tour made me very aware of how impossible the tours could be without a congenial companion. My worries were needless: I was introduced to a tall, redheaded young man who had a background of piloting B-29's as well as several years' experience with the FBI. He was put in charge of the tours and promoting the General Electric Theatre. We hit the sawdust trail for seven years and wound up with a deep and lasting friendship. George Dalen has the quiet efficiency that seems so typical of J. Edgar Hoover's elite corps but, in addition, this big, rugged redhead had a sense of humor that kept the whole business from breaking our backs.

Over those seven years the format could be described roughly as taking the train into the tour area, and then renting a car for the town-to-town hops. He delighted in teasing the enthusiastic GE executives who would be on hand to meet us at each new stop. For example, he could completely deadpan a conversation in a town in the Deep South when he would ask if there might be music where I was speaking, because at one point I spoke to a musical background of "The Battle Hymn of the Republic." Of course, the local management—usually Yankee transfers to Dixie—would cock a wary eye and get around to an elaborately casual inquiry as to what the subject of my speech might be. George, just as casually, would answer, "It's entitled 'Robert E. Lee—a Traitor to His Country.'" I never could sit through this without having to leave the room on some pretext or other.

Here, too, my memory begins to run together in a montage. There are a string of highlights on the pleasure side, because of the hospitality wherever we were that provided us with wonderful experiences. Salmon fishing on a yacht off Seattle, deep-sea fishing under the same luxurious conditions in the Gulf of Mexico, riding an Irish hunter over stone walls in Connecticut because the locals knew of my interest in horses, touring the bluegrass thoroughbred farms of Kentucky. Incidentally, that one time, even though it was spring in the South, more than the grass was blue: we were blue with cold. Kentucky turned on a record-breaking cold wave, with the thermometer at four above zero. Someday I'd like to go back and see the place without snow. George had an ability to schedule a trip that just happened to put us in Louisville at Derby time. He even booked us for a speech in Honolulu, and Nancy and I—as well as George and his wife, Gini—made our first visit to the land of Aloha.

As the years went on, my speeches underwent a kind of evolution, reflecting not only my changing philosophy but also the swiftly rising tide of collectivism that threatens to inundate what remains of our free economy. I don't believe it was all just a case of my becoming belatedly aware of something that already existed; the last decade has seen a quickening of tempo in our government's race toward the controlled society.

The Hollywood portion of the talk shortened and disappeared. The warning words of what could happen changed to concrete examples of what has already happened, and I learned very early to document those examples. Bureaucracy does not take kindly to being assailed and isn't above using a few low blows and a knee to the groin when it fights back. Knowing this, I have become extremely cautious in dealing with government agencies.

My speeches were nonpartisan as far as the two major political

266

parties were concerned, and I went out of my way to point out that the problems of centralizing power in Washington, with subsequent loss of freedom at the local level, were problems that crossed party lines. I emphasized the danger of a permanent structure of government grown so huge that it exerted power on the elected representatives and usurped their policy-making functions.

During that first couple of years I wasn't unaware that GE sometimes had to sell a few groups on taking a Hollywood actor as a speaker. I'm sure they thought I'd put on a canned pitch for the TV show, or try to sell them an electric washing machine. By the third year, however, the tours were being scheduled around the speaking engagements and the routine weekly luncheon clubs had given way to the more important annual events: state Chamber of Commerce banquets, national conventions, and groups recognized as important political sounding boards such as the Executives Club of Chicago, whose speakers have included Presidents and visiting heads of state. George had booked speaking dates for three years ahead. As a matter of fact, when GE Theatre was dropped in 1962, bookings had to be canceled for speaking tours as far ahead as 1966.

It would be nice to accept this as a tribute to my oratory, but I think the real reason had to do with a change that was taking place all over America. People wanted to talk about and hear about encroaching government control, and hopefully they wanted suggestions as to what they themselves could do to turn the tide. My story was really one available to anyone who wanted to look up a few facts and add them together. Government agencies own and operate thousands of businesses tax-free, rent-free, and dividend-free—in direct competition with private citizens who not only must survive in the face of this unjust monopoly, but must pay taxes to cover the losses incurred by these government-owned competitors.

Well, if I carry on in this vein, you'll be getting the speech. Pretty soon I began running into audiences already familiar with the speech so new versions had to be created, necessitating more reading and research until, like the journalist with a daily column, I too had a monkey on my back. I began to have recurrent nightmares between tours: in one I was struggling to get my bags packed and make a train, and in the other I was face to face with an audience and didn't know what to say. I told Nancy once that if she served hard rolls I'd probably stand up by automatic reflex and say, "Mr. Toastmaster, Ladies and Gentlemen."

The tragic and lonely Whittaker Chambers wrote that in turning his back on Communism he knew he was leaving the winning side, but he preferred to go down with the losers rather than continue supporting a cause he knew to be so evil. Commenting on the aftermath to his decision, he said, "When I took up my little sling and aimed at Communism, I also hit at something else. What I hit was the force of that great Socialist revolution which in the name of *liberalism,* spasmodically, incompletely, somewhat formlessly, but always in the same direction, has been inching its ice-cap over the nation for two decades. I had no adequate idea of its extent, the depth of its penetration, or the fierce vindictiveness of its revolutionary temper."

I am too optimistic to agree with his first statement, but I learned for myself the bitter truth of the latter. As my talks gained circulation, they didn't go unopposed.

In 1959 I was scheduled to speak at a convention being held in Los Angeles, sort of an extra added starter to the tours, when I received a phone call from George. He informed me that a government bureaucrat was on the warpath because of a paragraph in my speech wherein I used TVA (Tennessee Valley Authority) as an example of how government programs can grow beyond their original purpose. It was made pretty plain that I was to be fired, and there was pointed reference to $50,000,000 worth of government business that could be taken elsewhere.

I asked George what Ralph Cordiner, Chairman of the GE Board, had said, and he answered, "He hasn't said anything except that he'll handle it personally."

268

It was three days until my convention date. The next day George called and told me of Mr. Cordiner's answer. He had been polite but there was no hint of apology in his attitude. He was sorry if anyone decided to take its business elsewhere, but General Electric *would not tell any individual what he could not say*. The next day there was another call. They were spluttering: according to their view, my speeches were made while on trips sponsored by GE—therefore GE should be able to dictate the content of my speeches. This was a view GE politely but firmly rejected. Again I asked George if there had been any comment from Cordiner about my speech—now only one day away—and he replied, "Not a word."

Suddenly, realization dawned. There wouldn't be a word. Ralph Cordiner meant what he said and was prepared to back those words with $50,000,000 worth of business. Now the responsibility was mine. How free was I to embarrass or hurt the company, just because I had carte blanche to speak my mind? There was a certain austerity about Ralph Cordiner that made my next move not quite the easiest thing I've ever done. I picked up the phone and called him in New York. It was no time for chitchat—I plunged right in. "I understand you have a problem and it concerns me."

"I'm sorry you found out about that," he answered. "It's my problem and I've taken it on." Then he proceeded to fill me in on the exchange of views, not knowing George had kept me fully posted.

When he finished, I tried to tell him how much I admired his stand, but that I wouldn't want to think that someday they might have to lay off a few thousand men in the turbine plant because he had defended my right to speak. Still he didn't take advantage of this opening and hint that maybe I should change my lyrics. It was up to me. "Mr. Cordiner," I finally said, "what would you say if I said I could make my speech just as effectively without mentioning TVA?"

There was a long pause. Then a very human voice said, "Well, it would make my job easier."

Dropping TVA from the speech was no problem. You can reach out blindfolded and grab a hundred examples of over-grown government. The whole attempt only served to illustrate how late it is if we are to save freedom.

In spite of this attempted hatchet job, I didn't really feel the "vindictiveness of the liberal temper" until after January 20, 1961. Then, indeed, I became a target high on the priority list. The Committee on Political Education of the AFL-CIO—better known as COPE—had tagged me as a strident voice of right wing extremism, and under the accepted liberal practice of the end justifying the means, proceeded to issue bulletins long on name-calling and short on truth.

Early one winter morning in St. Paul, Minnesota, I stepped down from a train into a glare of flashbulbs, grinding newsreel cameras, and shouted questions. I turned around to see what high dignitary might be disembarking behind me, but all the fuss was for me. Someone shoved an early edition of the St. Paul paper in front of me and there was the answer. I was in town to ride in the Winter Carnival Parade and, as a kind of added appearance, to speak to the Central High School assembly. But there in the paper I read where the Teachers Federation had passed a resolution the night before, demanding that I not be allowed to speak to the students because I was a "controversial personality." This is the new gimmick: it isn't enough to meet you in debate and try to refute your ideas. There are campaigns to block you from being allowed to speak at all, and to that end there are compiled a whole list of speakers who are to be silenced by almost any means.

At ten o'clock that morning I stepped onto the stage of the high school auditorium, a little heartened because several teachers had managed to whisper in passing that they didn't agree with the resolution. Of course, it should give us all pause to think that these teachers had to get this word to me surreptitiously without being seen. I had no idea what the reaction of the students would be, but I wasn't long in finding out: they stood and cheered for five minutes. They damn well didn't want someone telling them whom they could or couldn't listen to. It was a heartwarming experience, even though that first glimpse of the newspaper had made me a little sick.

The windup took place the next night across the river in Minneapolis where I was a banquet speaker. During dinner a nice-looking man came up on the dais and asked the toastmaster for permission to say a few words. What happened then goes down in my list of unusual happenings—he introduced himself as a St. Paul teacher. He had followed me across the river to publicly apologize on behalf of the St. Paul teachers for the resolution passed by their federation. A newspaperman later told me that only a handful of teachers out of a membership of twelve hundred had attended the meeting where the resolution was passed. A few weeks later, a demand was made that Central High School allow the U. S. Communist party secretary, Ben Davis, to speak—the basis of the demand being that he was entitled to equal time because I had spoken.

Thank heaven for those hide-toughening experiences in the old CSU days—the arrows were coming in volleys. One of Drew Pearson's henchmen woke us out of a sound sleep one night, calling from Washington. His attitude couldn't have been friendlier as he questioned me about my criticism of the proposed compulsory government medical insurance. Somehow my answers must not have weathered the trip from Los Angeles by phone to Washington, and through Pearson's typewriter, because they came out turned around in a vitriolic attack against me and the American Medical Association. It made it easier to understand why three United States presidents of both parties had publicly questioned his tactics.

Except for the REA and TVA episodes, wherein they were resentful because of a direct reference, it was unbelievable how the same speech—which for six years during the Eisenhower

271

administration had only brought out some minor sniping—was now whipping up such turbulent winds. A couple of times I found myself going over it to see if someone had stuck some extra paragraphs in while I wasn't looking. I would have hated me too if I was making the speech they said I was making.

Our show had evolved into all film, and we completed our seventh year still the number one show at nine on Sunday night. Of course, it was something like waiting for the guy in the upstairs apartment to drop the other shoe. Every summer the other two networks got out the cookbook and stirred up some new recipes. When we finally dipped our colors, however, it was to another veteran. NBC moved TV's top-rated show, Bonanza, from its Saturday spot to Sunday, and in our eighth year we ran second most of the time. It doesn't make me flinch even a little to say this—to tell you the truth, Bonanza was a favorite of mine. Our half hour, black and white, was up against an hour color program with four permanent stars, plus a weekly guest star, all wrapped in a budget several millions of dollars greater than ours.

As that year drew to a close, a top-level shuffle in GE brought J. Stanford Smith back from plant management to public relations as a vice-president. I use the term *back* because he had been in charge of TV eight years earlier when GE Theatre was born. Now, understandably, he wanted a new look and asked us for ideas. I think we came up with a great one. It was obvious to us that the trend to longer shows was no temporary fad. We suggested the "Theatre" go to an hour every other Sunday, alternating with the Alcoa Theatre, hosted by that gentle genius, Fred Astaire. Frankly, my mouth was watering because both shows were Revue productions, which meant we could have worked out all kinds of co-starring gimmicks and exchanges to keep both shows sparking.

To this point there had been no indication that GE was seriously considering a real about-face. We had been patient to such an extent that we were well past the date when other opportunities were open to us for the year ahead. Then a strange thing happened: I received a call from an executive of the advertising agency. This in itself was strange, because my dealings for several years had all been on a first-name basis directly with GE. This man began to sound me out on how I'd feel about continuing the tours but limiting my speaking to commercial pitches about GE products. I thought about the dates already set up for three years ahead—the first one the annual dinner of the Indiana Manufacturers Association. I couldn't quite see myself spellbinding this group with a description of the new 1963 coffee pot. I told this gentleman that if the speeches were an issue I could see no solution short of severing our relationship.

Obviously GE couldn't call off the tours and tell important customers they were unable to deliver me as a speaker, and neither GE nor I could afford to send me out huckstering to an audience that was expecting a talk on "Encroaching Government Controls." Twenty-four hours later the GE Theatre was canceled. I don't know—maybe eight years was long enough. I do know that GE stood up against government threats in a day when government was less prone to use force and coercion. At any rate, I had spent eight wonderful years in a happy and worthwhile association, with some of the finest people I've ever met. I had enjoyed tremendous success, and was walking away with a choice of several directions.

I've dwelt a great deal on the show and the tours and once again I'm forced to recap, lest it seem that these were all of life for the eight years. Actually I wore several hats—including one that had to be dusted off and reclaimed from the discard—and a couple of hats were offered that I turned down as not my type.

The most important hat was the one marked "for home use only." Nancy and I had realized a dream in 1956 and built a home high on a hill overlooking the ocean and city. We moved Patti and a collie named Lucky (because that's the way I felt) into this house, which just happened to be the most electric house in the country. GE had played with it like a Christmas toy and we benefited no end from their generous intention to give us an

273

electric-powered home. As one department after the other got in its licks, the panel where the switches and circuit-breakers are began to outgrow the usual back porch cupboard. One day a truck arrived with a three-thousand-pound steel cabinet, twelve feet long and eight feet high. They mounted it outside one wall of the house on a concrete platform—this is where our electricity comes in. From there I'm sure we have a direct line to Hoover Dam.

There was an extra room in the new house because Nancy had decided Patti should have a brother. Personally I would have settled for the three of us: I grew frightened every time I remembered that long night when Patti was born, and didn't want to take chances with a happiness already so great I couldn't believe it. At the same time I knew Patti would have that brother, because I couldn't say no to the Nancy who'd decided this and if I did she'd probably get Mervin Le Roy to call me up again.

Sure enough, George scheduled a tour and made it come out so that I arrived home the day before she went into the hospital, this time for a planned Caesarean. No horse show this time—everything was on schedule, even including moral support for Papa. Nancy's mother, DeeDee, had come out and she and Ursula Taylor—Robert Taylor's beautiful wife—accompanied me to the hospital early in the morning.

The Taylors are neighbors and close friends, a treasured part of our pattern of living. Here again is one of those revealing differences between reality and the Hollywood of the press agent's dream. No one ever made a greater impact on the public or the movie industry than Bob Taylor: the perfect image of stardom—matinee idol, screen hero, and, incidentally, fine actor. Ursula came to this country a beautiful and glamorous import from the postwar German picture industry. To us they are friends who run like deer from the glamour spots and dressed-up shindigs. Like us, they have a horse ranch and know what to do about the livestock themselves. Bob is a handy man in a duck blind or on a hunt, and Ursula is a happy expert in the kitchen. When we have dinner together there or at our place, wardrobe is blue jeans.

Ursula and DeeDee stayed downstairs at the hospital while I went up to wait out my worry. No broom closet this time: Cedars had fancied up a special pacing room for papas, but it really didn't make much difference. Once again cold terror enveloped me, until I wished I could turn back the clock and cancel out this moment. Mercifully the pain was ended in a relatively short time. At 8:04 A.M. a nurse told me Ronald Prescott had arrived, weighing eight and a half pounds. Again that wasn't the first thing I wanted to hear. I'm in favor of a rule that, under the circumstances, nurses will begin their announcement with the words, "Your wife is all right."

One word here is appropriate about the fifth member of the family—Lucky, our female collie. She had come to us a puppy when Patti was a toddler able to navigate by clutching handfuls of tail and fur. In some mysterious law of baby communication, this established that Lucky belonged to Patti. Now the Skipper came along as the newest addition to a family of which Lucky was an established member and, by the same mysterious dog and baby grapevine, he belonged to her—he became her pup. There came a day when Lucky had to let me know this. Her almost daily routine included accompanying me to the ranch and she'd beat me to the car, eager to be under way. There came a day, however, when I stood by the door ready to go, and she made a choice in the clearest, most unmistakable language: she looked at me almost regretfully, turned, walked over to the door of the nursery, and stood there, watching me over her shoulder as if to say, "We mothers have other things to do." She goes to the ranch on weekends now when the children go too.

My old labor union hat hadn't been completely discarded. Nancy and I were both on the board of the Guild, but I had decided shortly after our marriage that it was time to let someone else wield the gavel. Walter Pidgeon had taken over as president, and a fine one he was until the gods of show business directed his

275

course toward Broadway, just as the 1959 contract negotiations loomed on the horizon. Unexpectedly, Jack Dales called one day to relay a question from the nominating committee: would I return for another term as president? Convinced as I was that my previous service had hurt careerwise, and feeling the upsurge of success in the GE Theatre after the lean period, I didn't want to answer the question at all—I just wanted to hide some place. Nancy was even more upset, and felt there was every justification for saying "No, thanks."

There were several restless days and sleepless nights. "No" was not an easy thing to say, knowing as I did that the Guild was coming to its moment of truth. We had lived ten years with the "stopgap" clause that had kept all pictures made after 1948 off television. Well, not all: some independent companies had sold post-'48's to TV and, in keeping with the clause, had negotiated settlements with the Guild, thus establishing in a way a recognition that actors did have a claim to additional pay if their pictures, made for (and paid for) theatrical use, found an additional market in television.

Our contention had been, and still is, that if a producer wants to use a film in theaters and then sell it to TV, the actor has a right to set a price for the two uses, or even refuse to sell TV rights. It is possible that a performer might have an exclusive TV contract and be legally unable to permit use of his screen performance on TV.

Finally I called my agent, Lew Wasserman—who else? I knew that he shared my belief that my career had suffered. To tell the truth, I was positive he'd reiterate that belief and I could say "no" with a clear conscience. Well, I pulled the ripcord and the chute didn't open. Lew said he thought I should take the job. It was still a satisfactory answer because down inside of me there was a certain knowledge that I wouldn't like me very much the other way.

There were two big issues in our contract demands: one, the end to the stopgap clause and the establishment of the principle of repayment for re-use; two, the setting up of a pension and

276

welfare fund. In those first weeks of negotiations we were like people being extra careful not to bring up an unpleasant subject. We haggled and bargained over minor changes in the contract until finally we had to say, "Look, we're all kidding ourselves. None of the things we are settling mean anything if we can't settle the big 'if.' " Then we were told by the men across from us—the men we'd always dealt with, the men who ran the studios—they could not even discuss the issue with us. For the first time in the history of our relationship, the presidents of the companies, almost all of whom ran the business from New York offices, had placed a restriction on the studio bosses' freedom to negotiate.

Then Jack and the late Ben Kahane went to the men's room. After the meeting broke up, Jack told me that Ben had said, "Call your strike—we'll never be allowed to negotiate until you do."

But before the strike took place there were more desperation passes and attempted field goals. We asked the producers if we could meet with the presidents, and this meeting was arranged. Our entire board, the producers' negotiating committee, and the several company presidents gathered two deep around the table. Incidentally, that table is something to see: it is a massive thing with a polished surface, fully thirty feet long and fifteen feet wide.

Each of the presidents made a hardship plea to the effect that his studio could only stay in business, giving jobs to actors, if it had free rein to sell its backlog of pictures to TV. This was the unvarying theme till they got to Jack Warner. He started out as if he'd sing the same song, but somehow the lyrics did a switch after the first eight bars, and the irrepressible Jack ended up telling how great business was for his company, and how little he had to worry about. We were grateful for the assist.

Spyros Skouras was general chairman and spokesman for their side, and he moved in fast to counter Jack's optimistic message. Mr. Skouras tends to be emotional, and as he really began to roll you could hear in the background the padlocks snapping on the studio gates as they went out of business. He was standing at the head of the oval table and I was seated just off the curve to his left at, say, the head of the stretch. Pretty soon he was leaning on the table, directing his entire pitch to me. I wasn't too happy about playing a solo role, as if the whole fuss were my personal hobby, but his throat was tightening up and there were tears in his eyes, so it wasn't an easy time to change seats or pretend I had another engagement. He concluded with the flat assertion that his company had to sell the pictures and keep all the money, or go out of business.

I told him that possibly everything he said was true, and if so, this would be revealed in negotiations. But then I asked, "Mr. Skouras, what if, as the result of negotiations, we asked only 1 per cent of the TV revenue for all of us—do you mean Twentieth could stay open with 100 per cent of the money but would have to close if you only got 99 per cent?"

His answer slammed that door. He said, "We won't discuss it."

A long time later, Y. Frank Freeman of Paramount, a fine and honorable gentleman, told me if I'd made that 1 per cent crack to him he'd have grabbed it and left me stuck with it.

In all fairness, I think we have to recognize that some of the companies were being pressured by new members of their boards of directors—Eastern investors who suddenly saw profit in the film backlogs and the studio real estate values that had skyrocketed in California's land boom. These individuals didn't want to make pictures—they wanted to cash in by going out of business and taking the capital gains tax break.

The strike lasted six months. It probably cost actors ten million dollars in lost income, and the studios five times that in lost production, and it really didn't have to happen at all. If only they had agreed to negotiate they would have found how reasonable our demands were. We settled for what we were always willing to settle for. Actually the strike wasn't over amounts or terms, but because they said, "We won't even talk to you." There is only so long you can keep knocking on a closed door.

Once the strike was on, the bitterness began as if our twenty-odd years of peaceful, friendly relationship had never taken place. A fellow with a small circulation sheet, Jaik Rosenstein by name, put me on his cover decked out in a Hitler mustache and hairdo over the caption "Heil!"

Nancy was the real sufferer. No doubt she could have taken the snide digs and anonymous column items in stride if they'd been directed at her, but she came unglued when I was the target. Actors may not have a monopoly on sensitivity and understanding, but they sure rank up front with all the others in that department. Every day during those long, bitter months, Nancy was sure of two morale-boosting phone calls a day—one each from John Wayne and Jimmy Cagney. They didn't talk to me, they talked to her, and I loved them for it.

Some old alliances came undone. Frank Sinatra, shooting a picture with his own company, called and said, "Where do I sign up? I'm on the Guild's side." This was, of course, the kind of thing that could splinter the solid front and end the strike.

In a matter of hours we had an agreement worked out. Before the ink dried, the roof fell in. An old ally, Richard Walsh of the IATSE, moved in—issuing an ultimatum to Frank and all other independents who had shown signs of going along. He made a demand for repayment for his people and said if they signed with the Guild, they'd give in on his demands in twenty-four hours or he'd strike their sets. His unions had a contract that wasn't up for renegotiation for several months. One of the producers' arguments had been that if they gave in to us, the door would be open to all kinds of demands from others. Our reply had been that we were prepared to take the lead in organizing the whole industry on this point, so that total repayment for everyone could be negotiated at once. In other words, if the unions and guilds could agree with the producers on some percentage of the TV revenue as a fair share, then we would work out among ourselves how the percentage would be split up. Of course, this too was met with the "we refuse to discuss it" line. Now we couldn't ask Frank to abide by his agreement with us because we would have destroyed him.

Walsh's act could hardly be excused. He had a signed contract with months to run. We resented the effect it had of interfering with our negotiations, and we didn't like it.

I put in a call to the AFL-CIO president, George Meany, and told him what had happened and what we thought it smelled like. He was angry and at the same time as puzzled as we were by an action that didn't seem to jibe with Walsh's previous record and known loyalty to the cause of labor. He said he'd get hold of Dick right away. In an hour he called back and said he couldn't find him, that Walsh's whereabouts was supposedly a mystery in IATSE headquarters. In another hour we called him with the information that Walsh was in the Knickerbocker Hotel in Hollywood, registered under an assumed name. Actors don't play private eyes without learning a few tricks.

Evidently Meany reached him because we received a call from a friendly-sounding Walsh who wanted to come by the Guild office the next morning. He arrived on schedule with the heads of three of his unions, all fine fellows, well known to us as sympathetic to our cause and strong in their belief that their people also had a claim against the TV revenue from old movies. This, as it turned out, was really a break for us.

Dick was genial and good-natured, and general in his approach. It was impossible to get down to specifics: he was all smiling sympathy and concern for our problem—until someone on our side blew his top.

"Damn it, Walsh," I screamed, "you are a lousy, damn strike-breaker!"

There may be a worse insult in labor language, but I don't know it. The reaction was predictable. Red of face, he shouted, "Do you really believe that repayment for re-use is a legitimate labor issue?"

We didn't have to answer. It was quite a tableau—the angry Walsh and his three stunned companions looking at him in

280

shocked disbelief. Finally one of them said, "Dick, we think it is a legitimate labor issue—enough so that our membership will also strike over it." That ended the "Affair Walsh."

Then came a real break in the solid front, and the first truly enjoyable moment we'd known in months. We received a call from Milt Rackmil, the president of Decca Records and Universal Pictures. He had gone along with the other studios as a good team member should, but he wryly explained he didn't think this meant "until death." As it developed, he had been trying to get the rest to end the ridiculous stopgap clause for years and negotiate a settlement. Maybe it was his experience with Decca, where the record business is based on the royalty payment idea, or just that he is a fair and capable businessman, but he made no secret of his belief that actors were entitled to a repayment and had not been properly compensated for TV use of theatrical pictures. Don't get the idea from this that he was a patsy who rolled over and played dead for us: he was a damn good, shrewd bargainer, but fair and honest—it was a pleasure to do business with him, and we made a deal.

Not long after the producers wheeled up new forces. It was announced that a former FDR cabinet member, Anna Rosenberg, had been employed as a public relations adviser in the strike.

Nancy and I were invited to one of those big Hollywood dinners where some two hundred guests prowl around tables for ten, looking for their own names on the place cards. And what do you know! There beside me as dinner partner was Anna Rosenberg. This was certainly a far cry from a men's room, but some tiny nerve that seems to develop with years of negotiating began to tingle—spiritually and mentally I was in the men's room.

She cleared the air for discussion by explaining her new position, and, as sort of a softener, told me the producers had shown her an advertising plan they had prepared, blasting actors individually and collectively. The pressure idea was that actors couldn't afford to have the public learn to hate them. She had called a halt to this, explaining to the producers that when the strike ended we were the very same people they'd once again depend on to sell tickets to the public. Then she edged up to the issue of what it would take to settle the strike. Of course, she had never been in a men's room, but she seemed to know the unwritten rule that declares this to be the moment of truth. Between soup and salad I laid out exactly just what the Guild would settle for. It was gratifying to see her astonishment.

"Do you mean," she demanded, "that this whole thing can be ended for just what you've told me?"

Very gently I answered, "It could always have been settled on these terms. As a matter of fact, it could have been prevented entirely for just what I've told you."

Forty-eight hours later we got a phone call at the Guild. We had often speculated on who the first one would be when the great day came, but curiously none of us had guessed right. It was Joe Vogel of MGM. Jack and I went to his room at the Beverly Hills Hotel and there, sitting on the edges of the twin beds, we hammered out a deal word for word as I'd described it to Anna. Joe said, "Can you deliver your people on such a basis?" We allowed we thought we could, and he seemed sure his group would come around. Actually we gave him our answer in four hours—it took him four days.

When the strike ended we settled on (1) the principle of extra payment for re-use; (2) a sound pension and welfare plan for the SAG membership; and (3) the sale of all TV rights for the 1948–59 pictures to the producers for a flat sum of $2,000,000 to get the pension plan moving immediately. The final agreement was a specific percentage of repayments to SAG members from films after that date.

The strike was over and my sixth term as president was almost over. Election of officers was only weeks away but, as fate would have it, I finally hung up that particular hat without waiting those extra weeks. A new deal had been worked out involving GE, Revue, and me—and for the first time I found myself with an ownership interest in the films we were producing for the

282

show. According to SAG tradition, my course was predetermined. I followed in the footsteps of all those other Guild officers who had stepped down when they acquired a financial interest on the other side of the labor management table.

I don't regret the years spent with the Guild—to the contrary, I'm a little proud of my association with the wonderfully zany yet remarkably common-sense people of show business, but still I hung up that hat with something of the same feeling I'd had the day Bob Sterling and I walked out of Fort MacArthur at the end of the war.

CHAPTER

18

Before my Guild hat hits the hook for good and all in this tale, a couple of loose ends should be neatly knotted. While Walter Pidgeon was serving his last term as president, a flare-up occurred in the old television controversy. With all of the NLRB elections decided in our favor and television coming out of the film factories in an ever-increasing flow of cans (film cans, that is), there was quiet on the Western front but evidently seething discontent in the East.

Our awareness of this discontent came through our New York membership who, again because of their multiple affiliations with the other performer groups, tended to vibrate like a tuning fork when those other unions rattled. In this case the noise started with AFTRA, which was AFRA—the radio guild with a T added for television, exactly the setup we had always thought should be the television answer in those hectic days of TVA strife. The magic word making the natives restless was "merger." The Screen Actors Guild and AFTRA should merge into one union. Almost before we knew it, we were back in the trenches, and on our part with a kind of weary here-we-go-again attitude.

There was no point in rehashing our previous efforts toward the "one card" Utopia: no one wanted to listen. Again thank heavens for the common sense of our own membership, who could wax as emotional as any group of performers but who also had a memory for battles past, so always kept at least one ear open and one foot earthbound. At a hectic and stormy membership meeting

284

we met an assault mounted by some of our members who were really AFTRA members in their primary role, up to and including membership on AFTRA's national board. We blunted their frontal attack by moving that SAG and AFTRA jointly hire an expert to work out a plan so that all our members could see exactly what merger would mean before voting aye or nay.

In choosing the expert a lot of names were thrown into the hopper, and the one that came out, David Cole, was so well received by AFTRA that I frankly wondered how we happened to have thought of him. He had an impressive list of credits in the field of arbitration, boards, commissions, and committees set up by government to "go into" the broad spectrum of problems government is always "going into."

Mr. Cole was to receive quite a chunk of money. When he arrived in Hollywood to pry into the innards of SAG, it was apparent to those of us who met with him (individually at his request) that his approach was not in any wonder-if-it-will-work way. Here was a man who knew merger was workable, and his job was to interpret the instruction sheet for us yokels.

No one likes to admit to a closed mind, but I must confess my session with our merger engineer narrowed mine down a lot. At a subsequent board meeting, Walter—trying to be fair—stressed the importance of awaiting the plan and viewing it without prejudice, even with the hope that it would be workable. His audience was understandably pessimistic: after all, we'd been through this twice before, and a lot of money's worth, without finding a workable plan. I couldn't resist saying, "Walter, I agree with you completely—I'm going to keep an open mind. I'm going to read his plan before I vote no."

As it turned out, I didn't have to regret my crack. His plan came down couched in some condescending words about us West Coast primitives, and the necessity for bracing ourselves to come out of our bucolic cocoon into the brave world of big labor, big government, one world and, of course, one union. The plan was complete with organizational charts so dear to the hearts of those who have breathed Potomac air even for a little while. Only one thing was clear and understandable in the whole unworkable manual for confusion: there weren't enough actors in the whole business to man the boards, sub-boards, and executive committees he'd lined up to make the wheels go round.

The merger-ites didn't give in easily—they came to the coast in force for a joint meeting to work out a simplification of our dearly bought plan. We figured we had finally come to the end of the long road of appeasement and accommodation. At the opening session we just said a plain "enough already." Then we laid out a schedule for intimate cooperation in all those areas where our paths were parallel and said, if we could work harmoniously there, perhaps we could find additional opportunities for joint action. The clincher to our argument was when we pointed out that both guilds had a pension and welfare fund managed by the same firm. There was no reason why we shouldn't turn that firm loose on combining these into one program. The benefits were obvious. Take myself, for an example: the SAG plan provided me with a health insurance policy; so did my membership in AFTRA. We'd all be money ahead if we ended that duplication. This particular story has a happy ending—cooperation is the policy and flowers grow on the battlefield. . . .

One last reprise ruffled the feathers in my Guild hat and even jiggled one or two other hats in my activity wardrobe. Revue— the TV producing subsidiary of MCA—had outgrown its parent and was by far the biggest part of MCA. A unique arrangement in Hollywood had for some years seen the agents voluntarily submitting to being franchised by the Guild. Rules governing their conduct and business practices were negotiated like labor-management contracts, only this time the Guild sat on the employer's side of the table. For MCA to be agent and producer required a waiver from the Guild. We had never withheld such waivers because we were in favor of anyone who wanted to give jobs to actors. Now, however, the tail was wagging the dog to such an extent that SAG and MCA came to an agreement that, at the end of about a nine-month period, MCA would decide on one business or the other. There wasn't much doubt which way they'd go: they acquired Decca records, giving them ownership of Universal International Pictures. As the day of decision drew near, MCA prepared to dispose of the world-wide agency business in a manner thoroughly consistent with their pattern of employee relations, which had always been generous and enlightened. The men who had staffed the agency formed a corporation, elected officers and directors; they (the employees) would wind up owning the agency.

Unfortunately for them, the clients, and the industry, government had a different idea. The Justice Department launched a grand jury investigation of possible anti-trust law violations. I was excused from the set as the result of a subpoena, and spent a long, unhappy afternoon being interrogated by a federal lawyer who'd seen too many Perry Masons. Feuding is a mild word to use when one is talking of our government's campaign against a private business concern.

An affable, friendly lawyer took me into a room with the explanation that another witness was still testifying, and identification of witnesses was being kept secret—so we'd play Blind Man's Buff until the coast was clear. Then for almost an hour this gentleman questioned me closely on whether I had been cheated for twenty-five years by those at MCA who had represented me. He explained that we were saving time because he was familiarizing me with the subject matter of the questioning I would undergo on the stand. Somewhere between that preliminary proceeding and the hearing room he switched story lines: he also lost his affability. Once on the stand, he launched into a series of questions such as, "Do you recall a discussion at a Guild board meeting the night of August 16, 1950 [ten years ago], regarding a waiver . . ."

Well, of course, I was not only caught off-guard but, as earlier chapters here indicate, I'd lived a lifetime of meetings, and to pick out one for specific questioning was like asking a fellow in a sawmill accident which tooth of the buzz saw cut him first.

Before the day ended I was pretty red-necked, but not half as burned as I would have been if I'd known then what I learned later.

My inquisitor had spent weeks at the Guild, prying through drawers and files and buttonholing secretaries on their way to lunch, to ask slyly if the Guild didn't have some secret files he hadn't been shown. The jury handed down an indictment. To those of you who have never had the experience, let me explain that a prosecutor has a free hand in such a hearing. There is no defense attorney, there isn't any representative or observer for the subject of the inquiry, and no way for a witness to volunteer information—he can only answer the questions propounded by the government attorney.

Of course, the theory is that indictment will be based on the jury's decision that a trial should be held and, in the event of a trial, then the defense will be heard. The matter never went to trial. Less than four days before MCA was to voluntarily divest itself of its agency, as per agreement with the Guild, orders were issued which not only wiped out the agency: they prohibited MCA from selling the agency to its employees, or anyone else, for that matter.

It was a fantastic situation. As of four o'clock on a Friday afternoon, hundreds of employees were guaranteed continuation of their jobs and livelihood; more than a thousand actors, writers, directors, and producers were assured of representation by the same individuals who had been guiding their careers for years. At 4:05 that same afternoon, the employees were without a future, the clients weren't allowed to get their agents on the phone, and the head, Jules Stein—who had created by his own genius an eight-million-dollar-a-year business—was told it wasn't an asset he could dispose of: it had to be thrown away.

One postscript is deserving of mention. Many of the veteran employees had a sizable stake in the company pension fund which had been wisely and judiciously invested. The blitz coincided with the stock market nosedive, but the government forced the

288

liquidation of the fund and its immediate distribution, with the result that individuals wound up with less than a third of what they thought they were worth. The guiding genius of the meat-ax operation issued a pontifical statement to the press that he had "freed the slaves." We, the clients—now without representation, many of us in the midst of negotiations regarding picture and theatrical work—were the supposed slaves. It's a good thing this legal emancipator didn't decide to visit the slaves personally —he'd have been beaten to death with "Oscars."

A lot of hat-changing took place. I went back to an old one— the movie hat I'd doffed when TV entered my life. Actually none of us had any idea that the GE Theatre would become a barrier to making pictures. As a matter of fact, we had an idea to the contrary. During the first year of the show I teamed with John Payne, Rhonda Fleming, and Colleen Gray in the Bret Harte story, *Tennessee Partner,* and a couple of seasons later Nancy and I made a Navy picture for Columbia called *Hellcats of the Navy.* This one could have been better than it was, except that the studio was more in love with the budget than the script. The story was from the factual account of a submarine operation in World War II, written by the Admiral who directed it. Navy co-operation in the filming was enthusiastic and without limit, but whoever said, "of all sad words of tongue or pen, the saddest are these: 'It might have been!' " would have been a good movie critic. Truth and the Navy went down in defeat before the production office string-savers.

Even so, there were some interesting moments making the picture. For one thing, we used no sets—everything was shot on location in "for real" scenery. There were several days when as many as sixteen of us were crammed in the tiny conning tower of a submarine, which was further cramped by our necessary lights, mikes, cameras. We did several "two-shots" in which each of us in the scene held a microphone under our arms on the side away from the camera—thus my lines were being picked up in my acting companion's mike and vice versa. Getting out of the cell

289

between shots was so difficult we just stayed there for hours at a time. I was worried about my own reaction to this imprisonment because of a lifelong tendency toward claustrophobia. I solved my problem by taking advantage of my role as skipper: I had access to the periscope. Between shots I'd run it up and spend my time watching all the outside activity in the harbor.

There is something about this crazy picture business that makes all of us, cast and crew alike, develop a chameleon quality. On a location like this we move in and become more Navy than the Admiral. It isn't phony or insincere either—for several weeks our life becomes the story with its locale and atmosphere. *Our* submarine was skippered by a wonderful commander, name of Kelly. I'm sure he and his charming wife were amazed to discover that they didn't get in on hours of Hollywood talk but found themselves talking seas and ships and submarines, more than they ever did at an Annapolis reunion.

Nancy played a nurse, and the love interest. As I say, there is a tendency to get more involved when the atmosphere is for real rather than the make-believe of a sound stage. We had a moonlight farewell scene on the eve of my departure for the dangerous mission which was the climax of the story. The first thing we all knew, Nancy was crying instead of saying the script lines, and then she was giggling between sobs, laughing at herself for having gotten so carried away that she was really saying good-by and sending me on a suicide mission.

That picture ended movies for me. Hollywood adopted an attitude that TV performers were *verboten* on the big screen, and once Hollywood starts believing its own cocktail party pronouncements, you just have to wait till they get off on a new kick. It didn't matter that my Sunday night stint was a quick forty-five seconds—I had a weekly show and that was that.

Now I'm back in a studio waiting to make a picture, and the prospect is as fresh and exciting as it was to an awestruck sports announcer in 1937. For this I am truly grateful. Some people have asked me when I've been out on the tours, "What's wrong with Hollywood?" The answer is easy: I don't know. Perhaps the question should be worded differently: "What's different about Hollywood?" That I can answer.

The first, most obvious, difference is of course due to the inexorable march of time. Nancy once gave me a birthday present I treasure above all others. She laboriously collected stills and had framed one still for each of the fifty movies I've made. A sadness and nostalgia goes with looking at those pictures today. There are so many faces we can only see in memory. "Muzzy" May Robson, Alan Hale, Lionel Barrymore, Ethel Barrymore, Zasu Pitts, Eddy Arnold of the booming laugh, kindly Paul Harvey, roistering, scratching Wally Beery, Charles Coburn, Adolph Menjou, and that greatest of all actors, Walter Huston. Some I had worked with, all I had known. Recent years have decimated the ranks of the greatest collection of exciting personalities ever assembled any place in the theatrical world: Ty Power, Errol Flynn, Bogey, Coop, Dick Powell, Wayne Morris, Clark Gable, Jack Carson. A special breed they were, sifted to the top in the highly competitive sweepstakes of Hollywood's golden era—the first decade of sound. The pattern seems to have been mislaid—certainly replacements of equal dash and color are sadly lacking.

Hollywood is far from the place it was when I first arrived, full of pith and vim, in 1937. The studios—seven majors—were the boss of the place. They controlled, within the limits of active competition, every major aspect of the industry. They accounted for more than 90 per cent of the pictures shown around the world. They had their own code of voluntary picture morals, contracts with the stars, publicity and advertising for their product. They controlled the theaters that showed their movies and, generally, could regulate the business as efficiently as De Beers today keeps up the artificial price of diamonds.

This virtual monopoly had both good and bad points. It supplied some deep needs in the public for entertainment; it rarely failed the half-billion people that went to the movies each week.

It created an industry worth nearly five billion dollars, out of thin blue sky and ideas, making people laugh and cry by no more than a shadow dance in a dark theater. It was made by men whose taste in drama was often questionable but who could justify drawing as much as a million dollars a year in salary. They had done this on their own. They had built up an empire by the use of faith and hope and a good deal of charity. When others had sneered at investing a nickel in the fantastic idea of such entertainment, they had justified their faith. If Louis B. Mayer could cash out his huge salary, he could also be remembered as the man in the early days that took his cans of film out on the desert and buried them to escape the sheriff seizing them in favor of his creditors.

The movies, from the beginning, were a pure American enterprise in the tradition of private thought and execution. More than any other industry, its founders worked with raw materials that had no other market than people's emotions. Their faults are buried with them; how much of the good remains?

Eleven years after I came to Hollywood, in 1948, the United States government invoked the anti-trust law against the motion picture studios. The studios were in the position of a candy manufacturer who has no store to peddle his product. Someone like Cecil B. DeMille could spend $13,000,000 in making *The Ten Commandments*—but if no theater owner wanted to show his picture, he was flatly forbidden from hiring a hall himself to show it. The studios rightly saw the truth of it; they were forced to take all the risk with an excellent chance of no return.

No longer could they choose young players and build stars. No longer could they estimate the demands of the public and release their movies according to the psychological audience peak. They could not take advantage of the habit of going-to-the-movies they had so laboriously built up. The careful campaigns of public relations—nonsensical as they often were—disappeared. The government had corrected the undoubted abuses and had left a commercial vacuum. It was filled almost instantly with foreign products that took advantage of what American initiative had created. That the movies had been sick, none of us doubted. But some of us felt that they might have been cured by another way than by slitting their throat.

Much of this attitude of government which contributed so materially to the decline of the movies has changed since 1948. In the summer of 1963, a federal district court approved a petition by the National General Corporation (which owns 225 theaters in seventeen states) to produce and distribute motion pictures. Wonderful to say, the United States Justice Department did not oppose the petition. Perhaps those who experimented in the "disintegration" of Hollywood have now decided to pick up the pieces—and return to the scheme of things that once made American pictures the envy of the world.

Today, no one can answer the question: "What's the telephone number of the movie business?" There is none. There are fifteen hundred independent producers registered by SAG. They have no agreed code of production, of quality, or of release. The big stars of yesterday are free lancers; but there are few stars coming up. Box office is an unknown quantity. The desires of the customers, always the prime factor in the considerations of a free industry, are unknown.

At the end of World War II, Hollywood was making five hundred pictures a year. It had more than 90,000,000 paying customers coming into the theaters every week. The 1948 decree plus TV intervened—and in ten years Hollywood came down to making fewer features than the British crown colony of Hong Kong.

So the Hollywood that I knew is gone. Not to Rome or Spain, or to the foggy, foggy dos-and-don'ts of London but to some fond nostalgic nook bathed in a golden haze.

Now that the past has boiled down to still photographs and passionate prose, the "art" of Hollywood is still a question. So is the way it was originally run. I've recently heard about the virtues of genius being best developed under a "creative bureaucracy"—at least that's what one of the numerous deans of the Uni-

293

versity of California has said. This kind of educational gobblede-gook is the art of saying nonsense in a way that makes it sound portentous. Actually, nothing is more opposed to creativeness than bureaucracy—and nothing is more opposed to bureaucracy than a really creative person.

The riotous success of Hollywood was always due to the role of the individual. It's easy now, looking back, to criticize the "taste" of the tycoons—but not many have done better. And it is instructive to recall that all of today's "new" and "daring" pictures of sex, intermarriage, horror, and new images were made a couple of generations back. You can duplicate all the most daring innovations of modern times with fuzzy negatives made sometime between 1910 and 1930.

The shape of television—except for its mammoth size—is not yet clear to me. I do not think it represents a new medium; it is, instead, simply a new kind of theater. It is the proscenium arch in miniature brought into the home. It can be compared, for example, to the drive-in theater, a device which answers the need of the time. No need to dress, no need for baby sitters, no need to do anything but sit and flick a knob. No need even to eat supper beforehand—it can be served *in situ*. The single stunning success of such things as TV dinners bears witness to the strength of television's grasp on the public—and upon me, as well. Maybe in a way we've come full cycle: the strolling players are back peddling their performance in the castle hall.

There are still a number of picture-makers making fine pictures of great quality because of their own pride in craftsmanship—Bob Arthur, Walt Disney, Ross Hunter, and a dozen others. My concern does not stem from any fear that weekly soap opera can outcompete them in quality. I can't help but feel that perhaps we are in danger of outcompeting ourselves.

The basis of the dramatic form of entertainment is the emotional catharsis experienced by the audience. Our lives have lost a certain amount of excitement since we quit having to knock over a mastodon for the family lunch or keep a sabertooth tiger

294

from having us for lunch. We've kept a little stardust in our mundane lives by identifying with make-believe characters in make-believe adventures in the house of illusion—the theater. The house lights dim, the curtains part, and for a few hours all women are again beautiful and beloved, all men brave and noble of character. We laugh, cry, know anger, grief, and triumph—then go home at peace with our corner of the world.

A few years ago we did this perhaps a half-dozen times a year. A privileged few on Broadway, many more in local stock theaters —the rest when Chautauqua or a traveling company came to town. Then the movies brought us this emotional experience once a week or, in the case of the majority, every two weeks. Now television is a knob within easy reach seven nights a week, and each night offers adventure, romance, comedy, and tragedy. Is it possible that TV isn't competing with movies, or movies with stage, but that we are overstuffing our audience to the point that we can no longer make them feel? A death scene could make a young actor a star as the viewers reached for their hankies: the death of George Gipp did that for me. Now the audiences have been asked to cry Monday through Sunday with victims of violence, disease (if Dr. Kildare doesn't get there in time), and mass slaughter in wide-screen spectacles.

Isn't this, in a much more real sense, what happened to the Roman orgies? They entertained the people with animals killing animals until the prospect palled—then it was animal against human, then human against human, until finally sadistic blood baths of scores of people could no longer give them that old feeling (the spectators, that is).

Being an actor, I can't believe the spoken drama, with its thousand years of history, will pass like the great auk or the carrier pigeon. While even free TV worries about the lost audience happily out boating, bowling, or camping, I wonder if a new technology on the horizon won't provide an economic barrier against satiation. Perhaps people will once again buy their emotional experience. I am, of course, speaking of pay television, that monster haunting the waking hours of all theater owners. It could work vast changes in the theater business because TV is in itself nothing more than a theater—brought to the customer. But it could also remove the bulk of dramatic entertainment from free TV, just as the television tube put radio into the music and news business. Conceivably, fine dramatic productions would go back to being a once-a-week emotional experience because the audience would once again be guided by desire plus a pocket-book limitation on how many times they could afford to look.

Let me digress for a moment to get in a mention here of old movies, and a word in their behalf to those who, lured by nostalgia, find them on the Late Late Show. So often, disappointed, they say, "It wasn't as good as I remembered it." Yes, it is: you just never saw it before with thirty or forty minutes scissored out of it so the sales department could get in a flock of used car ads. I saw *Knute Rockne* one night, and it was so hacked up, my eighty-yard run was a five-yard loss.

I have my movie hat on again—I hope for some little while: I've missed it. Still, eight years made a dent and I find my mind toying with television ideas. Another hat—a really new one—was displayed recently and, while it had some intriguing features, I decided it wouldn't be completely comfortable. A group of my fellow citizens were the designers and they did me a great honor, for which I am humbly grateful, even though the hat didn't fit. Their hat was the kind you throw into the political ring and they wanted me to do just that, for either governor or senator.

One does what he feels he can do best and serves where he feels he can make the greatest contribution. For me, I think that service is to continue accepting speaking engagements, in an effort to make people aware of the danger to freedom in a vast permanent government structure so big and complex it virtually entraps Presidents and legislators. Being an actor, I have access to audiences which might be denied an office holder or candidate. There is no point in saving souls in heaven; if my speaking is to serve any purpose, then I must appear before listeners who don't share my viewpoint.

It's a curious thing: I talked on this theme of big government during six years of the Eisenhower administration and was accepted as presenting a nonpartisan viewpoint. The same speech delivered *after* January 20, 1961, brought down thunders of wrath on my head, the charge that my speech was a partisan political attack, an expression of right wing extremism. My erstwhile associates in organized labor at the top level of the AFL-CIO assail me as a "strident voice of the right wing lunatic fringe." Sadly I have come to realize that a great many so-called liberals aren't liberal—they will defend to the death your right to agree with them.

The classic liberal used to be the man who believed the individual was, and should be forever, the master of his destiny. That is now the conservative position. The liberal used to believe in freedom under law. He now takes the ancient feudal position that power is everything. He believes in a stronger and stronger central government, in the philosophy that control is better than freedom. The conservative now quotes Thomas Paine, a long-time refuge of the liberals: "Government is a necessary evil; let us have as little of it as possible." The liberal ignores what that "radical," Chief Justice Oliver Wendell Holmes, said: "Strike for the jugular. Reduce taxes and spending. Keep government poor and remain free." The liberal wants a well-heeled government in a Big Brother image to buy for us the things "Big Brother" thinks we should have.

The conservatives believe the collective responsibility of the qualified men in a community should decide its course. The liberals believe in remote and massive strong-arming from afar, usually Washington, D.C. The conservatives believe in the unique powers of the individual and his personal opinions. The liberals lean increasingly toward bureaucracy, operation by computer minds and forced fiat, the submergence of man in statistics. The labels somehow have got pasted on the wrong people.

It is a fascinating phenomenon of our times. One of change, certainly; perhaps degeneracy. Our weaknesses have overnight become "strengths." What is denounced during political campaigns becomes the policy of the nation. Even when a scientific genius like J. Robert Oppenheimer, in the highest circles of top-secret confidence, admits under oath that he lied again and again about his association with the Communists, the chief complaints seem to be concerning the vigor of the prosecution that forced him to admit the damning facts.

We have prominent American newspaper commentators like John Crosby declaring that "to go to war under any circumstances for anything at all in the world in our time is utter absurdity." To this, such prominent English commentators as Kenneth Tynan add that "better Red than dead seems an obvious doctrine for anyone not consumed by a death-wish; I would rather live on my knees than die on my feet."

The trouble with such men is that they have never lived, either on their feet or their knees. They have lived on their fat fannies. They talk, with the fear of a child going into the dark, about dying, a death-wish in reverse. It may come as a surprise to them but the fact is—we will all die. It is the business of time to see to that. What makes the difference in the matter is what we die for. The noble standards set up by good men everywhere, in all nations, at all times.

It is not warmongering to say that some things are worth dying for. If this be not so—then write off the martyrs as fools. Christ should have refused the cross, and before him, Moses should have told the children of Israel slavery was better than risking death in the wilderness. Certainly those men at Concord bridge should have pretended they were just out on a squirrel hunt and no one should have lifted a hand against Hitler—or does that last stick in the liberal craw?

298

Lord Macaulay's *Horatio at the Bridge* asks:

> And how can man die better
> Than facing fearful odds
> For the ashes of his fathers,
> And the temples of his gods?

Or have the temples been brought down on our own heads? The ashes of our fathers scattered and debunked? Perhaps his Lordship should do a rewrite:

> For man lives all the better,
> When existing as a clod;
> Cringing beneath his daily fears
> And defiant of his gods.

Now, before someone says, "Ah ha! He *does* want a war," let me say, "No, I want and believe in peace—but we can't have it by telling the enemy we'll buy it at any price."

Punting from behind one's own goal posts is one of the most dangerous plays in football. We are trying to do the same thing in our international life and, at the same time, pretend that it is a winning touchdown play. It may be. But smart gamblers will give long odds that you will lose.

It is popular to talk about freedom, but how many of us in the world are sure we are talking about the same thing when we use the word? *Uhuru* in Africa is different from liberty in Philadelphia. Freedom in Hollywood is not quite what *liberté* is in Paris. Nor is freedom in Washington exactly what's meant by the word *svoboda* in Moscow, or *tszuyu* in Peiping. The truth is that here in America, as in almost no other place on earth, freedom means something that belongs to the individual by divine right, not a privilege granted by government. We here in the United States often fail to realize that we were born free in 1776, long before the rest of the world started talking about it.

299

The original government of this country was set up by conservatives, as defined years later by Lincoln, who called himself a conservative with a "preference for the old and tried over the new and untried." The setting up of our government was not, as it has been called, a great experiment. On the contrary, it was culling the best and the most stable elements from world history —from the experiences of Greece and Rome and England, to name three—in order to weld them into one "new" government. Today, more than ever, it is necessary to proceed with change with the greatest care. Experimenting with the lives of 200,000,000 people capriciously is much different than juggling test tubes in a laboratory. If damage is done to the nation, it is almost impossible to rectify; the bad drives out the good.

This peculiar word "freedom"—with hundreds of definitions— has been debased in the coinage of communications. It might be helpful to go back to the original derivation of the word—a dozen language roots with a common ancestry: always it springs from words that mean "peace" and "love." Strangely enough, the word "liberty" traced back to its roots means "growing up" or "maturing" or "taking responsibility." And therein lies the whole story— we can have peace and brotherly love by accepting our responsibility to preserve freedom here where it has known its longest run in six thousand years of recorded history.

So the part of me that puts up with rubber chicken along the banquet trail will continue to wear that hat out of gratitude for a way of life that could start above a general store in a little Illinois town, and lead to a view of the Pacific from a home in the Palisades. Indeed, I have to wear that hat because the most important part of me wears a hat I treasure above all others— designed by Nancy and well smudged by sticky little fingers. The owners of those fingers have a right to know the exciting freedom that make my memories so warm and pleasant.

Someone has asked, "Would you want your children to be in show business?" My answer: "Why not?" It has brought me everything I love, including those children and their mother. I am humbly grateful for the fact that I open my eyes every morning with a pleased anticipation of the day ahead. I can't conceive of a day filled with boredom. Does this business have heartache? Yes, a full measure. Probably the most tragic thing is to be denied the chance to practice your profession when someone handing out the parts decides against you—this too I have known. But if we do our job as parents, our children will take the bad with the good and not whimper. If Nancy passes on the lessons she learned from her mother (and I'm sure she will), Patti will know when to take off the make-believe hat and put on the one befitting her real role in life.

The days stretch ahead with promise. The city closes in on the ranch—we prowl the countryside scouting a new location. I should turn to the sages for some profound utterance to close out these words. Still, it is more fitting that a remark by The King of actors, Clark Gable, sticks in my mind. Clark said, "The most important thing a man can know is that, as he approaches his own door, someone on the other side is listening for the sound of his footsteps."

I have found the rest of me.

APPENDIX

An excellent summary of Mr. Reagan's political philosophy, derived from his own convictions on the functions of democracy, is contained in the speech below. It represents sentiments he has publicly expressed across the nation for the past fifteen years—regardless of political parties or programs that had happened to be in power.

—R.G.H.

I am going to talk of controversial things. I make no apology for this. I have been talking on this subject for ten years, obviously under the administration of both parties. I mention this only because it seems impossible to legitimately debate the issues of the day without being subjected to name-calling and the application of labels. Those who deplore use of the terms "pink" and "leftist" are themselves guilty of branding all who oppose their liberalism as right wing extremists. How long can we afford the luxury of this family fight when we are at war with the most dangerous enemy ever known to man? If we lose that war, and in so doing lose our freedom, it has been said history will record with the greatest astonishment that those who had the most to lose did the least to prevent its happening. The guns are silent in this war but frontiers fall while those who should be warriors prefer neutrality. Not too long ago two friends of mine were talking to a Cuban refugee. He was a business man who had escaped from Castro. In the midst of his tale of horrible experiences, one of my friends turned to the other and said, "We don't know how lucky we are." The Cuban stopped and said, "How lucky you are! I had some place to escape to." And in that sentence he told the entire story. If freedom is lost here there is no place to escape to.

It's time we asked ourselves if we still know the freedoms intended for us by the Founding Fathers. James Madison said, "We base all our experiments on the capacity of mankind for self-government." This idea

302

that government was beholden to the people, that it had no other source of power except the sovereign people, is still the newest most unique idea in all the long history of man's relation to man. For almost two centuries we have proved man's capacity for self-government, but today we are told we must choose between a left and right or, as others suggest, a third alternative, a kind of safe middle ground. I suggest to you there is no left or right, only an up or down. Up to the maximum of individual freedom consistent with law and order, or down to the ant heap of totalitarianism, and regardless of their humanitarian purpose those who would sacrifice freedom for security have, whether they know it or not, chosen this downward path. Plutarch warned, "The real destroyer of the liberties of the people is he who spreads among them bounties, donations and benefits."

Today there is an increasing number who can't see a fat man standing beside a thin one without automatically coming to the conclusion the fat man got that way by taking advantage of the thin one. So they would seek the answer to all the problems of human need through government. Howard K. Smith of television fame has written, "The profit motive is outmoded. It must be replaced by the incentives of the welfare state." He says, "The distribution of goods must be effected by a planned economy." Another articulate spokesman for the welfare state defines liberalism as meeting the material needs of the masses through the full power of centralized government. I for one find it disturbing when a representative refers to the free men and women of this country as the masses, but beyond this the full power of centralized government was the very thing the Founding Fathers sought to minimize. They knew you don't control things, you can't control the economy without controlling people. So we have come to a time for choosing. Either we accept the responsibility for our own destiny, or we abandon the American Revolution and confess that an intellectual belief in a far-distant capitol can plan our lives for us better than we can plan them ourselves.

Already the hour is late. Government has laid its hand on health, housing, farming, industry, commerce, education, and to an ever increasing degree interferes with the people's right to know. Government tends to grow, government programs take on weight and momentum as public servants say, always with the best of intentions, "What greater service we could render if only we had a little more money and a little more power." But the truth is that outside of its legitimate function, government does nothing as well or as economically as the private sector of the economy. What better example do we have of this than government's involvement in the farm economy over the last 30 years. One-fourth of farming is responsible for 85 per cent of the farm surplus. One-fourth of farming has seen a steady decline in the per capita consumption of everything it produces. That one-fourth is regulated and subsidized by government.

In contrast, the three-fourths of farming unregulated and unsubsidized has seen a 21 per cent increase in the per capita consumption of all its produce. Since 1955 the cost of the farm program has nearly doubled. Direct payment to farmers is eight times as great as it was nine years ago, but farm income remains unchanged while farm surplus is bigger. In that same period we have seen a decline of five million in the farm population, but an increase in the number of Department of Agriculture employees. There is now one such employee for every 30 farms in the United States, and still they can't figure how 66 shiploads of grain headed for Austria could disappear without a trace, and Billy Sol Estes never left shore. Three years ago the government put into effect a program to curb the over-production of feed grain. Now, two and a half billion dollars later, the corn crop is 100 million bushels bigger than before the program started. And the cost of the program prorates out to $43 for every dollar bushel of corn we don't grow. Nor is this the only example of the price we pay for government meddling. Some government programs with the passage of time take on a sacrosanct quality.

One such considered above criticism, sacred as motherhood, is TVA. This program started as a flood control project; the Tennessee Valley was periodically ravaged by destructive floods. The Army Engineers set out to solve this problem. They said that it was possible that once in 500 years there could be a total capacity flood that would inundate some 600,000 acres. Well the Engineers fixed that. They made a permanent lake which inundated a million acres. This solved the problem of the floods, but the annual interest on the TVA debt is five times as great as the annual flood damage they sought to correct. Of course, you will point out that TVA gets electric power from the impounded waters, and this is true, but today 85 per cent of TVA's electricity is generated in coal burning steam plants. Now perhaps you'll charge that I'm overlooking the navigable waterway that was created, providing cheap barge traffic, but the bulk of the freight barged on that waterway is coal being shipped to the TVA steam plants, and the cost of maintaining that channel each year would pay for shipping all of the coal by rail, and there would be money left over.

One last argument remains: The prosperity produced by such large programs of government spending. Certainly there are few areas where more spending has taken place. The Labor Department lists 50 per cent of the 169 counties in the Tennessee Valley as permanent areas of poverty, distress, and unemployment. Meanwhile, back in the city, under Urban Renewal, the assault on freedom carries on. Private property rights have become so diluted that public interest is anything a few planners decide it should be. In Cleveland, Ohio, to get a project under way, city officials reclassified 84 buildings as substandard in spite of the fact their own inspectors had previously pronounced these buildings sound. The owners stood by and watched 26 million dollars worth of property as it

304

was destroyed by the headache ball. Senate Bill 628 says, "Any property, be it home or commercial structure, can be declared slum or blighted and the owner has no recourse at law. The Law Division of the Library of Congress and the General Accounting Office have said that the Courts will have to rule against the owner."

Housing. In one key Eastern city a man owning a blighted area sold his property to Urban Renewal for several million dollars. At the same time, he submitted his own plan for the rebuilding of this area and the government sold him back his own property for 22 per cent of what they paid. Now the government announces, "We are going to build subsidized housing in the thousands where we have been building in the hundreds." At the same time FHA and the Veterans Administration reveal they are holding 120 thousand housing units reclaimed from mortgage foreclosure. Mostly because the low down payment, and the easy terms brought the owners to a point where they realized the unpaid balance on the homes amounted to a sum greater than the homes were worth, so they just walked out the front door, possibly to take up residence in newer subsidized housing, again with little or no down payment and easy terms.

Some of the foreclosed homes have already been bulldozed into the earth, others it has been announced will be refurbished and put on sale for down payments as low as $100 and 35 years to pay. This will give the bulldozers a second crack. It is in the area of social welfare that government has found its most fertile growing bed. So many of us accept our responsibility for those less fortunate. We are susceptible to humanitarian appeals.

Federal welfare spending is today ten times greater than it was in the dark depths of the depression. Federal, state, and local welfare combined spent 45 billion dollars a year. Now the government has announced that 20 per cent, some 9.3 million families, are poverty stricken on the basis that they have less than a $3,000 a year income.

If this present welfare spending was prorated equally among these poverty stricken families, we could give each family more than $4,500 a year. Actually, direct aid to the poor averages less than $600 per family. There must be some administrative overhead somewhere. Now are we to believe that another billion dollar program added to the half a hundred programs and the 45 billion dollars, will, through some magic, end poverty? For three decades we have tried to solve unemployment by government planning, without success. The more the plans fail, the more the planners plan.

The latest is the Area Redevelopment Agency, and in two years less than one-half of 1 per cent of the unemployed could attribute new jobs to this agency, and the cost to the taxpayer for each job found was

305

$5,000. But beyond the great bureaucratic waste, what are we doing to the people we seek to help?

Recently a judge told me of an incident in his court. A fairly young woman, with six children, pregnant with her seventh, came to him for a divorce. Under his questioning it became apparent her husband did not share this desire. Then the whole story came out. Her husband was a laborer earning $250 a month. By divorcing him she could get an $80 raise. She was eligible for $350 a month from the Aid to Dependent Children Program. She had been talked into the divorce by two friends who had already done this very thing. But any time we question the schemes of the do-gooders, we are denounced as being opposed to their humanitarian goal. It seems impossible to legitimately debate their solutions with the assumption that all of us share the desire to help those less fortunate. They tell us we are always against, never for anything. Well, it isn't so much that Liberals are ignorant. It's just that they know so much that isn't so.

We are for a provision that destitution should not follow unemployment by reason of old age. For that reason we have accepted Social Security as a step toward meeting that problem. However, we are against the irresponsibility of those who charge that any criticism or suggested improvement of the program means we want to end payment to those who depend on Social Security for a livelihood.

Fiscal Irresponsibility. We have been told in millions of pieces of literature and press releases, that social security is an insurance program, but the executives of Social Security appeared before the Supreme Court in the case of Nestor v. Fleming and proved to the Court's satisfaction that it is not insurance but is a welfare program, and Social Security dues are a tax for the general use of the government. Well it can't be both, insurance and welfare. Later, appearing before a Congressional Committee they admitted that Social Security is today 298 billion dollars in the red. This fiscal irresponsibility has already caught up with us.

Faced with a bankruptcy we find that today a young man in his early twenties, going to work at less than an average salary, will with his employer pay into Social Security an amount which could provide the young man with a retirement insurance policy guaranteeing $220 a month at age 65, and the government promises him $127.

Now are we so lacking in business sense that we cannot put this program on a sound actuarial basis, so that those who do depend on it won't come to the cupboard and find it bare, and at the same time can't we introduce voluntary features so that those who can make better provision for themselves are allowed to do so? Incidentally, we might also allow participants in Social Security to name their own beneficiaries, which they cannot do in the present program. These are not insurmountable problems.

306

Youth Aid Plans. We have today 30 million workers protected by industrial and union pension funds that are soundly financed by some 70 billion dollars invested in corporate securities and income earning real estate. I think we are for telling our senior citizens that no one in this country should be denied medical care for lack of funds but we are against forcing all citizens into a compulsory government program regardless of need. Now the government has turned its attention to our young people, and suggests that it can solve the problem of school dropouts and juvenile delinquency through some kind of revival of the old C.C.C. camps. The suggested plan prorates out to a cost of $4,700 a year for each young person we want to help. We can send them to Harvard for $2,700 a year. Of course, don't get me wrong—I'm not suggesting Harvard as the answer to juvenile delinquency. We are for an international organization where the nations of the world can legitimately seek peace. We are against subordinating American interests to an organization so structurally unsound that a two-thirds majority can be mastered in the U.N. General Assembly among nations representing less than 10 per cent of the world population.

Is there not something of hypocrisy in assailing our allies for so-called vestiges of colonialism while we engage in a conspiracy of silence about the peoples enslaved by the Soviet in the satellite nations? We are for aiding our allies by sharing our material blessings with those nations which share our fundamental beliefs. We are against doling out money, government to government, which ends up financing socialism all over the world.

We set out to help 19 war ravaged countries at the end of World War II. We are now helping 107. We have spent 146 billion dollars. Some of that money bought a $2 million yacht for Haile Selassie. We bought dress suits for Greek undertakers. We bought 1,000 TV sets, with 23-inch screens, for a country where there is no electricity, and some of our foreign aid funds provided extra wives for Kenya government officials. When Congress moved to cut foreign aid they were told that if they cut it one dollar they endangered national security, and then Senator Harry Byrd revealed that since its inception foreign aid has rarely spent its allotted budget. It has today $21 billion in unexpended funds.

Some time ago Dr. Howard Kershner was speaking to the prime minister of Lebanon. The prime minister told him proudly that his little country balanced its budget each year. It had no public debt, no inflation, a modest tax rate and had increased its gold holdings from $70 to $120 million. When he finished, Dr. Kershner said, "Mr. Prime Minister, my country hasn't balanced its budget 28 out of the last 40 years. My country's debt is greater than the combined debt of all the nations of the world. We have inflation, and we have a tax rate that takes from the private sector a percentage of income greater than any civilized

307

nation has ever taken and survived. We have lost gold at such a rate that the solvency of our currency is in danger. Do you think that my country should continue to give your country millions of dollars each year?" The prime minister smiled and said, "No, but if you are foolish enough to do it, we are going to keep on taking the money."

9 Stalls for 1 Bull. And so we built a model stock farm in Lebanon, and we built nine stalls for each bull. I find something peculiarly appropriate in that. We have in our vaults $15 billion in gold. We don't own an ounce. Foreign dollar claims against that gold total $27 billion. In the last six years, 52 nations have bought $7 billion worth of our gold and all 52 are receiving foreign aid.

Because no government ever voluntarily reduces itself in size, government programs once launched never go out of existence. A government agency is the nearest thing to eternal life we'll ever see on this earth. The United States manual takes 25 pages to list by name every Congressman and Senator, and all the agencies controlled by Congress. It then lists the agencies coming under the Executive Branch, and this requires 520 pages.

Since the beginning of the century our gross national product has increased by 33 times. In the same period the cost of Federal government has increased 234 times, and while the work force is only 1½ times greater, Federal employees number nine times as many. There are now 2½ million Federal employees. No one knows what they all do. One Congressman found out what one of them does. This man sits at a desk in Washington. Documents come to him each morning. He reads them, initials them, and passes them on to the proper agency. One day a document arrived he wasn't supposed to read, but he read it, initialled it and passed it on. Twenty-four hours later it arrived back at his desk with a memo attached that said, "You weren't supposed to read this. Erase your initials, and initial the erasure."

While the Federal government is the great offender, the idea filters down. During a period in California when our population has increased 90 per cent, the cost of state government has gone up 862 per cent and the number of employees 500 per cent. Governments, state and local, now employ one out of six of the nation's work force. If the rate of increase of the last three years continues by 1970 one-fourth of the total work force will be employed by government. Already we have a permanent structure so big and complex it is virtually beyond the control of Congress and the comprehension of the people, and tyranny inevitably follows when this permanent structure usurps the policy-making function that belongs to elected officials.

One example of this occurred when Congress was debating whether to lend the United Nations $100 million. While they debated the State Department gave the United Nations $217 million and the United

308

Nations used part of that money to pay the delinquent dues of Castro's Cuba.

Under bureaucratic regulations adopted with no regard to the wish of the people, we have lost much of our Constitutional freedom. For example, federal agents can invade a man's property without a warrant, can impose a fine without a formal hearing, let alone a trial by jury, and can seize and sell his property at auction to enforce payment of that fine.

Rights by Dispensation. An Ohio deputy fire marshal sentenced a man to prison after a secret proceeding in which the accused was not allowed to have a lawyer present. The Supreme Court upheld that sentence, ruling that it was an administrative investigation of incidents damaging to the economy. Some place a perversion has taken place. Our natural unalienable rights are now presumed to be a dispensation of government, divisible by a vote of the majority. The greatest good for the greatest number is a high-sounding phrase but contrary to the very basis of our Nation, unless it is accompanied by recognition that we have certain rights which cannot be infringed upon, even if the individual stands outvoted by all of his fellow citizens. Without this recognition, majority rule is nothing more than mob rule.

It is time we realized that socialism can come without overt seizure of property or nationalization of private business. It matters little that you hold the title to your property or business if government can dictate policy and procedure and holds life and death power over your business. The machinery of this power already exists. Lowell Mason, former antitrust law enforcer for the Federal Trade Commission, has written "American business is being harassed, bled and even black jacked under a preposterous crazy quilt system of laws." There are so many that the government literally can find some charge to bring against any concern it chooses to prosecute. Are we safe in our books and records?

The natural gas producers have just been handed a 428-page questionnaire by the Federal Power Commission. It weighs ten pounds. One firm has estimated it will take 70,000 accountant man hours to fill out this questionnaire, and it must be done in quadruplicate. The Power Commission says it must have it to determine whether a proper price is being charged for gas. The National Labor Relations Board ruled that a business firm could not discontinue its shipping department even though it was more efficient and economical to subcontract this work out.

The Supreme Court has ruled the government has the right to tell a citizen what he can grow on his own land for his own use. The Secretary of Agriculture has asked for the right to imprison farmers who violate their planting quotas. One business firm has been informed by the Internal Revenue Service that it cannot take a tax deduction for its institutional advertising because this advertising espoused views not in the public interest.

309

A child's prayer in a school cafeteria endangers religious freedom, but the people of the Amish religion in the State of Ohio who cannot participate in Social Security because of their religious beliefs have had their livestock seized and sold at auction to enforce payment of Social Security dues.

We approach a point of no return when government becomes so huge and entrenched that we fear the consequences of upheaval and just go along with it. The Federal government accounts for one-fifth of the industrial capacity of the nation, one-fourth of all construction, holds or guarantees one-third of all mortgages, owns one-third of the land, and engages in some nineteen thousand businesses covering half a hundred different lines. The Defense Department runs 269 supermarkets. They do a gross business of $730 million a year, and lose $150 million. The government spends $11 million an hour every hour of the 24 and pretends we had a tax cut while it pursues a policy of planned inflation that will more than wipe out any benefit with depreciation of our purchasing power.

We need true tax reform that will at least make a start toward restoring for our children the American dream that wealth is denied to no one, that each individual has the right to fly as high as his strength and ability will take him. The economist Sumner Schlicter has said, "If a visitor from Mars looked at our tax policy, he would conclude it had been designed by a Communist spy to make free enterprise unworkable." But we cannot have such reform while our tax policy is engineered by people who view the tax as a means of achieving changes in our social structure. Senator Clark (D.-Pa.) says the tax issue is a class issue, and the government must use the tax to redistribute the wealth and earnings downward.

Karl Marx. On January 15th in the White House, the President told a group of citizens they were going to take all the money they thought was being unnecessarily spent, "take it from the have's and give it to the have-nots who need it so much." When Karl Marx said this he put it: ... "from each according to his ability, to each according to his need."

Have we the courage and the will to face up to the immorality and discrimination of the progressive surtax, and demand a return to traditional proportionate taxation? Many decades ago the Scottish economist, John Ramsey McCulloch, said, "The moment you abandon the cardinal principle of exacting from all individuals the same proportion of their income or their property, you are at sea without rudder or compass and there is no amount of injustice or folly you may not commit." No nation has survived the tax burden that reached one-third of its national income.

Today in our country the tax collector's share is 37 cents of every dollar earned. Freedom has never been so fragile, so close to slipping from our grasp. I wish I could give you some magic formula, but each of us must find his own role. One man in Virginia found what he could do, and dozens of business firms have followed his lead. Concerned because his 200 employees seemed unworried about government extravagance he conceived the idea of taking all of their withholding out of only the fourth paycheck each month. For three paydays his employees received their full salary. On the fourth payday all withholding was taken. He has one employee who owes him $4.70 each fourth payday. It only took one month to produce 200 Conservatives.

Are you willing to spend time studying the issues, making yourself aware, and then conveying that information to family and friends? Will you resist the temptation to get a government handout for your community? Realize that the doctor's fight against socialized medicine is your fight. We can't socialize the doctors without socializing the patients. Recognize that government invasion of public power is eventually an assault upon your own business. . . . If some among you fear taking a stand because you are afraid of reprisals from customers, clients, or even government, recognize that you are just feeding the crocodile hoping he'll eat you last.

If all of this seems like a great deal of trouble think what's at stake. We are faced with the most evil enemy mankind has known in his long climb from the swamp to the stars. There can be no security anywhere in the free world if there is not fiscal and economic stability within the United States. Those who ask us to trade our freedom for the soup kitchen of the welfare state are architects of a policy of accommodation. They tell us that by avoiding a direct confrontation with the enemy he will learn to love us and give up his evil ways. All who oppose this idea are blanket indicted as war-mongers. Well let us set one thing straight, there is no argument with regard to peace and war. It is cheap demagoguery to suggest that anyone would want to send other peoples' sons to war. The only argument is with regard to the best way to avoid war. There is only one sure way—surrender.

Appeasement or Courage? The spectre our well-meaning liberal friends refuse to face is that their policy of accommodation is appeasement, and appeasement does not give you a choice between peace and war, only between fight or surrender. We are told that the problem is too complex for a simple answer. They are wrong. There is no easy answer, but there is a simple answer. We must have the courage to do what we know is morally right, and this policy of accommodation asks us to accept the greatest possible immorality. We are being asked to buy our safety from the threat of the Bomb by selling into permanent slavery our fellow human beings enslaved behind the Iron Curtain. To tell them to give up their hope of freedom because we are ready to make a deal with their slave masters.

Alexander Hamilton warned us that a nation which can prefer disgrace to danger is prepared for a master and deserves one. Admittedly there is a risk in any course we follow. Choosing the high road cannot eliminate that risk. Already some of the architects of accommodation have hinted what their decision will be if their plan fails and we are faced with the final ultimatum. The English commentator Tynan has put it: he would rather live on his knees than die on his feet. Some of our own have said "Better Red than dead." If we are to believe that nothing is worth the dying, when did this begin? Should Moses have told the children of Israel to live in slavery rather than dare the wilderness? Should Christ have refused the Cross? Should the patriots at Concord Bridge have refused to fire the shot heard round the world? Are we to believe that all the martyrs of history died in vain?

You and I have rendezvous with destiny. We can preserve for our children this the last best hope of man on earth or we can sentence them to take the first step into a thousand years of darkness. If we fail, at least let our children and our children's children, say of us we justified our brief moment here. We did all that could be done.

INDEX

Abel, Walter, 220
AFL-CIO, 220, 270
AGVA, 220, 223
Albert, Eddie, 87
Alexander, Ross, 76
Altschuler, Sid, 42–45, 58
American Federation of Labor, 127, 130, 132, 136, 150–152; see also AFL-CIO
American Federation of Radio Artists, 199, 221, 222, 227, 230
American Federation of Television and Radio Artists, 222, 230, 284–286
American Veterans Committee, 165
Ames, Leon, 131
Arnold, Edward, 132, 154, 175, 179, 204
Arnow, Max, 71–74
Arthur, Bob, 215, 241, 294
Associated Actors and Artistes of America, 219, 228–230

Bacon, Lloyd, 85–86
Barrymore, John, 87
Barrymore, Lionel, 99, 100
Beery, Wallace, 99–100
Berlin, Irving, 121, 122
Beverly Hills, Treaty of, 146
Bioff, Samuel, 159–160, 180
Birthright, W. C. See "Three Wise Men"
Bogart, Humphrey, 85, 86, 100–101, 186
Booker, Phillip, 107–113
Boyer, Charles, 132, 177
Bracken, Eddie, 204–205
Brent, George, 81, 101
Brewer, Roy, 147, 159, 199
Bridges, Harry, 161, 163–164
Broderick, Helen, 133
Browne, George E., 159–160, 180
Burkhardt, Franklin, 63–64

Burns, George, 250
Byington, Spring, 215

Cagney, James, 80, 86, 87, 101, 102, 132, 177, 279
Calhoun, Rory, 193
Cambiano, Joe, 147
Cantor, Eddie, 131–132
Carson, Jack, 182, 204
Case, Nelson, 227–228
Catlett, Walter, 87
Chambers, Whittaker, 268
Chevigny, Jack, 94
Cleaver, Margaret, 21–23, 31, 45
Coburn, Charles, 215
Cole, David, 285
Cole, Enos ("Bud"), 35–36, 43, 50
Committee for the First Amendment, 200
Communism and the movie industry, 157–159, 161–164, 170–184, 199–201, 264–265
Conference of Studio Unions, 135, 143–144, 146, 153, 156, 161, 162, 176, 179–184
Congress of Industrial Organizations, 137; see also AFL-CIO
COPE, 270
Cordiner, Ralph, 268–269
Cromwell, John, 167
Crosby, John, 298
Curtiz, Mike, 96–97

Dalen, George, 265–268
Dales, Jack, 173, 179, 182, 183, 221, 225, 276
Davis, Bette, 101–102
Davis, Edith (Edith Luckett), 236, 240, 274
Davis, Nancy. See Reagan, Nancy
Day, Doris, 215, 239
Dead End Kids, 101

313

314

315